THINKING MACHINES
THE SEARCH FOR ARTIFICIAL INTELLIGENCE

THINKING MACHINES

THE SEARCH FOR ARTIFICIAL INTELLIGENCE

IGOR ALEKSANDER
AND
PIERS BURNETT

Illustrations by 4i Design Partnership at Imagine

OXFORD UNIVERSITY PRESS
1987

Oxford University Press, Walton Street, Oxford OX2 6DP
Oxford New York Toronto
Delhi Bombay Calcutta Madras Karachi
Petaling Jaya Singapore Hong Kong Tokyo
Nairobi Dar es Salaam Cape Town
Melbourne Auckland

and associated companies in
Beirut Berlin Ibadan Nicosia

Oxford is a trade mark of Oxford University Press

This book was created and produced by Roxby Science Limited
a division of Roxby Press Limited
98 Clapham Common North Side
London SW4 9SG

Editor: Deborah Blake
Art Direction: David Pearce
Design: Michelle Barnacle
Typesetting: Tradespools Limited, Frome, Somerset
Reproduction: Minervascan Ltd, London

British Library Cataloguing in Publication Data
Aleksander, Igor.
Thinking machines: a search for artificial intelligence.
1. Artificial intelligence.
I. Title.   II. Burnett, Piers.
006.3   Q335

ISBN 0-19-217755-9

Printed in Italy

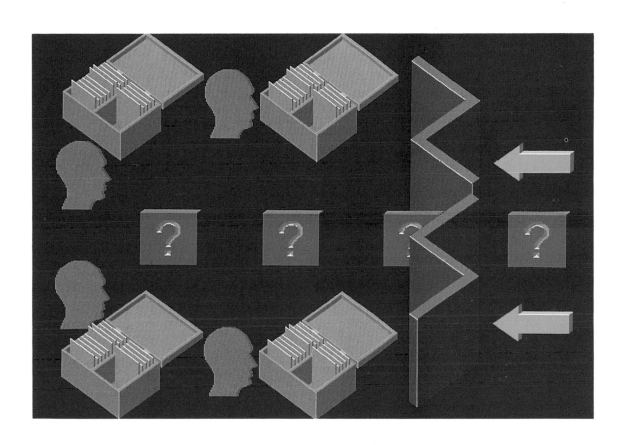

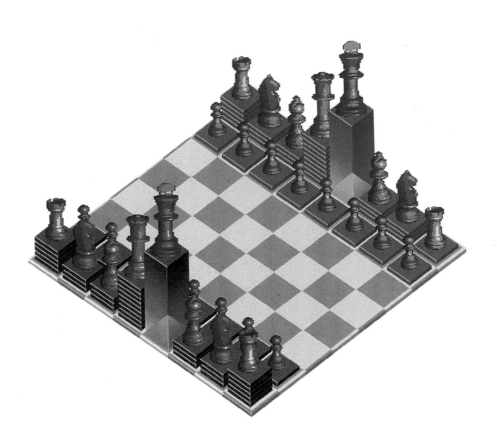

CONTENTS

INTRODUCTION

'I think that . . .', 'You know about . . .', 'She is intelligent . . .', none of us would raise an eyebrow on hearing any one of these phrases in the course of everyday conversation. But if we replace 'I', 'You' and 'She' with 'The machine', 'The computer', or simply 'It', the effect is distinctly disconcerting.

However, although we may feel uncomfortable at the idea of talking about boxes full of silicon chips in the same terms as we talk about our fellow human beings, we can no longer feel quite certain that it is, and always will remain, utterly inappropriate to apply such language to machines. For the fact is that major corporations, hard-headed bankers and sober-minded bureaucrats, as well as scientists and engineers, are taking the possibility of artificial intelligence very seriously indeed. They are already looking forward to the day when, it is claimed, our lives will be transformed by machines that will think about problems, dispense expertise, take decisions and express opinions.

Such a prospect raises issues that must concern us all — as human beings as well as potential purchasers, users or customers of mechanized intelligence. What exactly do we mean by a thinking machine? How does artificial intelligence differ from human intelligence? Can computers ever know things in the same sense as we know them? If we do succeed in building intelligent machines, what purposes will they serve?

These are the sort of questions that we have had in mind while writing this book. But we do not pretend, indeed we have not sought, to provide conclusive answers to them. Instead we have tried to demystify a subject that is all too often discussed in terms both obscure and intimidating to the lay reader. It is our hope that by explaining in plain language and as clearly as possible how the technology works and how even relatively simple machines can be made to seem intelligent, we may help people to decide for themselves whether, and to what extent, the claims made for artificial intelligence can be justified.

Our approach is, therefore, both cautious and sceptical. This is not to say that we regard artificial intelligence as either unimportant or uninteresting — quite the contrary. But we do feel that the subject is too often discussed in terms which suggest that it is somehow *more* interesting and *more* important than human intelligence, when in fact much of the fascination of the endeavour lies in the light which it casts upon the original, and still by far the most advanced 'thinking machine' — the human brain.

Although artificial intelligence has only lately begun to hit the headlines, it is a comparatively well-established field of research going back more than thirty years. The first pioneers were primarily concerned to show that the computer was more than just an extremely fast calculating device — that it could manipulate symbols and perform logical operations as well as adding, subtracting, multiplying and dividing. In fact, the subject that eventually became known as artificial intelligence could have been given a dozen different names – non-numerical computing, logic calculation, symbolic processing, etc. – which would have attracted little attention and raised no eyebrows in the wider world beyond the computer laboratory.

However, once it had been given the title of artificial intelligence, it was almost inevitable that the field would become the subject of controversy and that people's perceptions of its aims and potential would become polarized. As a result those who look forward to the advent of intelligent machinery with enthusiasm have tended to overestimate the chances of success, while those who view the prospect with foreboding have tended to underestimate the benefits success might bring. In this book we have tried to avoid both extremes and to take a cool look at what has so far been achieved and what may realistically be expected.

One of the best possible examples of what may turn out to be the real value of intelligent machines is provided by the illustrations in this book, which were all produced by computer graphics. It is certainly fair to say that had we been trying to prepare a similar set of illustrations twenty years ago the task would have been infinitely more arduous and the results far less satisfactory. But it is also true to say that, for all its ingenuity, the graphics computer provided no more than an immensely fast and adaptable tool which would have been useless had it not been for the intelligence of Mark Norton of the 4i Design Partnership at Imagine, whose skill, patience and enthusiasm are beyond the scope of any imaginable machine.

I.A.

P.B.

February 1987

CHAPTER 1

WHAT DO WE MEAN BY INTELLIGENCE?

It would be difficult to discuss the workings of even relatively simple machines, such as washing machines say, or sewing machines, unless we understood the functions they were designed to perform. Since artificial intelligence is concerned with perhaps the most complex kind of machines we can envisage, 'intelligent machines', prudence suggests that we should begin by trying to define what we expect such machines to do. Obviously, we expect them to be intelligent. But what do we mean by 'intelligence'?

If we turn to a dictionary we find that intelligence is defined as 'the faculty of understanding' and that to understand something means to comprehend it or to recognize its significance. This is a concept that seems clear enough when we apply it subjectively – that is, it seems to correspond reasonably accurately to our own individual experience of what it is like to be intelligent or to use our intelligence. Unfortunately, however, it begins to fall apart as soon as we try to apply it objectively, to consider intelligence as a faculty which might be shared by other entities, whether living or mechanical.

Part of the problem is that while we know what it feels like to understand something, and are generally willing to credit other people with sensations similar to our own, the feeling is one that can, in the final analysis, only be attested to by the person who achieves the understanding. If we want objective evidence that something has been understood by someone – or something – other than ourselves then we must look for it in their behaviour. A teacher, for example, will only be satisfied that his pupils have really understood long division or the proper use of the past present tense in French if they can successfully complete a test on the subject.

However, even though we may doubt that understanding exists unless it has been demonstrated by intelligent behaviour, we do not always accept apparently intelligent behaviour as conclusive proof that something has been understood – and we are likely to be especially sceptical where machines are concerned. To take a simple example, consider a familiar piece of machinery, the thermostat in a central heating system. It does not just recognize when the temperature falls below or rises above a certain level, it responds by taking the appropriate action. In a single, admittedly very limited, respect it seems to possess understanding and to demonstrate this in the clearest possible fashion, by behaving intelligently. But if we concede that elementary devices like thermostats are intelligent, we devalue the word to the point at which it becomes meaningless.

The issue can, of course, be sidestepped in several ways. It could be argued that a device which behaves intelligently in one respect, and one respect only, is so limited that its claims to be intelligent can safely be disregarded. A more sophisticated argument would be that if the device *seems* to behave intelligently this is due in part to the ingenuity of its designer and in part to the judgement of the householder who has set the dial to the desired temperature. The thermostat is not intelligent, in short, because its operations are predetermined and entirely 'mechanical'.

A similar argument is employed by those who seek to explain away apparently intelligent behaviour on the part of other creatures, the main difference being that the design of the mechanism is now attributed, according to the beliefs of the individual, either to God or to evolution.

This argument faces us with formidable difficulties no matter whether we reject it or accept it. If we reject it we find ourselves in a position which most people would consider absurd. We would, for example, logically be forced to conclude that insects, which often behave in ways that are, from an objective point of view, highly intelligent, do so because they understand the situation in which they find themselves and work out what to do about it. This seems unlikely, to say the least. But if we accept that behaviour on the part of some creatures – or machines – which seems to be intelligent is entirely mechanistic, where do we draw the line?

If ants build their intricate nests as the result of some sort of evolutionary pre-programming, what about birds? And if the birds, too, are simply following instructions 'wired into' their brains, what about the beaver's dam? And, ultimately, what about our own behaviour as builders of homes?

If, on the other hand, we do not believe that the sort of understanding that is possessed by other creatures, or by machines which maintain the sitting-room temperature at a comfortable level, constitutes intelligence, we have to ask ourselves in what sense a truly intelligent machine would understand things. The answer that comes most readily to mind is that it would do so in the same sense as we do.

But are we really clear about the nature of our own understanding and how it relates to our behaviour? Does the experience of being intelligent provide us with a bedrock upon which we can build a more useful definition of the word? Unfortunately, we again find that the concepts begin to slip through our fingers when we try to analyse them in everyday terms.

We would all agree, for example, that in many instances understanding is synonymous with knowledge – there is no useful distinction between 'knowing' how to tie a shoelace, or that Mount Everest is the highest mountain, and 'understanding' the same things. But most of us would instinctively resist the idea that simply knowing more than other people justifies a claim to be more intelligent. Since some people clearly have more opportunity or inclination to acquire knowledge than others, this would seem patently unfair. It would, for example, lead us to the conclusion that the winners of the TV quiz shows, who have clearly demonstrated that they know more than the losers, have also proved themselves to be more intelligent.

It was because the simple equation between knowledge and intelligence is so clearly inadequate that psychologists tried to develop techniques for measuring 'pure intelligence': tests in which the subject's success did not depend upon the amount of knowledge that he possessed. The underlying assumption was that there was a 'thing' called General Intelligence, or g, which some people had more of than others, and that a subject's 'intelligence quotient', or IQ, was a measure of that individual's g in exactly the same way as an engine's horsepower is a measure of the energy it is able to generate.

General Intelligence, however, turned out to be a concept of dubious value when applied in practice, and the whole question of using IQ tests to measure people's worth or suitability for a job has become extremely controversial. In part this is because the tests, especially when applied to children, were suspected of producing results that were anomalous and unjust; and in part because, over the past thirty years, the theoretical assumptions on which the tests are based have come to look less and less secure.

Some critics have argued that, rather than being a quality like, say, physical strength, which can be measured and quantified, g is merely a statistical abstraction. On this view, to take the results of a series of tests, each designed to measure a different kind of skill, and factor them together to produce a single figure – the subject's IQ – is as meaningless as it would be to time a runner over every distance from the 100 metres sprint to the marathon, calculate his average speed, and then say that the resulting figure represented his 'athletic quotient'. The mathematical technique used by the intelligence testers, known as factor analysis, is considerably more complicated than simple averaging, but the conclusions it leads to are, the critics claim, even more fallacious in that there is no evidence that the thing they set out to measure actually exists. The obvious conclusion of this line of argument is that if IQ tests measure anything, it is the capacity to do IQ tests!

But if the concept of a unified General Intelligence is abandoned, what we left with? Should we break intelligence down into separate faculties such as perception, reason, creativity? And if so, where do we stop? If we grant that a concert pianist has the faculty of 'musicality', then can we deny that a plumber or a polo-player also have faculties of equivalent status? We cannot argue that it takes more intelligence to be a good pianist than to be a good plumber because we have started from the premise that intelligence, in the abstract, is no more than a convenient fiction.

The critics have also focussed on the growing volume of evidence that seems to show that, whatever intelligence might be, it is not a quality that is innate and invariable. A person is not, it is argued, allotted a predetermined ration of intelligence at birth by 'nature', as some are allotted blue eyes and others red hair. Instead intelligence is a potential which people realize to differing degrees according to their 'nurture'. On this view, people who grow up in an environment which favours the development of intelligence are more likely to become highly intelligent for much the same reasons that people born in Switzerland are likely to become good skiers.

HOW COULD WE TELL IF A MACHINE WAS INTELLIGENT?

Rather than becoming embroiled in the controversies which surround the nature of human intelligence, the practitioners of artificial intelligence have generally chosen to define their goals in empirical or operational terms rather than theoretical ones. An intelligent machine, they suggest, is one that is able to do things which, if done by people, would be judged to require intelligence. On this basis, a definition of intelligence becomes unnecessary: the researcher simply choses a task that seems to require intelligence (playing chess, say, or recognizing visual images) and tries to build a machine that can accomplish it. If the attempt is successful, the machine will have shown itself to be intelligent. This seems, at first sight, a workmanlike and commonsense approach. After all, even if we cannot agree what intelligence *is*, we have no difficulty in recognizing when other people are behaving intelligently – why should we not apply the same standard to a machine?

Unfortunately, it turns out that this argument can easily be turned upon its head by people who, for one reason or another, dislike and distrust the prospect of artificial intelligence. To the proposition that if people need intelligence to perform some function, then a machine that can duplicate the feat must be intelligent, sceptics can respond with the argument that once it has been shown that a machine can do something then, whatever was previously believed, it is now obvious that the task is entirely 'mechanical'. If we can explain *how* the machine works then we have explained away its apparent intelligence.

Human intelligence thus becomes an 'explanation' that cannot itself be explained, since it is only invoked to account for behaviour which would otherwise be inexplicable. Put in those terms the argument sounds transparently silly. But to see how seductive it is we need only look at an activity which has been of great interest to artificial intelligence researchers – chess-playing. Most people would accept that this is something which requires intelligence; indeed we commonly think of a good chess-player as someone who is, almost by definition, highly intelligent. Yet it has proved possible to construct machines which can compete successfully against all but the very best human players. Surely we cannot deny that such machines are intelligent?

In practice, we do just that. For someone who walks into the games department of a store and buys a chess-playing machine does not think of it as an intelligent machine, but simply as an ingenious piece of gadgetry. In part this may be because many people so dislike the idea of an intelligent machine that they will refuse to acknowledge any evidence for artificial intelligence, however convincing it may be. Certainly some researchers have come to believe that such 'human chauvinism' makes it impossible for them ever to satisfy the sceptics; every time it looks as if they might get the ball in the net, they say, their opponents move the goal posts.

Even if we put aside the possibility of prejudice, however, there are still at least two very significant questions which we must answer if we are to satisfy ourselves that a chess-playing machine is indeed intelligent. The first is this: even if we admit that such machines behave intelligently, may it not be that the intelligence we witness is a property of the people who program them and not of the machines themselves? We will pass over this point for the moment because we will be returning to it in Chapter 2. But the second question is, if anything, even more fundamental: might there not be a distinction that can be drawn between intelligent behaviour and behaviour which merely *appears* to be intelligent?

Even to ask this question is, obviously, to challenge the very assumptions upon which most work in artificial intelligence has been based. Indeed, if we are not prepared to accept intelligent behaviour at face value and acknowledge that it is evidence of intelligence, then the people who are engaged in artificial intelligence might very well ask what evidence we *would* accept. Nevertheless, the issue is a genuine one and it lies at the very heart of the controversy between the proponents of 'hard AI' – the people, mostly involved in the field, who argue that if a machine behaves intelligently then only a pedant would deny that it is intelligent – and their critics, usually from other disciplines, who say that such arguments are simplistic and naive.

This debate has very strong parallels with the controversy that has raged between the behaviourist school of psychology and its opponents over the past half century. The behaviourists argue that if psychology claims to be the *science* of the mind, it can only concern itself with those aspects of the mind which can be observed, that is, with people's outward behaviour. What goes on inside their heads cannot be observed or measured objectively, therefore it is irrelevant – or, in the view of the more extreme behaviourists, merely a subjective illusion. Those who dispute the behaviourist case, on the other hand, point out that a psychology which limits itself to the study of what people do and ignores what they think is hardly worthy of the name.

A behaviourist, clearly, would accept that if a machine is able to duplicate intelligent behaviour then there can be no possible grounds for refusing to acknowledge its intelligence. But if we take the view that intelligent behaviour is merely the outward manifestation of internal processes, and that it is those processes that actually constitute intelligence, then we must consider the possibility that a machine might merely simulate the appearance of intelligence without actually *being* intelligent.

Naturally, since we do not know what goes on inside our heads, acceptance of this argument implies that our own intelligence may also be in some fashion illusory – perhaps we only *think* we are intelligent. In the case of a machine, however, we *can* establish the nature of the internal processes. As we shall see in Chapter 2, this raises another fundamental question: if a machine and a person display similar behaviour, is it legitimate to assume that the internal processes which produce that behaviour are in some way comparable?

To return to the controversy over the status of machine intelligence, we can illustrate the opposing points of view by looking at two famous 'experiments'. The first of these, the Turing Test, was originally proposed in 1950 by one of the prophets of artificial intelligence, the British mathematician Alan Turing, in a paper entitled 'Computing Machinery and Intelligence'.

The experiment, as Turing envisaged it, is shown below. His idea was that if a human being was unable to determine, from an exchange of dialogue on any subject he chose to explore, whether he was talking to a machine or another human being, then it would be 'unfair' to deny that the machine was intelligent.

If behaviour were the sole criterion of intelligence it would be hard to fault the Turing Test. For if the machine was to be successful it would not only have to cope with questions like 'What is the square root of 144?' or 'Can you tell me the population of Rio de Janeiro?' which could be answered by any computer with an appropriate program and access to a substantial database; it would also have to be able to improvise convincing lies when asked 'What did you have for breakfast?' or 'Do you find computers scary?' and therefore know how a human being could be expected to respond and behave accordingly.

But what about understanding? Is it safe to assume that because a machine behaves as if it understands things, it understands them in

The Turing Test. The 'interrogator' sits on one side of a screen equipped with a teletype terminal connected to two other terminals, one operated by a human being, one by a machine. Both 'witnesses' must provide answers to any and every question the interrogator cares to put to them. The machine will have passed the test if, at the conclusion of the experiment, the interrogator is unable to say which of the two witnesses is the machine and which the human being.

Turing suggested that by the year 2000 it would be possible to program computers so well that the average interrogator would not have more than a 70 percent chance of making the right identification after five minutes of questioning.

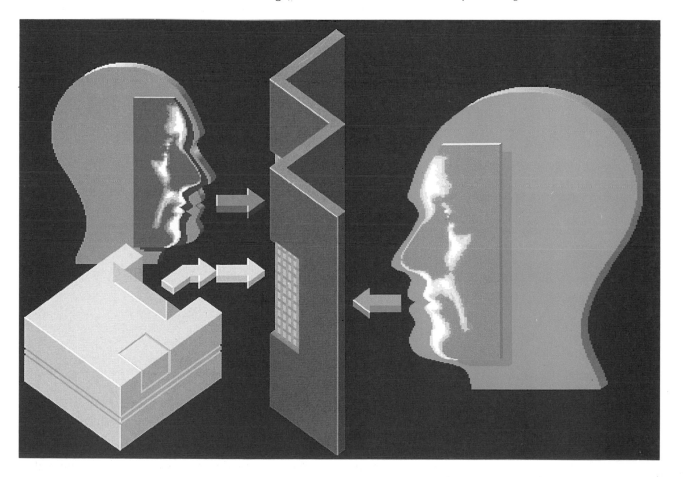

The Chinese Room, a thought-experiment in which we are asked to imagine a room containing a complete set of instructions for manipulating and combining Chinese characters. These instructions are written entirely in English and can be implemented by any group of people who can follow them and match one Chinese character against another simply on the basis of their appearance. Now suppose that a story written in Chinese is passed into the room through a hatch (below), followed by a series of questions about the story, also written in Chinese (opposite top). By referring to their rules the people inside the room, none of whom know Chinese, should in principle be able to produce a third set of Chinese characters, representing the answers (opposite bottom).

The programs produced by researchers trying to enable computers to use natural language operate in just this way. They are simply sets of rules which may be applied to one set of symbols in order to produce another set.

the same sense as we do? Some of those who accept Turing's argument have suggested that such a question is meaningless. The American philosopher Daniel Dennett, for example, has said that if a chess-playing machine appears to be trying to win a game, then there is no point in asking whether it really *wants* to win. The issue arises because, as we shall see in Chapter 3, the programs that such a machine runs do not embody the concept of 'winning' in any form which a human player would find recognizable, but Dennett's case is that, whether or not we are aware that this is so, it is irrelevant since we could not deduce it from the machine's behaviour. If the machine *seems* to be trying to defeat us then we might as well assume that it is.

It was in order to expose what he sees as a basic fallacy in such arguments that another American philosopher, John Searle, devised the 'thought experiment' shown here. The particular target Searle had in mind was not game-playing machines but the branch of artificial intelligence concerned with trying to develop machines that can use 'natural language' (see Chapter 5). He showed that it is possible to envisage, in principle though not in practice, circumstances in which people might behave as if they were perfectly fluent in a foreign language while, in reality, not being able to understand a word of it. Artificial intelligence researchers, he suggested, had totally failed to appreciate that there was a fundamental difference between their machines, which behave as if

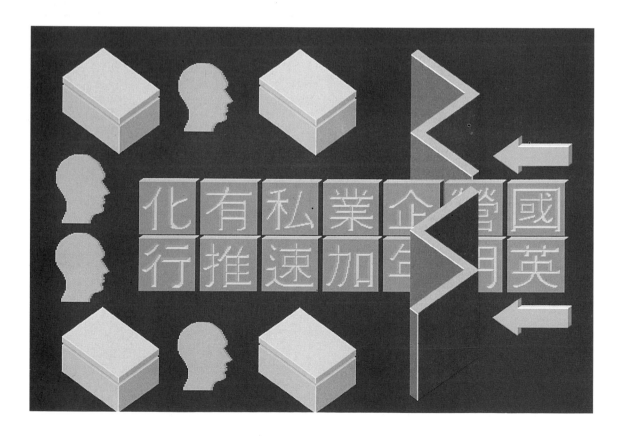

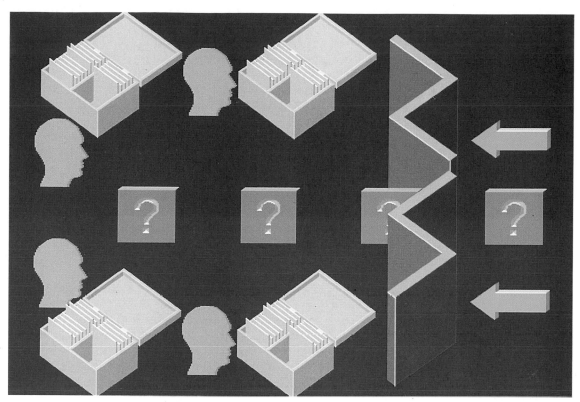

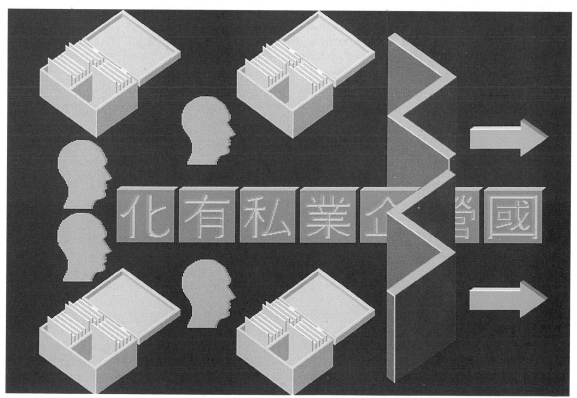

they understand things, and people, who genuinely understand them.

The crux of Searle's argument is that when we say that we understand a language we mean that we can relate the symbols – the print on the page, the sounds coming out of a loudspeaker – to objects and events in the real world. We are able to do this, he claims, and machines cannot, because we possess the quality of 'intentionality'.

Intentionality is such a crucial concept that it is worth pausing to try to see exactly what it means. Certainly, as Searle and others use it, it amounts to something far more than simply having intentions or being able to express them. Perhaps the best way of describing it is to say that it is the quality of 'knowing what one is talking (or thinking) about'. It is because we possess intentionality, for example, that we can empathize with the characters in a story and understand what is meant when they are described as angry or hungry or frightened – the words are not just sets of symbols on the page which can be defined in terms of other sets of symbols in a dictionary, they evoke images or emotions which relate to our own experience.

We can see the significance of intentionality if we consider how difficult it is to describe an unfamiliar object without referring to familiar ones. Consider, for example, how indispensable we find phrases like pear-shaped, mushroom cloud, hairpin bend, Vee formation or razor-sharp which can be relied upon to conjure up an image in the minds of our audience.

Searle's case is that, in the absence of intentionality, words are ultimately meaningless, for they can only be defined in terms of other words. Thus, even though a machine may have mastered all the grammatical rules that govern the way in which words may be combined, it will still only be employing a sort of verbal algebra, manipulating abstract symbols according to a set of formal rules. It will never understand why it is meaningless to talk of mushroom bends or describe a knife as pear-sharp.

KNOWING ABOUT REALITY

In the case of human beings intentionality depends upon our ability to construct internal representations of the external world. We could not understand what the phrase 'mushroom-shaped' meant unless some sort of mental image of a mushroom was already stored inside our heads, and we would not possess a mental image of a mushroom if we had never seen one, or at least a picture of one. Our understanding of reality, and thus our ability to think and talk about it, ultimately depend upon the fact that we have experienced it through the medium of the senses.

Much work is currently being done, as we shall see in subsequent chapters, on equipping machines with sensors that will allow them to experience reality at first hand. But the general assumption in artificial intelligence has been that, rather than trying to get machines to construct their own internal representations on the basis of their own experience, much time and effort can be saved by providing them with a pre-packaged version of reality. Even if we understood the mechanisms by which we translate sensory data into experience, why should we attempt to reproduce them? Why not simply tell machines what they need to know about reality in order to perform their allotted functions?

On the face of it, the distinction between first-hand experience and knowledge passed on at second hand might seem unimportant. After all, even human beings frequently apply their intelligence to aspects of the world which they only know about from other people's reports. We can, for example, plan a touring trip by looking at a road atlas. The images on the page may only be symbolic representations of reality, but they conveniently summarize all we need to know about the real landscape we will be traversing. Why should a machine be considered any less intelligent because it reasons about a 'map' of reality rather than a reality which it has itself experienced?

However, a moment's consideration will show us that our ability to understand the information in the road atlas depends entirely upon the fact that we can attach meanings to the symbols that represent the various features of the terrain. Unless we had seen forests and rivers and driven along roads, the big green patches and the blue and red lines on the map would be no more than marks on paper. We could, of course, be provided with instructions to tell us that our route must follow the red lines, that it can only cross a blue line where there is a bridge symbol, and that the green patches are likely to be good places in which to have a picnic lunch. But at that point, surely, we have stopped planning a real journey through a real landscape and are merely playing a formal game. Our intelligence has ceased to have intentionality because it is no longer being applied to a representation of reality but to a series of problems that are wholly artificial: the rule that says we cannot travel along the blue lines has become as arbitrary as the rules that govern the movements of the various pieces on a chessboard.

Even so, if all reality, or even some aspects of it, could be accurately represented by sets of formal rules such as those that apply to chessmen, then the difference between human intelligence, anchored to the real world by intentionality, and an artificial intelligence which manipulated pre-packaged versions of reality, might be considered purely academic. The distinction between *being* intelligent and *seeming to be* intelligent would become a mere semantic quibble which had no practical implications, in that an intelligent being and a being capable of mimicking intelligence would behave in exactly the same way.

In practice, however, it has proved remarkably difficult to pre-package reality in this fashion. True, some limited aspects of the real world have proved amenable to the treatment, notably those we have already described in a highly formalized way for our own purposes. The movement of the planets or the workings of a national economy, for example, are phenomena which we ourselves can only understand in terms of abstract mathematical or logical rules which allow us 'model' their workings. Yet all the evidence suggests that, although we may make use of such formal representations of reality when seeking to understand very complex phenomena which we cannot experience at first hand through the senses, our understanding of the everyday world is based on very different principles.

Consider, for example, a commonplace skill which most children master between the ages of five and ten – catching a ball. At the age of five a child may well have difficulty in catching a beach-ball tossed gently at the range of a couple of yards, yet a few years later he will probably be able to catch a tennis ball lobbed high in the air from twenty yards away. Obviously, the improved dexterity of the older child is an important factor, but how do we account for the fact that he is also able, as the younger child is not, to calculate very rapidly indeed where the ball is going to land and move to intercept it?

A scientifically-minded visitor from a planet where ball games were unknown might well conclude that this was a piece of strikingly intelligent behaviour, demonstrating that human children mastered the mathematical technique for calculating a ballistic trajectory at an impressively early age. We, on the other hand, having been through the experience in our own childhood, are well aware that the ten-year-old has probably never heard of ballistics, indeed we know that children were successfully catching balls for centuries before Newton formulated the laws which govern the trajectory of a missile in free flight.

To put it another way, we could say that the child's feat is comparable in principle to that of the computers linked to a ballistic missile warning system which are designed to calculate, on the basis of information from radar sensors, where and when an approaching warhead is going to land. But, clearly, even though we might say that somewhere in the child's mind there must be a representation of 'The rules governing the behaviour of balls', it is quite unlike the rules for calculating missile trajectories which have been programmed into the computers. Not only are the two kinds of understanding couched in different terms – one intuitive and not capable of being expressed in any formal language, the other rigorous and mathematically explicit – they have been acquired in totally different ways.

The child's understanding has been gained by *induction*. It is as a result of watching the trajectories of many balls and trying, with varying degrees of success, to catch them, that the ten-year-old has become capable of predicting the trajectory of the next ball he wants to catch. The computer, by contrast, has been provided with a program that enables it to *deduce* the flightpath of a missile by reference to a set of formal mathematical rules.

Thus, although a neutral observer might conclude that the behaviour of the two 'systems' was comparable and that, by Turing Test criteria, both were equally intelligent, we can see that the representations of reality which they rely upon are not just different in nature, they have also originated in very different ways.

It might seem that an intelligence which operates on deductive principles, employing formal and explicit rules, must be superior to one which relies upon vague and informal rules of thumb derived from experience by means of induction. After all, few people would dispute the proposition that calculating a ballistic trajectory mathematically requires more intelligence than simply being able to catch a ball.

Indeed education, which could be thought of as one of the means by which nurture makes us more intelligent, is very largely concerned with fitting knowledge that was originally acquired through inductive learning into a deductive framework – as is the case with ten-year-old children, already good at catching balls, who subsequently go on to master Newton's laws. But although knowledge which has been systematized and made explicit in this way gains a new status, in that it allows us to understand in principle what we previously grasped only intuitively, it is far from clear that it always becomes more useful or more accessible in practice. Even a mathematician does not solve equations in his head as he runs for a difficult catch.

It is also becoming clearer, largely as a result of research into artificial intelligence, that a good deal of the knowledge which we garner through the rough-and-ready process of induction cannot satisfactorily be expressed in the precise and logical language of deduction. Often, this knowledge is so familiar to us that we take it for granted and barely consider it the province of intelligence; and yet it is precisely the kind of knowledge upon which we rely most heavily in the course of our daily lives.

We have no difficulty, for example, in picking one particular object out of a jumble of objects loosely piled into a box. Indeed we would probably say that we do it 'without thinking'. But it has so far proved impossible to write a program – provide a set of formal, deductive rules – that will enable a robot to duplicate the feat. Similarly, we can distinguish, let us say, a peach from a plum, a poodle from a pekinese or a Peugeot from a Pontiac without, apparently, applying any intelligence to the question at all. Yet programmers are as yet finding it very difficult to devise rules that will allow artificial vision systems reliably to distinguish nuts from bolts.

These are in fact just two instances of a paradox which, it is now evident, presents artificial intelligence with a major challenge. Even if, as seems entirely possible, we are able to build machines that behave in ways which in human terms might be said to require a high degree of intelligence, it does not follow that they will be capable of performing simple, everyday tasks which we scarcely rate as intelligent at all. It begins to look as if, far from being a ramshackle, improvised and inferior way of learning, induction may allow the brain to deal with complexities and resolve ambiguities which a system based on deductive principles simply cannot cope with.

If this is indeed the case, then we shall have to revise our ideas of what constitutes intelligence. And we may find that rather than being the starting point for a discussion of artificial intelligence, a precise answer to the question, 'What do we mean by intelligence?', is one of the most important of the goals that artificial intelligence researchers should be striving to attain.

CHAPTER 2

A UNIVERSAL MACHINE

Starting from the premise that intelligence should be defined as the quality which enables human beings to behave intelligently, there are two ways in which artificial intelligence researchers might set about the task of producing intelligent machines. They can, as we have already suggested, select particular instances of intelligent behaviour and try to design machines that can replicate that behaviour. Alternatively, they can study the biological mechanisms that underlie human intelligence and try to build machines which work on similar principles, in the expectation that those machines will share the property of being intelligent.

These two approaches, known respectively as 'top-down' and 'bottom-up', are fundamentally different: they start from different assumptions, they pursue different research strategies and, in some respects at least, they have different goals. These differences have divided the people who work in the field into two opposing schools of thought right from the start – indeed, the lines upon which the rift was to open up could be discerned even before the term 'artificial intelligence' had been coined.

Until comparatively recently, however, the scales seemed to be weighted heavily in favour of the advocates of a top-down approach; so much so that there are still many people who would define artificial intelligence exclusively in top-down terms and would regard the bottom-up approach as being something very close to heresy. This book will not take sides in the dispute – though it does aim to redress the balance somewhat, by showing that the bottom-up approach has now advanced to the point at which it can make contributions of real significance.

INFORMATION MACHINES

Before we discuss the two approaches and the theoretical assumptions that underlie them, we must go back to look at the watershed from which both have sprung. This is the idea of an 'information machine'. A machine which, unlike the majority of machines that are designed to generate energy or to transform one kind of energy into another, operates in the medium of information: given inputs of information it processes them into outputs of information and the fact that it consumes energy in the process is irrelevant to its primary function.

In order to design an information machine, no matter whether it be an adding machine or a supercomputer, it is necessary to find some way in which information can be represented by the 'state' of a mechanism. The basic idea of using the state of a mechanism to represent information, especially numerical information, has been exploited in a hundred and one familiar devices. Consider, for example, the dashboard of a car: each of the instruments, the speedometer, the fuel gauge, the rev counter, the various warning lights and so on, conveys information to the driver by changing the state of its components – by moving needles or switching bulbs on and off. But these devices are scarcely information processors, their function is to respond to an input of energy by producing an output which conveys information to the driver, usually when read off against some scale. Their functions are, moreover, very specific – an oil pressure gauge is useless other than as a means of monitoring oil pressure.

There is a far more ancient device, the abacus, which can be used to represent numerical information in the abstract – the numbers represented by the state of the beads may themselves represent anything we please. But although an abacus may be said to store numbers it barely qualifies as a machine since the beads must be manipulated by hand and the accuracy of a calculation is determined not by the device itself, but entirely by the skills of the operator.

The first true information machines were the mechanical calculators which appeared in seventeenth-century Europe. The inventors of the earliest machines, the philosophers Pascal and Leibnitz, used a series of interlinked wheels, each of which could be rotated through ten states representing the digits from 0 to 9, and this idea continued to form the basis of all calculating machinery for the next two centuries. Even today, despite the fact that electronic calculators have supplanted mechanical ones, the principle is still employed in a host of familiar devices.

From Blaise Pascal's invention of the mechanical calculator in 1642 until the revolutionary developments in electronics during the Second World War, wheels were the primary means of representing numerical information in terms of the state of a mechanism. Far and away the commonest arrangement, used in everything from adding machines to mileometers, is the one shown here. The circumference of each wheel is divided into ten segments, representing the digits from 0 to 9. If a set of such wheels rotate about a common axle it is comparatively easy to arrange matters so that whenever a wheel passes from 9 to 0 a ratchet moves the next wheel to the right on by one digit. Rather more complicated systems involving stepped gearwheels are required to deal with multiplication and division and to compute mathematical tables such as logarithms. Charles Babbage's 'difference engine' (seen here in the background) employed tiers of interlocking gearwheels.

Far and away the most ambitious scheme for a machine of this kind was that proposed by the nineteenth-century English scientist Charles Babbage. His projected 'analytical engine' has indeed often been described as a direct precursor of the computer because it embodied so many of the ideas which would finally be realized, in electronic form, a century later – most notably the division of the mechanism into two parts: a 'store', or memory, and a 'mill', or processor. Like many of the computer's immediate predecessors, it was designed to read its inputs off a series of punched cards and, like the computer itself, it would have 'printed out' the results of its operations. But Babbage's visionary design was far ahead of its time, and it was never brought to fruition largely because it demanded a degree of precision in its construction that was beyond the capacity of contemporary engineering.

Although faster and more elaborate calculating machines continued to appear throughout the nineteenth and early twentieth centuries, the next real breakthrough in information machines came in the 1930s. It followed the realization by a few engineers that there was another commonplace mechanism, the switch, which might replace the wheel as the basic element in a calculator. At first glance the advantages of a switch may seem far from obvious: it has, after all, only two states, *on* and *off*, whereas a wheel that rotates in a series of 'clicks' can, in principle, have ten, a hundred or even a thousand different states. Or, to put it slightly differently, a rotating wheel moves through a continuum of states which may, in principle, be divided and subdivided *ad infinitum*; though in practice the number of states will be limited by the precision with which the movement of the wheel can be regulated.

The difference between devices like switches which are confined to a limited range of *discrete* states, and something like a wheel which has an infinite continuum of states is crucial. For the former are inherently *digital* – their very nature makes them suitable for representing information that is divided into separate, evenly-sized and irreducible chunks. Wheels, on the other hand, can be used, as a series of switches cannot, to represent *analogue* information.

The distinction between analogue and digital information can be illustrated by a simple example. Suppose that a carpenter wants to replace a damaged bookshelf with another piece of wood of exactly the same size. He may measure the new timber in two ways. If he lays the old piece on top of it and marks off the position of the ends he will have made an analogue measurement, and the new shelf will, at least in theory, be exactly the same length as the old one. But if he takes a measuring tape and determines the length of the old shelf to the nearest inch or centimetre and then marks off that dimension on the new timber, he will have made a digital measurement. Analogue measurements can of course be converted to digital ones, but the conversion will always involve a degree of arbitrariness, of rounding off to the nearest unit or sub-unit. In mathematics, for example, there are 'real numbers', such as π or the square root of 2, which are infinite decimals and can never be expressed in digital form with complete accuracy.

The 1930s saw the development of a whole variety of analogue devices, often designed to solve complex mathematical problems, some of them entirely mechanical, others using electrical currents to represent numerical information. Even today, there are many applications in which computers that use voltages or currents as analogues of physical quantities are preferable to digital systems – a typical example is the equipment used to monitor and control flow processes in the chemical industry. But since analogue information is, by definition, an analogy of some physical quantity, analogue machinery is generally limited to specific functions. Even when a general-purpose device can be thought of as being either analogue or digital – and the best example of this is probably the brain itself, as we shall see in subsequent chapters – it will nearly always be easier to think of it in digital terms.

In the case of calculators, digital systems are obviously preferable to analogue ones because arithmetic itself is digital. But the real advantage of using switches rather than wheels to represent numerical information only becomes apparent when we abandon the idea that the familiar decimal system is the only, or even the best, way of expressing numbers. For it will be clear that, using ten digits, the simplest possible system will require nine switches to represent a single digit – when all are set to 'off' the state of the combination will represent 0, when all are set to 'on' it will represent 9.

But if we turn to the binary system, where there are just two digits, 0 and 1, the switch comes into its own – one switch can be used to represent one binary digit, or *bit*. (Those unfamiliar with the binary system may find it helpful at this point to glance at the diagram on the next page). The earliest switch-based systems were those built in the late 1930s by two American teams led by George Stiblitz of Bell Telephone and Howard Aitken of Harvard University and by the young German engineer, Konrad Zuse. All employed electro-mechanical relays: switches in which one electrical current is used to open or close a circuit through which another electrical current flows – the most familiar example of such a switch is probably the solenoid which switches on the starter motor of a car when the ignition key is turned.

Relays can be switched on and off several times a second, but their operating speed is limited by the fact that the circuit is opened or closed by the movement of mechanical components. The real breakthrough came when engineers began to consider the possibility of electronic switching systems which, because they contain no mechanical elements, can operate within thousandths, even millionths, of a second. It was already well-known in 1940 that the valves or vacuum tubes used in radio sets could, if wired up in combination, operate as electronic switches; the problem was that the valves were highly sensitive devices, prone to frequent failure and producing a great deal of heat. The war, however, proved an enormous stimulus to the development of electronics, and the urgent need for high speed calculators – for calculating artillery range tables, code breaking and, latterly, the designing of the atomic bomb – encouraged engineers to put caution aside and experiment with systems incorporating thousands of valves. The result was that, as the war drew to an end, a whole new breed of

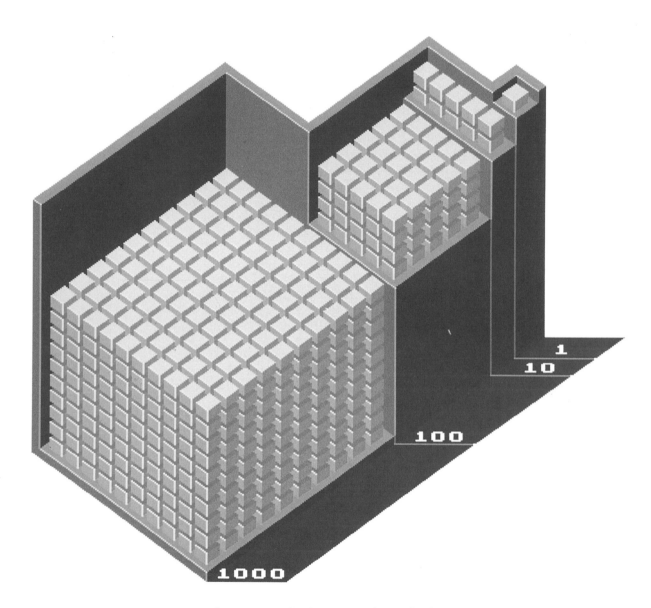

1

10

100

1000

electronic calculating machines had come into existence. Some, like the 'Colossus' machines used at Bletchley Park, the British code-breaking establishment, had already proved their worth; others, like the American ENIAC, were still under construction. Overall, there was no doubt that the use of electronics opened up a host of possibilities for the next generation of information machines.

THE CYBERNETIC REVOLUTION

Initially, everything seemed to point in a direction which favoured the development of what would later be called the bottom-up approach. Those with a speculative turn of mind could already see intriguing parallels between electronic switching systems and the

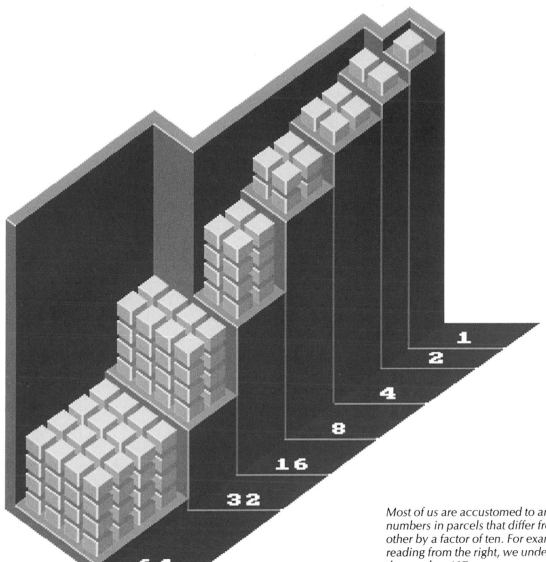

neurons, or nerve cells, which are the basic building blocks of the brain. For W.S. McCulloch and W. Pitts of the University of Illinois had, in 1943, published a paper in which they proposed a model of the neuron's logical function (see Chapter 9) and it was already apparent that the processing circuitry at the heart of a binary calculator could be seen in logical as well as arithmetical terms.

This had in fact been pointed out in 1938 by Claude Shannon in a paper entitled 'A Symbolic Analysis of Relay and Switching Circuits'. The essential point is that the state of a switch can be seen as representing a 'yes' or 'no', a 'true' or a 'false' just as readily as it can be thought of as representing a '1' or a '0'. Thus the *logic gates* which are used to add, multiply, or apply other arithmetical operations to binary digits (see next page), can also be thought of as

Most of us are accustomed to arranging numbers in parcels that differ from each other by a factor of ten. For example, reading from the right, we understand the number 467 as seven ones, six tens and four hundreds. In the binary system there are just two digits, 0 and 1, and the parcels therefore differ from each other by a factor of two: binary 10 (equal to decimal 2) is twice 1, and binary 100 (equal to decimal 4), is twice 10. In order to think in binary we must stop counting in tens, hundreds, thousands, etc., and instead count in their binary equivalents: twos, fours, eights, sixteens, thirty-twos, etc. Thus decimal 467 becomes binary 111010011 or, reading from the right as before, a one, a two, no four, no eight, a sixteen, no thirty-two, a sixty-four, a one hundred and twenty-eight, and a two hundred and fifty-six.

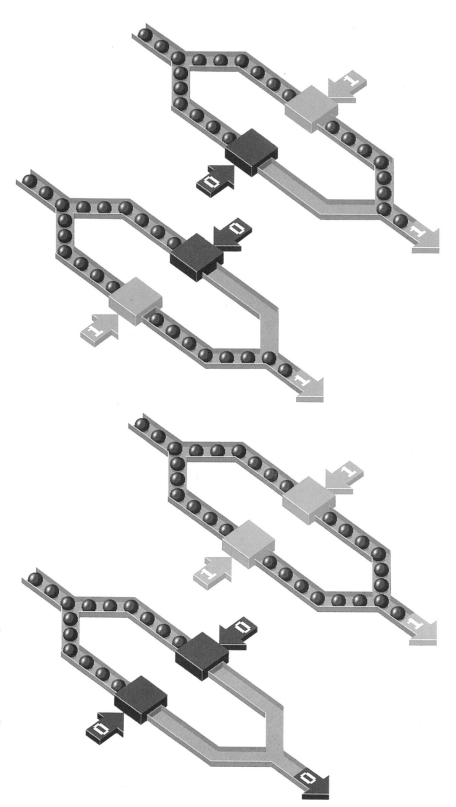

The arithmetic and logic unit of a computer, the bit which actually performs the computations, is made up of thousands of 'gates' – combinations of electronic switches which are turned on or off by inputs of information. There are several different kinds of gate, each designed to implement one particular arithmetical or logical function.

These four pictures show the operations of one of the simplest kinds of gate, an OR gate. When either or both the switches are set to 'on', representing the input of a binary 1, the current will flow from left to right, producing an output that also represents a 1. But if both switches are set to 'off', representing the input of two binary 0s, the output will also be a 0.

implementing logical functions such as 'and', 'or', 'not' etc. Even more importantly, Shannon showed that a circuit which is arranged so that the output of one logical operation is 'fed back' to provide one of the inputs to the next operation will be capable of implementing the 'if' function (see next page).

This last point is crucial because a computation of any complexity will almost always involve what is known as 'conditional branching'. That is, there will come a stage at which the nature of the next step in the calculation will depend upon the result of some previous step. In fact, it is obvious that, unless an information machine can follow instructions which take the form 'If... then...', it will always operate in a fashion that is transparently 'mechanical'.

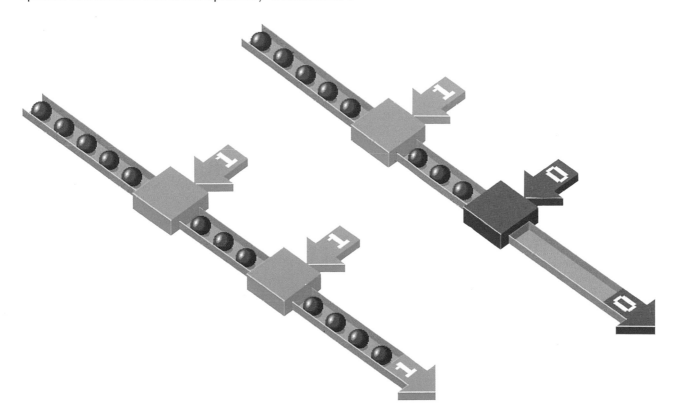

In the late 1940s, Shannon took things even further by developing a theory of information which showed that the binary code is, in principle, universal: that any message, no matter how complex, can be encoded in a string of 1s and 0s and that there is a direct relationship between the number of digits in the string and the amount of information conveyed. Since, according to McCulloch and Pitts' model, messages within the brain and nervous system were passed from neuron to neuron in the form of binary signals (see Chapter 9), this again opened up intriguing possibilities. All in all, it began to look as if the resources required for a bottom-up assault on intelligence were coming together in an extremely promising fashion.

These pictures represent the operations of an AND gate. In this case, if both inputs are 1 the output will be a 1, while all other combinations of input will result in the output of a 0.

Any system of logic gates in which the output of one cycle of operation is fed back as an input into the next cycle will be capable of implementing the IF function. The example shown here, known as a 'latch', is one of the simplest systems of this kind. It is essentially an OR gate in which one of the inputs is provided by the gate's own output. The latch's function is as follows: if the input in the current cycle is a 1, then the output in the next cycle will always be a 1 regardless of the input; but if the input in the current cycle is a 0, then the output in the next cycle will be the same as the input – a 1 input will produce a 1 output, but a 0 input will produce a 0 output.

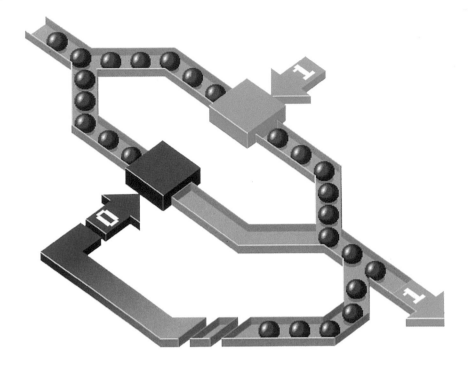

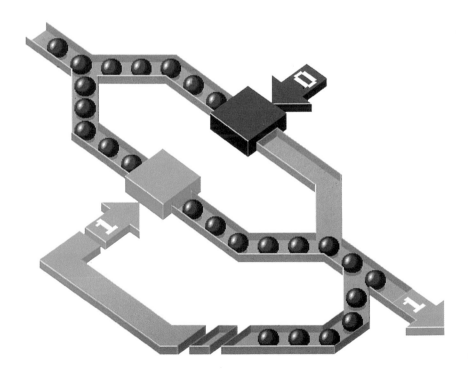

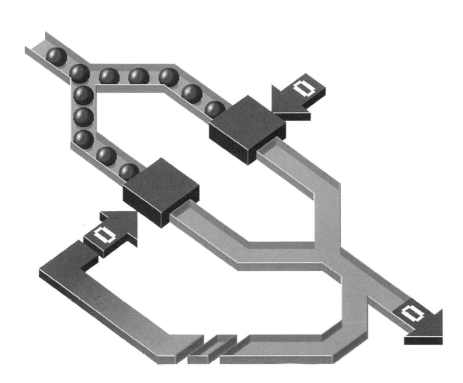

The amount of information that can be conveyed by a string of binary digits is proportional to the length of the string. Here the message to be conveyed is the identity of a single playing card, the 5 of diamonds. Reading from left to right the first digit, a 1 or Yes, represents the answer to the question, 'Is the card red?'; the second digit, a 0 or No, answers the question, 'Is it a heart?'. The remaining four questions, with their answers in brackets, are: 'Is it less than 7?' (Yes); 'Is it less than 4?' (No); 'Is it less than 6?' (Yes); 'Is it the 4 of diamonds?' (No). Therefore, by a process of elimination, it must be the 5 of diamonds. Thus, using this code, the 5 of diamonds is represented by the string 101010, and all the other 51 cards in a pack can be represented by other six digit combinations.

In fact six bits of information can convey 64 different messages. If another digit is added, the number of possible messages doubles to 128, but if a digit is removed, limiting the string to 5 bits, only 32 different messages can be conveyed.

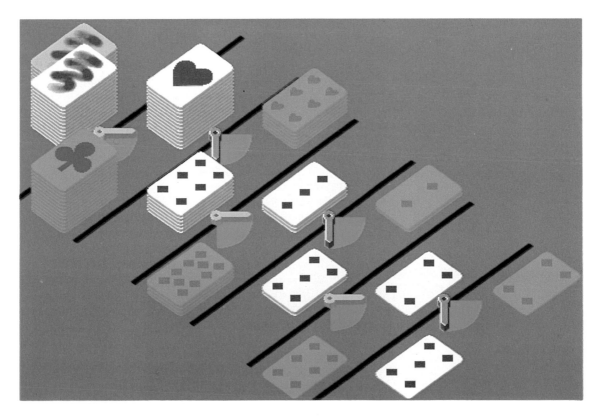

The rising tide of expectation reached a peak in 1947 with the publication of Norbert Weiner's *Cybernetics*, in which he proposed the institution of a new science devoted to the study of control (that is, information) mechanisms in man *and* machine. As a mathematician, Weiner was primarily interested in the theoretical parallels between devices, such as servo-mechanisms, that could be used to regulate and control other machines, and the biological machinery which allowed the brain to regulate and control the body. But he also foresaw the day when it might be possible to build 'working models' of at least some small part of the brain, so-called neural networks. In view of the disrepute into which cybernetics subsequently fell as the result of the naivety and over-optimism of some of Weiner's followers, it is worth remembering that Weiner himself was quite clear that the point of such experiments would be to discover more about ourselves, not to build machines that would supplant human beings.

THE VON NEUMANN MACHINE

For the future science of artificial intelligence, however, the cybernetic revolution of the late 1940s proved to be a false dawn. This was partly due to practical difficulties which we shall look at when we return to the subject of neural networks in Chapter 9, but even more important was the fact that one particular specimen of the new breed of electronic information machines – the stored-program digital computer – quickly achieved pre-eminence. The crucial factors were, firstly, the stored program and, secondly, the fact that the machine turned out to be something a great deal more significant than a mere 'super calculator'.

The idea of storing a program of instructions internally originated as little more than an additional convenience. If a calculator capable of performing thousands of arithmetical operations each second had constantly to mark time while it waited for new instructions from its operator, its speed was largely wasted. But if such a machine could store data – the figures that were fed into it and the intermediate results of its computations – internally, in terms of the states of combinations of electronic switches, why should it not also store its instructions in the same way, thus making them instantly accessible? Thus the idea of a computer program, a series of instructions that can be stored inside a machine and implemented one by one as a task progresses, was born.

Given that the computer was originally conceived as a machine for 'doing arithmetic', it was natural that its inventors, led by the great American mathematician, John von Neumann, should have visualized a program as a linear sequence. After all, every mathematical operation proceeds in a step-by-step fashion; indeed, it is very difficult to envisage any formal, explicit process of reasoning that is not modelled in this way. This requirement, in turn, dictated the design of what we now know simply as the computer, the 'von Neumann machine' as it is sometimes called.

What was needed was a central processing unit (or CPU) consisting, basically, of a processor (sometimes called an arithmetic and logic unit, or ALU) and a control unit which told the CPU what step it was required to take next and regulated the delivery of data to it; a memory which could be used to store both data and program information: and input and output mechanisms. Although developing technolgy has altered the appearance and improved the performance of successive generations of computers almost beyond recognition, this basic structure (see below) has remained unchanged for 40 years. Only now are computer engineers seriously starting to examine the possibility of 'alternative architectures'.

The reasons for the success of the von Neumann machine are very evident. Far from being simply a bigger and better calculator, it has turned out to be a veritable jack of all trades, revolutionizing the factory floor and the games arcade, the secretary's desk, the pilot's cockpit, even the artist's drawing board – as the illustrations in this book make plain. From the present point of view, of course, the vital question is whether the computer can add 'intelligence' to the myriad feathers which already adorn its cap.

The architecture of the traditional von Neumann computer contains three basic elements: a central processing unit, or CPU (red box); a memory (green box) which can store both programs and data; and a control unit (blue box) which takes program information out of memory, tells the CPU what it must do next, and regulates the flow of data back and forth between the memory and the CPU. There are also input and output mechanisms of various kinds.

The essential feature of this architecture is that because the CPU can only deal with information in small chunks of 8, 16 or 32 bits at a time, the computer can only operate in a serial, step-by-step fashion. The CPU of a modern computer can perform hundreds of thousands of logical operations a second, and this often disguises the fact that it deals with large computations by breaking them down into thousands of separate steps, each of which would seem trivial to a human being. But in many branches of artificial intelligence the sheer volume of data that must be processed makes it very difficult for a serial machine to operate in real time, i.e. keep pace with events as they happen in the real world.

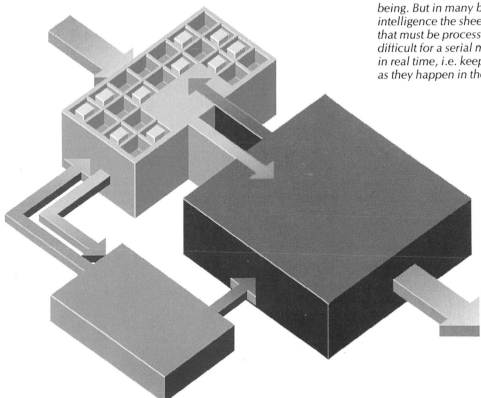

The idea that computers might one day master intelligent behaviour was mooted almost as soon as the first machines had taken shape. For example, Turing's classic paper, 'Computing Machinery and Intelligence', in which the Turing Test was outlined, appeared barely two years after the world's first computer ran the world's first stored program in a laboratory at Manchester University on 21 June 1948. Why was such optimism expressed so early? What reasons are there for supposing that the computer is, at least potentially, intelligent? Essentially they fall into two groups: those that derive from the fact that a computer is a 'universal machine' and those that are based on the supposition that intelligence can be defined working from the top down.

THE IDEA OF THE UNIVERSAL MACHINE

Since the concept of the universal machine provides top-down artificial intelligence with many of its theoretical, even philosophical, foundations, we must examine it with care. First: what is meant by a universal machine? Basically a machine which can replicate the behaviour of all machines, both machines that actually exist and machines that do not exist but whose behaviour can be specified formally and in detail.

When we say that a computer can replicate the behaviour of other machines we are, of course, talking of other information machines. Obviously a computer, by itself, cannot act upon the physical world like, say, a crane or a food processor. But it is worth reminding ourselves that computers can, and do, *simulate* the behaviour of many other machines and, indeed, that of systems of all kinds. Most TV weather forecasts, for example, now include 'predictive sequences' in which computers simulate the way in which the current meteorological situation is expected to develop. In just the same way economists can use computers to simulate the behaviour of a market or even a whole economy under different conditions or with varying parameters.

Perhaps the best known case of computers being used to simulate the behaviour of other machines is that of aviation, where flight simulators have now developed to the point at which pilots can familiarize themselves with a new type of aircraft, or practise approaches to an airport on the other side of the world, without ever leaving the ground. Very similar techniques are also used in computer-aided design in order to simulate, say, the operation of robots, thus allowing an entire automated production line to be planned on the display screen.

The essence of the computer's universality, therefore, does not lie in an ability actually to perform functions in the physical world, but in its capacity to reproduce the *logical* characteristics of other systems. As far as artificial intelligence is concerned, the crucial point is that a computer can simulate the operations of any other mechanism that processes information – and it is clear that, whatever else it may be, the brain is such a mechanism.

The fact that a machine could, in theory, enjoy this quality of universality was in fact established long before the first computer was built, indeed before anyone had even considered the possibility of building a computer. For it was in 1936 that Alan Turing first conceived the idea of a universal machine. He was not, at that time, greatly interested in the practicalities of such a thing; he was simply concerned to show that it was, in principle, possible to envisage a device which, using purely 'mechanical' methods, could perform any and every mathematical or logical process which was 'computable'. (Having shown that this was so, Turing was then able to go on to prove that there were problems to which the machine could not produce a definite answer and which were, therefore, 'uncomputable').

In order to demonstrate that a universal machine could be defined in rigorous mathematical terms, Turing described a hypothetical device, the Turing Machine, which was made up of just two elements: an endless paper tape and a 'head' which moved along the tape, reading symbols written on it and adding or deleting them (see next page). Such a device is, of course, no more than a basis for 'thought experiments'; in practice it would be hopelessly clumsy and slow. But in principle, for all its apparent simplicity, a Turing Machine embodies the essential features of its infinitely more elaborate descendant, the digital computer.

All that a machine of this kind requires in order to perform a computable process is what Turing called 'a definite method', that is a set of instructions that describe, step by step, the sequence of logical operations which it must implement. Since the process of reading such instructions and implementing them is itself computable, they can be encoded on the tape and read by the machine (just as a computer reads the instructions, or program, contained in its own internal memory). Thus it is, in theory, possible to envisage a Turing Machine equipped with a tape containing the instructions for every possible computable problem – a truly universal machine which would, in due course, plod its way through every conceivable operation in every conceivable mathematical or logical calculus.

It was more than ten years, and a world war, after the publication of Turing's paper, 'On Computable Numbers', that the first digital computers actually appeared on the scene, and they were naturally very primitive by current standards, though infinitely superior to the Turing Machine in every practical respect. Nevertheless, they could in principle be said to enjoy the quality of universality. In practice, of course, severe limits were imposed by their lack of memory space and their relatively slow speed of operation. Similar limitations would be shared by all computers for many years to come – but those who believed that in the long run such handicaps would be removed have, by and large, been proved correct.

For the field of artificial intelligence, which was to come into existence a few years later, the crucial point was this. Unless we are prepared to resort to mystical or magical explanations in order to account for human intelligence, it is undeniable that it must be a computable process. The 'definite method', the set of logical instructions, that a computer would require in order 'to be intelligent' would, clearly, be immense; but, in theory at least, such

The Turing Machine consists of a 'head' which travels back and forth along an endless paper tape which is divided into boxes. These may either be blank or contain a single character. The head can read the contents of a box, write a character in a blank box, and delete the character in a box either leaving it blank or substituting another character. In order to perform any given task, all the machine needs is a table of instructions which tell it what it should do next and what 'state' it should be in.

Here a Turing Machine is checking whether or not a sequence of letters forms a palindrome (i.e. reads the same both backwards and forwards). The first instruction tells it to enter state 1 and move to the right. The head will continue to move along the tape from left to right, reading the contents of the boxes as it goes, until it encounters a box containing a character. As soon as it does so it deletes the character, in this case an A, replaces it with an X, and changes to state 2. In this state it will continue to move from left to right until it encounters a blank box (see page 38). It then moves back to the left and changes to state 3. In this state it reads the character in the box and if, as in the illustration, it is also an A, the machine deletes it and replaces it with an X before changing into state 4, in which state it moves back along the tape looking for the X at the other end. Proceeding in this laborious fashion the machine will eventually replace all the pairs of As and Bs at either end of the string with Xs and thus prove that the string does indeed form a palindrome. But if at any point it finds that the character at the right-hand end of the string does not correspond with the one which it last deleted and replaced at the left-hand end it will immediately come to a halt, signalling that the sequence has failed to pass the test.

The crucial point is that, no matter how complicated the problem it is dealing with, the Turing Machine's next output and its next state can always be defined in terms of just two factors, its current state and its current input. Thus the 'program', the set of instructions, can be set out as a table in which the machine can always 'look up' its next output and its next state.

a thing is conceivable. And in practice, of course, even if only very limited aspects of intelligence could be captured a breakthrough of great significance would have been achieved.

The crux of the matter could be put like this. A digital computer that has been switched on but, as yet, contains no program can be thought of as a machine with the potential for becoming – that is, simulating the behaviour of – any other machine, even a biological machine like the brain. Only when a program has been loaded into its memory does the computer cease to be a universal machine and become one particular kind of machine. This concept will be familiar to anyone who owns even the most modest of home computers. For they will know that they can determine, by selecting one piece of software rather than another, whether their personal

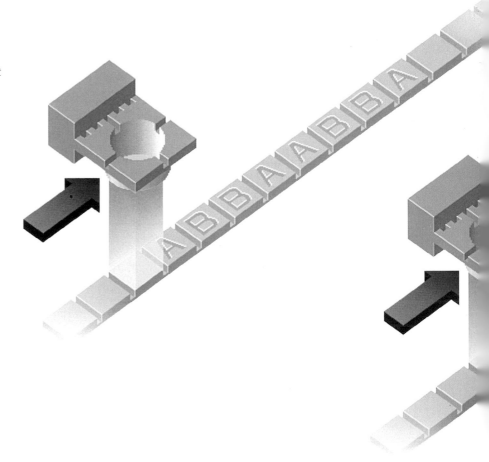

'universal machine' will be transformed into a word processor or a device for playing Space Invaders or indeed, if they know how to write programs for it, a unique machine which they themselves have specified.

It thus becomes clear that the key factor which determines what any particular universal machine can do in any particular situation is not the design of the hardware, the machine itself in the traditional sense of the word, but the nature of the instructions, the software or programs, with which it is equipped. The logical structure of the hardware is a function of the software and one can think of a computer as a general-purpose device, little more than a collection of components which is reconfigured every time a new program is loaded into it.

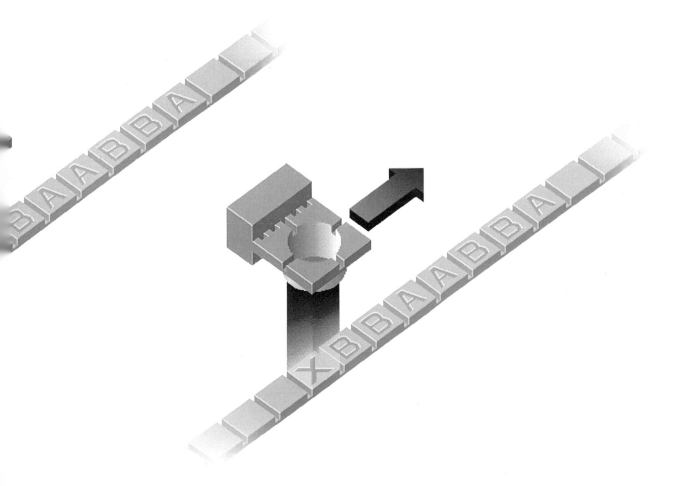

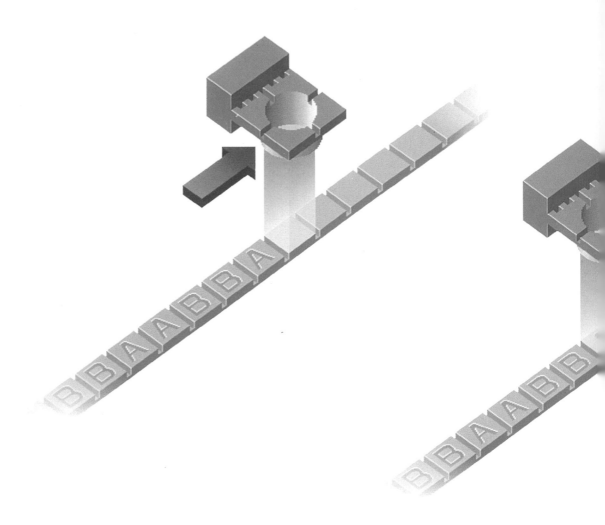

Since it is the program which specifies the behaviour of the machine on which it runs, a program itself is in some sense a machine. This idea, widely used in artificial intelligence where scientists frequently refer to a program or a part of a program as a 'machine' or an 'engine', is a rich source of confusion for the uninitiated. Most of us are, after all, accustomed to thinking of a machine as a bit of ironmongery with levers to be pulled and knobs to be pushed, not as something that can enjoy an entirely abstract existence. Yet it is essential to realize that when people in artificial intelligence talk of an 'intelligent machine' they may mean no more than a set of instructions – maybe not even written out as a formal program – which, when implemented on a computer, would cause it to simulate some aspect of intelligence.

In principle, it is possible to envisage an intelligent machine consisting of a computer program which simulated intelligence, the operations of a brain, in a completely literal fashion. But in order to

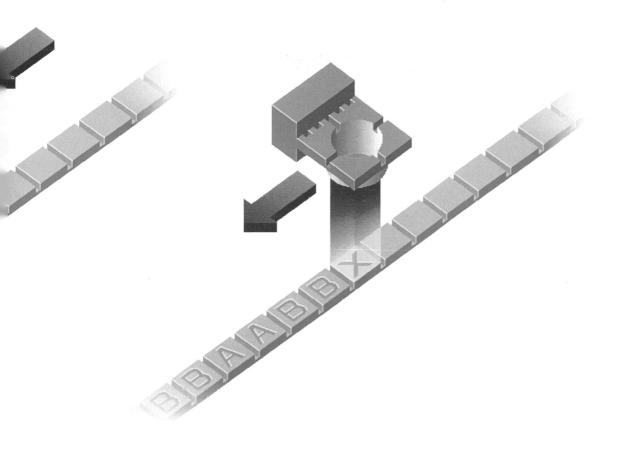

do this it would be necessary to determine exactly what went on inside a brain at the most detailed level: which nerve cells fired under what circumstances and with what consequences. In the 1950s and, it must be said, even today, this seems a very remote prospect. What is feasible, however, is to simulate the behaviour of brain-like mechanisms on a computer, and we shall be looking at some examples of this when we discuss the bottom-up approach in more detail in later chapters.

MODELLING INTELLIGENCE

The mainstream of artificial intelligence research, however, developed along rather different lines. The essential proposition upon which it is based is that it is more practicable, and perhaps more useful, to 'model' intelligent behaviour from the top down.

When contemporary science talks of 'modelling' a process it uses the term in a very specific sense. A model is a description, often mathematical in form, which summarizes a working hypothesis about some aspect of reality. It provides a general framework that is logically self-consistent within which we can make predictions and test them, but it does not necessarily claim to provide us with a complete picture of the process in every detail, let alone with the sort of final 'explanations' that were offered by nineteenth-century science. In order to describe different aspects of a phenomenon, or to explore what happens at different levels, it may be necessary to employ more than one model. In the case of intelligence, for example, a neurophysiologist might insist that the behaviour of rats in a laboratory experiment could ultimately be explained in terms of the firing of nerve cells in the brain; a behavioural psychologist might argue that everything could be accounted for by the conditioning to which the creatures had been subjected; and a layman might say that a rat produced the predicted response because it had the intelligence to realize that this would result in it being rewarded rather than punished. The subsequent arguments between the three observers would be quite fruitless because each would be arguing in the context of a different model, and while each model may be perfectly valid, none can be reduced to, that is explained in terms of, the others.

The basic assumption that underlies the top-down approach is that intelligence can be modelled in terms of formal *algorithms*. This is such a key word in all branches of computer science that it is worth pausing to define it with some care. Essentially an algorithm is the procedure that must be followed in order to solve a problem or perform a task. The algorithm for obtaining an average, for example, could be summarized as follows:

1. Count the number of figures to be averaged, call that number x.
2. Add up all the individual figures, call the total y
3. Divide x into y in order to obtain the average

An algorithm, in other words, is another word for the definite method which must be specified before a computable problem can be tackled. In the context of computing, it is obviously very closely related to a program, in that it consists of a set of instructions to be implemented in a given order, but it is not quite the same thing. For whereas every program must be based upon some underlying algorithm, any algorithm can provide the basis for an almost infinite variety of programs.

An analogy from everyday life may help to illustrate the distinction. Think of a familiar dish, say beef stew. Clearly, there are a number of standard ingredients – beef, onions, carrots, etc. – which will be found in all beef stews and a basic procedure involving slow cooking in a low oven which all cooks will follow. These common factors could be described as the algorithm for beef stew. Yet if you looked up 'Beef Stew' in half a dozen different cookery books you would find six recipes, or programs, each of which differed in one minor respect or another from the others.

The way in which an algorithm is translated into a program will depend upon which computer language is being used, the idiosyncracies of the machine upon which the program is to be run and the ingenuity and personal preferences of the programmer. But the intricacies of the program itself are usually of interest only to those who concern themselves with such technicalities; the real issue is the nature of the algorithms employed. For it is very tempting to assume that the algorithms which are devised are, at some level, models of the processes that take place in our own minds when we perform similar tasks and to describe the algorithms used in artificial intelligence as models of how we think. But there is also a possibility that they are something rather different – models of how we *think* we think.

However, as we saw in Chapter 1, artificial intelligence is very largely concerned with mechanizing processes which we do not fully understand even though we may routinely perform them without apparent effort or difficulty. Over the next four chapters, we shall look at some of the aspects of human behaviour which artificial intelligence has tried to model using a top-down approach. In each case we shall ask not just whether the algorithms are effective and efficient, but also whether they are recognizable – whether they reflect the way we actually think or just the way we think that we think.

There is, however, a further question which must be considered. If the algorithms used in top-down artificial intelligence have been devised by human beings, then, even if they cause machines to behave intelligently, why should we concede that the machines are intelligent? Surely, they are simply 'playing back' the intelligence of their programmers, much as a record player plays back the voice of a singer. One answer is, of course, that much of our own intelligence is derived from other people, in the sense that it is the product of a formal education. On this view, the programmer's relationship to the computer is simply that of teacher to pupil. Granted, the teacher has to explain things in far greater detail than would be necessary in the case of a human pupil. But, on the other hand, it must also be granted that the machine can be relied upon to follow its instructions with a fidelity that would cause many a schoolteacher to envy the programmer's good fortune.

However, as we have already seen, there are many good reasons for believing that the capacity to learn, and especially to learn by induction, is an essential feature of human intelligence. Surely a machine which simply follows a prescribed set of rules with blind obedience cannot be described as intelligent? Again the objection can be met, in theory at least. If learning is a computable process, then it should be possible to create 'learning algorithms' and a good deal of ingenuity has, as we shall see, been devoted to just this issue. Given algorithms of sufficient subtlety, advocates of the top-down approach argue, a machine will in time learn to behave in ways which even the person who programmed it may not be able to explain. Once that stage has been reached, they go on to ask, if the machine's behaviour is not attributed to its own intelligence, then how else can it be accounted for? This question should be kept in the forefront of the reader's mind as we move on to consider some specific instances of intelligent behaviour and to examine the ways in which top-down artificial intelligence has modelled them.

CHAPTER 3

THE RULES OF THE GAME

Game-playing has been one of the most successful branches of artificial intelligence, as witness the success of the chess-playing machine. It was also one of the first to be explored. Indeed, the possibility that machines might be capable of playing games such as chess had been mooted long before artificial intelligence emerged as a discipline in its own right, even before the first primitive computers had been built and tested.

Many of the people involved in designing and building the first computers including Alan Turing, were fascinated by chess and tried to devise systems of rules which would allow a human player to determine the 'best move' at any stage of a game. Any such set of rules is a computer program in all but name, and in 1950 Claude Shannon published a paper entitled 'Programming a Computer for Playing Chess' which made the connection quite explicit and set out many of the basic ideas which are still used in today's chess-playing programs.

But in the early 1950s, when the number of computers in the world had barely reached double figures, and those machines that did exist had a capacity that was trivial by current standards, the prospects of devising a workable chess-playing program still seemed remote. Yet, by the end of the decade it had been established beyond doubt that machines could be programmed to play chess of an impressively high standard. And twenty-five years later only a player of grand-master status can feel confident of consistently outwitting some of the more advanced systems.

It is easy enough to see why game-playing, and chess in particular, attracted the attention of so many of the pioneers of computing. We commonly think of chess as an activity which demands a high degree of intelligence, indeed the skilled chess-player is almost a stereotype of the 'intellectual' in many people's eyes. It seemed to follow that if machines could demonstrate an ability to compete successfully at chess they would have taken a major step towards establishing their claim to intelligence. At the same time the target did not seem impossibly ambitious. For it was clear that playing chess, or other games such as draughts or checkers, was essentially a matter of applying logical rules. Back in the 1930s John von Neumann himself had shown that in any 'game of perfect information' (i.e. a game like chess, where all the relevant information is available to both players, as contrasted to a 'game of imperfect information' like poker, where an element of bluff is involved) there will always be an optimum strategy that can, in principle, be logically determined.

The problem was (and still is) that for most of the game that optimum strategy will lie beyond the reach of even the most powerful computer imaginable. For the number of possible 'states' of a chess game (the number of different ways in which the pieces can legitimately be arranged on the board) is vast beyond conception. This is but one example of a phenomenon, known as the 'combinatorial explosion', that we shall be meeting again and again throughout this book. The point is that even in the simplest conceivable game of this kind, one where a player has to choose between only two possible moves, 'looking ahead' to calculate the consequences of a move will involve considering a range of possible states that grows exponentially each time the player looks one move further into the future. Thus, looking two moves ahead, the game may be in any one of four states; looking three moves ahead, there are eight possible states; looking four moves ahead, sixteen – and so on. In chess, where there are, on average, about thirty-five moves open to each player whenever it is his turn to move, looking two moves ahead will involve the consideration of over a thousand possible states and after three moves the number of states will have increased to over 40,000.

Nevertheless, the fact that game-playing posed problems which could, if only in theory, be solved by following some definite method, or set of logical rules, seemed at least to offer a foothold for the programmer. There was one further factor which made the field enormously attractive. The number of different states of the pieces on a chess board may be, to all intents and purposes, infinite, but each state can be clearly defined and relatively easily described in a fashion that would be intelligible to a machine – indeed any one who reads chess books will, for example, know that squares on the board are commonly identified by use of a system of grid references, so that square A1 is in the bottom left-hand corner of the board and square H8 is in the top right-hand corner of the board. Similarly, the rules that govern the movement of the pieces, the ways in which the state may legitimately be changed, can readily be expressed in logical terms.

LOOKING AHEAD

This concept of a game (or a task or problem of any kind) being in a certain *state* which can be transformed, within a given set of rules or logical constraints, into a variety of alternative states (see next page) is fundamental to all game-playing programs and is indeed central to many branches of artificial intelligence. In areas other than game-playing the major difficulty is frequently that neither the state of the problem nor the rules which govern the changes of state are easily described in well-defined and logical ways – as we shall see in subsequent chapters. But representing the present state of a board game (and a range of possible alternative states that may occur in the future) in terms of the internal states of a machine poses relatively few problems. In other words, it is relatively easy to find ways in which the machine may be furnished with an internal representation of the 'world' it is required to 'think about'. The real challenge is to devise algorithms which will enable the machine to decide what moves it should make, or, to put it a different way, which future states of the game are, from its point of view, most desirable in that they represent a winning position.

In the game of noughts and crosses, or tic-tac-toe, shown here, the first player has put an X in the central square of the grid and his opponent has countered by placing an O in the square above it, producing the present state (see top left). It is now X's turn to move and he can transform the grid into any one of the four next states (see top right). The range of possible next states is limited here because after the first two moves the state of the grid is still symmetrical, so putting an X in any of the three squares on the left-hand side is exactly equivalent to putting an X in the corresponding square on the right-hand side.

The state of the chessboard (below), with only four pieces left in play, also reduces the range of next states which can follow White's move, this time to five. In practice, however, most board states which occur during a chess game can be followed by between 30 and 40 next states.

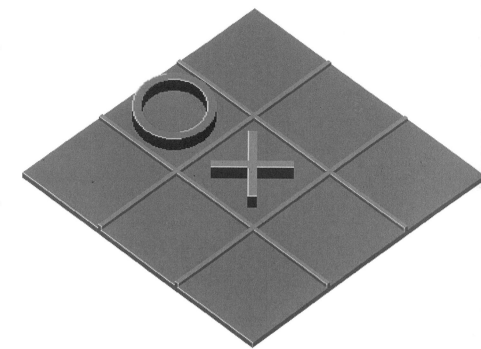

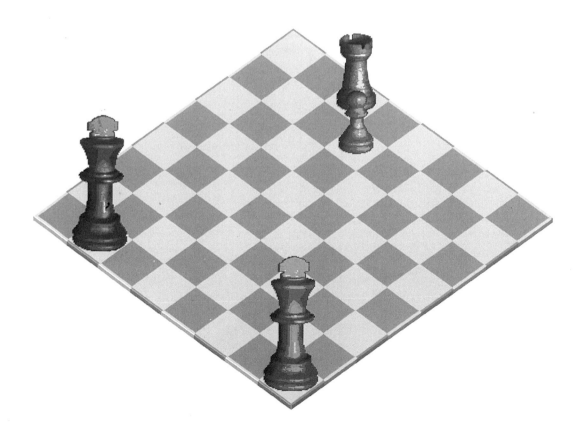

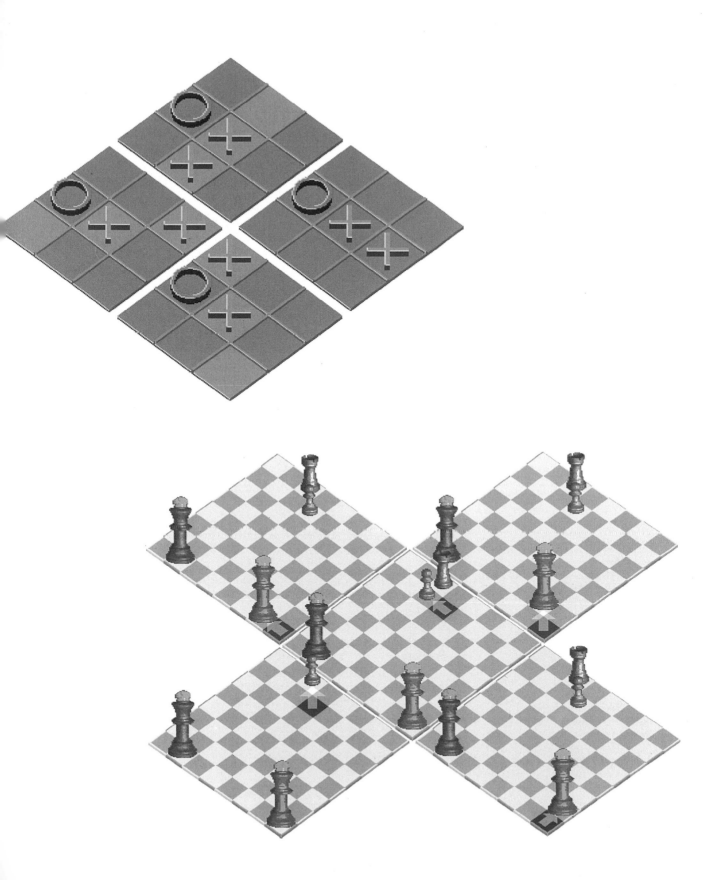

Any game-playing algorithm must, clearly, be based upon the principle that making a choice between the moves that are currently available will involve looking ahead. The player must consider each move in turn, and pursue the implications of the counter-moves and counter-counter-moves that might follow from it. The results of this sort of analysis can be set out in the form of a *decision tree* (see opposite), with branches radiating from a single 'root node', representing the present state of the game, and dividing and subdividing at further nodes, each of which represents one of the states which may be reached as a result of further play.

In order to construct a decision tree, the machine is provided with a set of 'production rules' which it applies first to the description of the current board state, i.e. the root node. Each production rule has two halves. The first, the left-hand side, has the form '*If* pawn now on square G4 and square G5 vacant . . .', and the right-hand side continues, '. . . *then* pawn on square G5'. The description of the current board state simply lists the position of all the pieces plus all the vacant squares. By comparing this list with the left-hand side of each production rule in turn, the machine can identify the rules which are applicable and, by substituting the right-hand side of the rule for the appropriate entry in the list, generate the description of a 'next state', i.e. one of the 'successors' of the root node. Once all the possible successor nodes have been generated, the machine can then move on to generate all *their* successors, and so on.

Obviously, the further ahead the machine looks, the greater the number of possible states that must be considered. In theory, a decision tree can be extended until a 'winning state' appears at the tip of one of the branches. But in practice, as we have seen, such a 'brute force' approach is impossible until a game enters its final stages. Before that, both time and the amount of memory space available will limit the extent to which the decision tree can be expanded. So, once the tree has been extended as far as possible, the machine will require an algorithm that allows it to 'search' the nodes at the extremities of the decision tree – sometimes called 'leaves' – in order to establish which of the future states that can be foreseen is, from the machine's point of view, most desirable.

Any such algorithm must take account of two factors. First, some scoring system is required, a value must be attached to each of the leaf nodes in order that they may be compared. Secondly, it would be futile simply to select the 'most valuable' of the leaf nodes and initiate the sequence of moves which leads to it, for this would be to ignore the fact that the opposing player will naturally seek to frustrate the plan at every stage.

IDENTIFYING THE 'BEST' STATE

Given that the states of the game which have to be evaluated are, by definition, at the limits of the machine's vision (i.e. it cannot look even further ahead to examine the states that might follow from them), any scoring system has to rely on what are known as

Opposite: In this decision tree each of the nodes (the points where the branches divide) represents one state of the game. Thus the single root node at the top of the tree represents the present state, and the leaf nodes at the tips of the branches represent all the possible states that might occur after five further moves. In this highly simplified example each player must choose between just two options each time it is his turn to move, so that each ancestor node has only two successor nodes. In the case of chess, however, where a player may have to consider at least 30 possible options each time he makes a move, decision trees rapidly expand to a colossal size and the final level may contain many thousands of leaf nodes.

A decision tree is, of course, no more than a convenient means of representing the reasoning processes that are employed. No such structure actually 'exists' inside the computer, where the same data might be represented in a variety of ways. If, for example, the nodes in this tree were labelled from left to right, level by level so that the root node was 1–1 and the leaf nodes were 6–1 to 6–32, the structure of the entire tree could be represented using a system of nested brackets: (1–1(2–1(3–1(4–1(5–1(6–1, 6–2))5–2(6–3, 6–4)))4–2(5–3(6–5, 6–6)) . . . 6–32)))))).

heuristics — another key term in many branches of artificial intelligence. A heuristic is best defined as a 'rule of thumb' which can be used to decide an issue or select a course of action when the optimum choice cannot be discovered by means of exhaustive search or rigorous calculation. A moment's reflection will show that we ourselves constantly make use of heuristics in the course of our everyday lives. If the sky is grey we conclude that it will be better to put on a coat before going out; we book a holiday in August because that is when the weather is usually at its best, and so on.

Human game-players, like machines, must perforce rely upon heuristics. In chess, for example, it is only when the end-game is reached that a player can actually envisage the exact sequence of moves that will lead to checkmate. For most of the game he will be following strategies that are aimed at achieving a position, or board state, which, on the basis of experience, reasoning or intuition, he feels will be advantageous to him. Thus a chess-player's thinking is not unlike that of a military commander who constantly manoeuvres his forces to maintain what he considers to be a strong position — strength being defined in terms of heuristics covering such things as the desirability of good communications and available lines of retreat and the dangers of exposed flanks, etc. — even though he cannot know when and where the

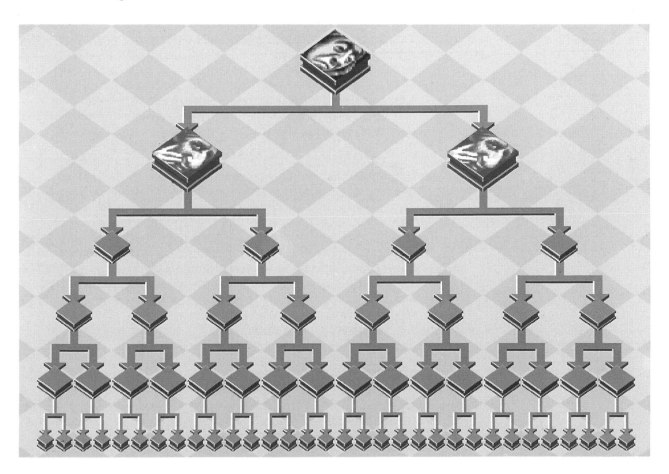

decisive battle will take place or how he will fight it.

Human chess-players may describe the heuristics that they employ both in technical language – talking of gambits, forks and skewers – and in more general terms – emphasizing the need to maintain a strong position in the centre of the board or to guard one's queen. But, however they are expressed, these ideas are not easily reduced to a set of hard and fast rules – if that were feasible, then chess-playing would indeed be a more or less 'mechanical' process; whatever state the game was in it would only be necessary to look up the appropriate rule in order to decide upon the best move.

It is, however, worth noting that the early stages of the game often involve well-established patterns of move and counter-move – there are, as every chess-player knows, a limited number of classical opening gambits to each of which there is a tried and tested response. Many of the commercially available chess-playing programs therefore incorporate 'look-up tables', which are in effect lists of standard moves together with the standard responses. This allows them to play the first few moves without having to look ahead at all. Thus, until their opponent makes a move which breaks the pattern, they are able to respond almost instantaneously and anyone playing against them will notice a perceptible lengthening of the response time when the machine is first forced to abandon its look-up tables and starts to construct and search decision trees.

The heuristics used in chess programs are complicated, since evaluating a single board state will involve taking account of many different factors (see pages 50–1). Indeed, with two decades of experience behind them, today's programmers have developed heuristics which are almost certainly more elaborate than those used by even the very best human players – which does not mean that their programs will play better chess than a grand-master, simply that their judgements are based on calculations of a complexity which no human being could possibly perform under similar circumstances. It is, however, worth adding that the performance of commercial chess-playing programs is determined very largely by how far ahead they look. When a machine is reset to play at a higher level of skill, for example, all that happens is that its program is adjusted to look, say, seven moves ahead instead of five.

But although the capacity to look further ahead is obviously valuable, a 'deeper' search involves no new principles, it simply demands increased processing power and greater amounts of memory space and, of course, more computer time before it can be completed. Given that all programs employ very similar algorithms (though there are significant differences in search strategies which we shall examine shortly) their intelligence, if they are deemed to be intelligent, is mostly embodied in the heuristics that they employ.

LEARNING TO PLAY A BETTER GAME

If these heuristics are provided by the programmer, as a complete prepackaged set of rules, then, clearly, it can be argued that the intelligence is a property of the programmer and not the machine.

But in the early days of artificial intelligence and still, to a lesser extent, today, those who concerned themselves with game-playing were intrigued by the possibility that machines might be able to construct new heuristics for themselves, to enlarge and amend their programs on the basis of the 'experience' gained in the course of successive games.

For example, a program might start with a relatively simple set of heuristics, embodying the sort of short-term thinking that leads a novice player to believe that any move which results in the capture of an opponent's piece must always be 'good'. But if the programmer has built in some sort of 'learning mechanism', then when the machine falls into the traps which a sophisticated player can easily contrive for such a simple-minded opponent, the heuristics can be modified and elaborated by the machine itself to reflect the experience that has been gained.

Ultimately the value that should be attached to a particular board state can only be determined on the basis of the final outcome of the game. For unless the game ends in either victory or defeat for the machine, the only way of evaluating the states that occur in the course of play is to apply further heuristics. This means that a program can only educate itself if it is matched against a human player. All that will happen if two programs are set to play against each other is that they will swop their existing heuristics.

There are essentially three strategies that can be used to enable a program to learn from a human player. The first and most obvious method involves co-opting a human to act as a collaborator, so that when it is the machine's turn to move it simply asks advice and modifies its heuristics if that advice differs from its own conclusions. But this process can scarcely be described as learning, for it amounts to little more than an alternative method of transferring knowledge from programmer to machine. In effect, rather than trying to construct heuristics in the abstract, the programmer is teaching the machine by taking it through a range of actual examples and showing it what he would do in a variety of different circumstances. The problem is that there is no way in which the human collaborator can explain to the machine *why* he chooses one move rather than another, nor is it possible for the machine to improve upon the heuristics used by its teacher.

A rather more subtle variation of this technique depends upon the fact that the algorithm used to search a decision tree involves the assumption that the machine's opponent will always make what is, from the machine's point of view, the 'worst' move. This means that it is possible for the machine to learn by taking note whenever its opponent makes a move which is unexpected. If, in other words, the machine had calculated that its opponent would make move A, which, on the basis of its existing heuristics, it reckoned to be the most damaging move available, and it turns out that the opponent chooses move B, then it can amend its heuristics to account for the fact that the states resulting from move A were 'better' than it previously believed whereas those resulting from move B were 'worse'.

The second method is quite straightforwardly based on trial and

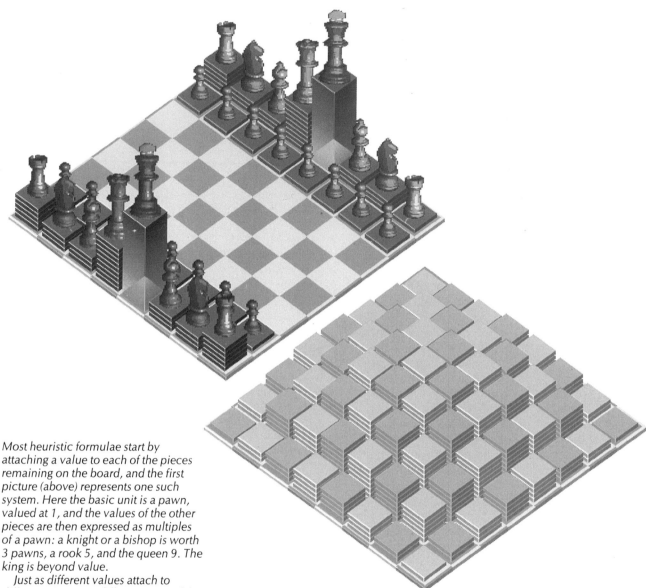

Most heuristic formulae start by attaching a value to each of the pieces remaining on the board, and the first picture (above) represents one such system. Here the basic unit is a pawn, valued at 1, and the values of the other pieces are then expressed as multiples of a pawn: a knight or a bishop is worth 3 pawns, a rook 5, and the queen 9. The king is beyond value.

Just as different values attach to different pieces, so different areas of the board are worth more or less according to the amount of freedom for manoeuvre which a piece situated in that area will enjoy. The second picture (below) shows one possible scheme for dealing with this aspect of the game. The four central squares are valued at 10 and the values then fall away towards the edges of the board. But the squares on or adjacent to the middle of the edges, where it is still possible to move freely on three axes, are more highly valued than the corner squares, which have the minimum value of 1, and their neighbours.

error. The program simply modifies its existing heuristics in the light of the final outcome of a game – reinforcing those that lead to victory and discarding those that result in defeat. But this has the disadvantage of being a very hit-and-miss technique. It is, for example, perfectly possible for the machine to win despite having made a number of moves that an experienced human player would recognize as 'bad', but it will nevertheless reclassify as 'desirable' the states that resulted from its bad moves along with those achieved by its good moves. Conversely, the machine may make a number of 'good' moves in the course of a losing game and, as a result, actually eliminate valuable heuristics from its repertoire.

In the case of the third strategy, originally developed for a checker-player program by A. L. Samuel of IBM, the program does not have to await the final outcome of the game, but constantly modifies its heuristics as play progresses. As has already been explained, each time the machine has to make a move it uses its existing heuristics to evaluate each of the leaf nodes at the extremities of the decision tree; then, following a process which will be described shortly, it selects the highest scoring node which it can reach despite the best efforts of its opponent, and makes the move that leads towards that node, the 'best node'. The value of the best node thus represents the best score that the machine can foresee at the current state of the game. It follows that, if the heuristics are

The third picture (above) shows how this scheme might be modified to create a program which will play aggressively. The value of each of the squares in the second picture has now been increased by adding another figure representing the rank in which the square falls, so that the value of the squares on the near side of the board has been increased by 1 while that of the squares on the other side, the opponent's back rank, has been increased by 8. It would be possible to create a program that played defensively by reversing these weightings.

The fourth picture (below) represents a scoring system that encourages the program to attack the opposing king by attaching the highest value, 7, to the square where it is currently situated plus the adjoining squares, and the lowest value, 1, to the ranks of squares furthest away from the king.

good ones, they should yield exactly that score when they are applied to the root node at the top of the tree.

The learning process therefore involves comparing the value of the best node with the value of the root node, as determined by the machine's current heuristics. If the two values are the same no changes are made. But if the value of best node is higher than that of the root node, then the heuristics are modified to give more weight to those factors which tend to raise the score; if, on the other hand, the value of the best node is lower than the value of the root node more weight is given to the factors which tend to lower the score. At the next move, these modified heuristics are then used to evaluate the new set of leaf nodes, and the whole process is repeated. Unfortunately, while Samuel's techniques were extremely effective in the case of checkers – his program was ultimately able to compete successfully at the very highest level – it has proved difficult to apply them to the very much more complicated heuristics used in chess.

Interest in new learning methods for chess-playing has, however, revived of late, mostly as a result of work on expert systems (see Chapter 6). Attention is now concentrated on programs which learn by induction, and it is argued that a machine which is allowed to 'observe' the ways in which a variety of human players deal with a particular problem can make inferences about the players' strategies which may not have been apparent before, even to the players themselves.

Obviously, whatever the strategy that is adopted, the learning process is going to take a long time. The program will have to incorporate the lessons of many games before the heuristics are reliable and comprehensive enough to cope with a representative range of play – but then even a very gifted human player has to gather a good deal of experience before his play reaches a high standard. And the machine does have one great advantage over its human counterpart, once the program has accumulated the necessary 'experience' it can be duplicated and reduplicated rapidly and cheaply.

We shall be returning to the subject of learning, and especially inductive learning, in later chapters; for it seems clear that the ability to infer general principles from specific instances is a crucial factor in human intelligence. But in order to complete the discussion of game-playing we must now turn from the issue of heuristics to consider the second problem involved in the basic decision-tree algorithm – the need to take account of the fact that an opponent will be trying to frustrate the machine's plans.

MINI-MAXING AND ALPHA-BETAING

Once the decision tree is complete and the leaf nodes at its extremities have been evaluated, the machine must determine which of the leaf nodes is the best node, representing the board state it should be trying to bring about, and which of the options that presently confront it will lead to that state. This task involves 'backing up' the scores from one level to another. Since each level

of the tree contains fewer nodes than the one below it, the range of
scores to be considered will be reduced at each stage of the process
until, when the root node is reached, just one score remains,
representing the best result that the machine can foresee itself
achieving. Since the leaf nodes always represent the results of
moves on the machine's part, the first stage in this process presents
few problems. It is only necessary to select the best score from each
cluster of leaf nodes and back it up to the ancestor node on the level
above – this is simply to make the assumption that, if and when the
game reaches the state represented by one of the ancestor nodes,
the move which currently appears to be the best, on the basis of the
heuristics that have been applied, will still be the best.

But the next stage in the backing-up process is not so simple. For
the now-reduced list of scores on the penultimate level of the tree
are attached to nodes which represent the results of moves made by
the opposing player and the only safe assumption is that he will seek
to minimize the machine's chances of winning. So this time it is the
worst score in each group which must be selected and backed up to
the next level. This process, known as mini-maxing (see next
page), is continued until, in the final stage, a single maximum score
is backed up to the root node. The zig-zag path through the tree
traced by the backing up of alternating maximums and minimums
now represents the machine's current strategy. Accordingly, it will
now take the first step towards retracing that path.

The mini-max algorithm is the basis of all chess-playing programs, for it implements a common-sense principle that must be
basic to any look-ahead system: when trying to forecast what an
opponent may do, the only safe assumption is that he will make the
move that is least advantageous to the machine. The business of
constructing a decision tree and then backing up the scores is,
however, a laborious one, and much ingenuity has been applied to
devising algorithms which can cut short one or both stages of the
process. The business of actually backing up the scores can be
shortened by employing a refinement of the mini-max technique
known as 'alpha-betaing'. The mathematics of this may seem
slightly complicated (see page 56), but the principle is very simple.
Essentially the machine abandons the search along any limb of the
tree if and when it becomes apparent that the result will be less
favourable than one which can be obtained from a limb that has
already been partially searched. Alpha-betaing is, however, by no
means a guaranteed way of achieving economies. Its success
depends very largely on the order in which the tree is searched – if a
promising result shows up early on in the search much time may be
saved, but if the best results are discovered only towards the end
few benefits will have been achieved.

Both mini-maxing and alpha-betaing were described by Claude
Shannon in his 1950 paper, before anyone had actually sat down to
write a game-playing computer program. But once programmers
began to study game-playing as a serious possibility it became clear
that the most important need was to find some way of limiting the
size of a decision tree; for the process of looking even a few moves
ahead rapidly absorbed all the available memory space in the early

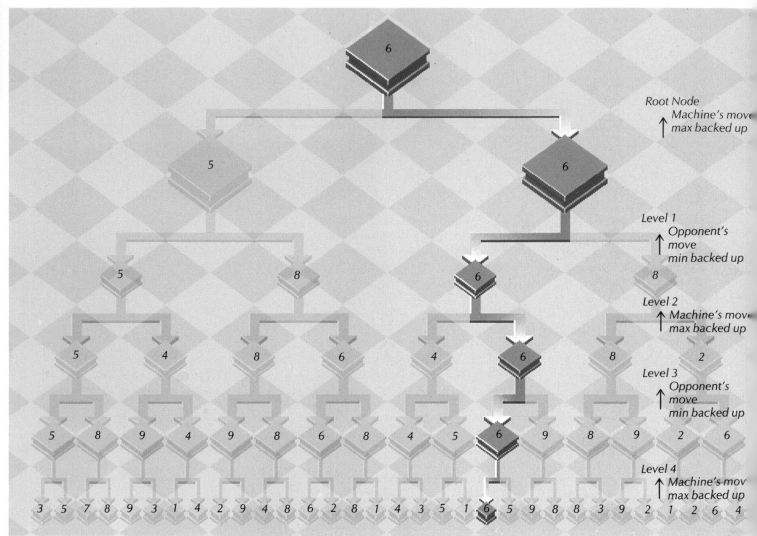

Root Node
Machine's move
↑ *max backed up*

Level 1
Opponent's move
↑ *min backed up*

Level 2
↑ *Machine's move*
max backed up

Level 3
Opponent's move
↑ *min backed up*

Level 4
↑ *Machine's move*
max backed up

Level 5 (Leaf Nodes)

machines, while the task of assessing the scores and backing them up could occupy many minutes of processor time.

One way of dealing with the problem is to concentrate on limited areas of the board, perhaps sixteen or twenty-four squares, if necessary considering two or more such areas one after another. The sectors to be examined can be chosen, or given priority, on a variety of grounds. In chess, for example, it could be argued that the position in the centre of the board should always be explored before considering the sides; or that the squares in the immediate neighbourhood of the king merit priority.

This sort of technique has certainly proved very powerful in that it allows a machine to look further ahead, to search in greater depth. But this is achieved at the cost of sacrificing breadth. To some extent, there can be no doubt, this mirrors techniques used by human players – even a grand-master will concentrate on certain areas of the board and ignore others which are not relevant to the strategy he is developing. But for a human player such rules are made only to be broken, and there is always the possibility, kept open somewhere in the back of the player's mind, of an opportunity opening up in an unexpected direction.

MAN v MACHINE

There is no doubt that the sophisticated heuristics employed by the best contemporary chess programs, coupled with the computer's ability, based on its sheer number-crunching capacity, to look further ahead in greater detail than even the best human player, has given chess-playing machines an impressive power. Even grand-masters can no longer feel quite secure from the threat of mechanical competition.

Computer chess has also become well-established as a game in its own right. Tournaments are held on a regular basis and successful programs attract *aficionados* who show quite as much enthusiasm as the followers of Boris Spassky or Bobby Fischer. A recent game in which a humble personal computer defeated a mighty VAX minicomputer was even reported in the national press. But, for our purposes, the really interesting question is this: do the algorithms employed in computer chess reflect accurately – or even partially – the sort of processes which take place in the mind of a human player?

The two are clearly related in some way. The need to look ahead, for example, is fundamental to any board game, as is the need to take account of the fact that the opposing player will seek to frustrate your strategy. There do, however, seem to be some major, and perhaps highly significant, differences. To begin with, any accomplished human chess-player will look for weaknesses in an opponent's game and seek to exploit them. He may, for example, recognize that while one player is by nature reluctant to take risks and can, therefore, be relied upon to err on the side of caution, a different opponent, who is by nature a gambler, can far more easily be provoked into making a rash move. But no one has yet devised a program that can evaluate and capitalize on this sort of psycho-logical factor. A human player might, to take another example, quickly realize that an opponent attached a great deal of importance to making captures and might then look for ways of turning this to his advantage by laying traps baited with a relatively unimportant sacrifice. But machines have not, as yet, been endowed with the ability to reason in this fashion; they must apply exactly the same algorithms no matter whether they are competing against a grand-master or a raw beginner.

It may, it is true, be possible to vary the level at which a chess program plays, but this is a decision that is taken by its human opponent, not by the machine itself. It has no means of weighing up an opponent's play and saying to itself, after the first few moves, 'This person is really pretty hopeless, I will save myself some

The mini-max algorithm (see left). Once a decision tree has been generated and the values of the leaf nodes calculated, the machine can move on to determine which of the possible next states is the most desirable. This involves 'backing up' the values of the leaf nodes, level by level, until, when the root node is reached, only one remains. The leaf nodes at the final level, level 5 in the case of this tree, represent the board states that would result from the machine's move at level 4, so each cluster of leaf nodes at level 5 (limited to just two nodes in this simplified example) is examined in turn and the highest value, the 'max', is backed up to the common ancestor node at level 4. Then the process is repeated, but this time it is the lowest score, the 'mini', which is backed up, for the nodes on level 4 represent board states resulting from a move by the opposing player at level 3, and it must be assumed that he will choose the option that is least advantageous to the machine.

Once the process has been completed, with a single score being backed up to the root node, the path followed by that score, highlighted here, represents the most advantageous sequence of moves and counter-moves that the machine can currently foresee.

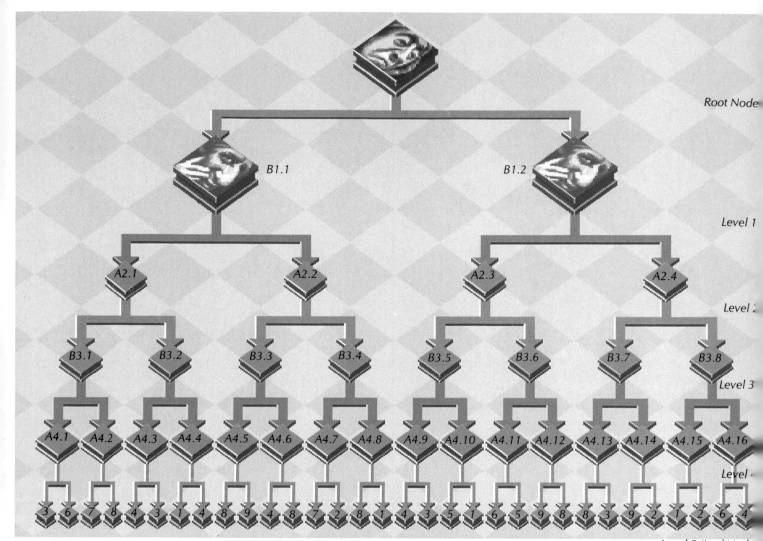

B1.1 B1.2

Level 1

A2.1 A2.2 A2.3 A2.4

Level 2

B3.1 B3.2 B3.3 B3.4 B3.5 B3.6 B3.7 B3.8

Level 3

A4.1 A4.2 A4.3 A4.4 A4.5 A4.6 A4.7 A4.8 A4.9 A4.10 A4.11 A4.12 A4.13 A4.14 A4.15 A4.16

Level 4

3 6 7 8 4 3 1 4 8 9 4 8 7 2 8 1 4 3 5 1 6 5 9 8 8 3 9 2 1 2 6 4

Level 5 (Leaf Node)

trouble from now on by looking only five moves ahead instead of seven.'

There also seem to be some fundamental differences between the methods by which a program looks ahead and calculates a sequence of possible board states and those used by people. A machine, as we have seen, proceeds by a process of exhaustive search. It may concentrate on one area of the board, or opt to pursue one sequence of moves in depth at the expense of making a shallower breadth-first search, but within those limits it must follow every sequence of moves in a step-by-step fashion. But, if we listen to a grand-master explaining his reasoning, we often find that he can 'see' that a particular move is 'good' or 'bad' without going through a similarly laborious calculation.

This facility for weighing up the essential features of the board, which could be compared to a military commander's 'eye for ground', seems to be based on experience. The player will recognize that the particular board state with which he is now confronted is 'like' one he encountered in a game five years ago, even though the position of every piece is not identical, and will select his move accordingly. It is very difficult indeed to see what sort of algorithm might be used to give a machine this capacity for seeing the strategic woods without bothering too much with the precise position of the individual trees.

What the human player does is clearly closer to the use of look-up tables than to an exhaustive calculation of future board states. For it is by referring to a body of past experience that he determines that, if the game has reached *this* sort of board state now, *that* sort of board state is both desirable and achievable. The catch lies in the concept that states can be similar without being identical; how 'like' is 'like'? How, in computational terms, do you define a 'sort of state'?

Many aspects of human intelligence seem to depend upon the ability to recognize, match and manipulate highly generalized patterns that defy precise definition and can only be described as being 'like' or 'unlike' other patterns. We can see this principle in action in many other spheres of human activity. Consider, for example, the tennis player who, having played a passing shot down one side of the court, calculates almost instantaneously that the other player is going to have to counter with a backhand return across the court and starts moving in anticipation even before his opponent has hit the ball. In computational terms, the task of assessing the situation and calculating the required response is awe-inspiring in its complexity and yet, somehow, the player recognizes that the game is in a certain 'sort of state' and initiates the appropriate action within a fraction of a second. In just the same way, a good football player can 'read the game' and move into position to receive a pass almost instinctively.

It seems likely that it is this ability to think in terms of generalized patterns that enables us to avoid the worst implications of the 'combinatorial explosion'. For it is certain that in the case of chess and similar games, no human player, however talented, constructs a decision tree containing hundreds of nodes, evaluates them all and then backs up the scores. Instead it seems that the human brain has a facility for recognizing board states that are 'like', but not identical to, states that are 'known', in that they are familiar from past experience. It can then make very rapid associations between those states and a range of likely outcomes.

The algorithms required to capture this sort of thinking are, clearly, very different from those used in existing game-playing programs. It may even be that, in order to implement them efficiently, it will be necessary to use machines that operate on principles quite unlike those of the von Neumann computer. This is a question we shall be considering in the latter part of the book when we examine alternatives to classical, top-down artificial intelligence. But first we must move on to look at how the top-down approach has fared in other fields.

The alpha-beta algorithm (see left). Suppose that we are faced with the task of backing up the values shown on the leaf nodes of this decision tree, where each ancestor node has just two successors. Using an A (or the Greek character alpha) to represent the value of a node where a maximum is backed up and a B (or beta) to represent a node where a minimum is backed up, the nodes can be labelled, level by level from left to right, as shown here.

If, starting from the left, we now look at the first pair of leaf nodes, valued at 3 and 6, we can immediately set the value of node A4.1 to 6 and, provisionally, give its ancestor node, B3.1, the same value. Continuing, we examine the next pair of nodes, valued at 7 and 8. But we do not need to back up the 8 to node A4.2 because it is obvious that neither of these figures will alter the value of node B3.1 and, since all the latter's successor nodes have now been examined, it can be set permanently to 6, and its ancestor, node A2.1, can provisionally be given the same value.

If we now look at the next four leaf nodes, all of which are descended, via B3.2, A4.3 and A4.4, from node A2.1, we see that none has a value which exceeds 6. It is therefore unnecessary to back up these four nodes and, as all the successors of A2.1 have now been examined, we can fix its value at 6. We can, moreover, now provisionally give the same value to the node above, B1.1, before moving on.

The next two pairs of leaf nodes have to be backed up to A4.5 and A4.6, giving those nodes values of 9 and 8 respectively. But when, as a result, the value of their common ancestor, B3.3, is confirmed at 8 it is immediately clear that this exceeds the provisional value of its ancestor, B1.1, and that the next stage of the backing-up process can therefore be abandoned.

CHAPTER 4

WHAT'S THE PROBLEM?

The ability to solve problems of one sort or another is widely used as a yardstick of intelligence in many different contexts. Experimental psychologists devise problems that will measure the intelligence of pigeons, rats and even earthworms; educational psychologists rely upon verbal, mathematical or spatial problems to measure the IQs of school children; and most of us would acknowledge skill in coping with the problems of everyday life to be an indication of cleverness or quickness of wit. In the case of intelligent machines, it is rather obvious that such things are unlikely to serve any practical purpose unless they are capable of coping with at least some of the myriad simple, and not-so-simple, problems which people overcome as a matter of routine.

But, as every human problem-solver knows, problems come in a bewildering variety of shapes and sizes. There are problems which can only be solved with patience and perseverance, and others which require flair and intuition. There are formal, abstract problems, like those involved in game-playing, the solution of which may be of little more than academic interest; but there are also many problems which are practical and urgent, matters of life and death even. There are some problems that will yield to elementary common sense; and others that can only be solved with the help of obscure expertise. There are problems that may, literally, drive us to distraction; and others that we actually invent or seek out for the sheer fun of trying to solve them.

It is, however, worth noting at the outset that there are many problems, of great concern to people, which machines may never be able even to consider, let alone solve. When the issue turns upon human needs or emotions it is reasonable to assume that only an intelligence which can experience, and therefore share, those feelings can be expected to grasp 'what the problem is'. For this reason those who imagine that computers, or any other mechanical devices, can offer solutions to political, social or economic problems are dangerously deluded. Such problems are of our creation and we are being naively optimistic if we expect that machines are going to sort them out on our behalf.

There is nevertheless a vast range of problems that should, in principle, yield to artificial intelligence as readily as to natural intelligence and it is not surprising that problem-solving should have been one of the first fields to be systematically tackled by the founding fathers of artificial intelligence. Indeed, the development of artificial intelligence as a discipline in its own right is usually traced back to a problem-solving program called LOGIC THEORIST that was developed at Stanford University in the late 1950s. As the name suggests, this program was designed to deal with problems of a highly formalized kind: given a set of axioms it could prove the theorems that could logically be derived from them. But the creators of LOGIC THEORIST, Alan Newell and Herbert Simon, subsequently went on, with J. C. Shaw, to develop a much more ambitious program, the GENERAL PROBLEM SOLVER. The GPS, as it became known, provided the basis for most of the work done in the field of problem-solving over the following twenty years, until the new and rather different methods associated with logic programming and knowledge-based systems took over at the end of the 1970s (see Chapter 6).

RULE-BASED SYSTEMS

The GPS and its successors are all examples of what are known as rule-based systems, and before we look at the GPS itself we must examine the principles that are common to all such programs and at some of the basic techniques employed.

The fundamental idea underlying all problem-solving algorithms is the concept that a problem, like a game, can always be thought of as being in a certain state. In essence, the task of the problem-solver is to discover a sequence of state changes that will lead, as quickly and economically as possible, from the 'starting state' (the form of the problem as originally posed) to a solution or 'goal state'.

This search can be conducted with the help of the same decision-tree algorithm as is used in game playing. Starting from a single node, representing the initial state of the problem, a machine expands the tree, generating successor nodes that represent possible transformations of that state by applying a set of production rules. A production rule, in its most basic form, consists of a description of two problem states prefaced by the word *if* and linked by the word *then*. This can be interpreted as an instruction that *if* the node currently being considered corresponds to the description of the first state (the 'left-hand side'), *then* the rule may be applied, generating a new node which will correspond to the second half of the rule (the 'right-hand side'). Thus the machine proceeds by comparing the current state of the problem to the states listed on the left-hand side of its rules and, whenever it finds a match, generating a new node corresponding to the right-hand side of that rule (see next page).

This process may however be complicated by a whole variety of difficulties. There are, for example, many cases where great ingenuity will be required merely to find a way in which the state of the problem can be represented efficiently and economically or, indeed, in any intelligible fashion at all. The need for economy arises because most search strategies require the machine to keep a list of 'known states', representing the nodes that have been generated to date, as well as maintaining a record of the paths which link each known state to both its successors and its ancestors. If this is not done, then even if the machine does reach a solution state, it will be unable to 'remember' how it got there! For the same reason it is also necessary to record the action that is taken when one state is transformed into another.

Thus far, the processes employed in problem-solving are very similar to those used in game-playing. But now we come to a very significant difference. In the case of the great majority of problems the goal state can be defined at the outset and is therefore already

In this familiar children's puzzle eight numbered tiles, initially arranged at random as in the starting state at the top of the decision tree, must be moved around the nine available spaces in order to reach the goal state shown at the bottom. In order to identify the nine spaces, they have been labelled A to I as on the blank grid at the top of the page. Using this convention, the goal state can be described as state A1B2C3D4E5F6G7H8 Iblank. The production rules required to deal with this problem are extremely simple. The left-hand sides take the form: 'If A blank...', 'If B blank...', and so on; and the right-hand sides simply list the way in which the state will change if the rule is applied '... then Ab and B blank' (b representing the number of the tile previously in space B), or '... then Ba and A blank'. Thus, starting from the current state shown in the illustration – state A3B7C6D1E2F8G5Hblank I4 – there are just three production rules which can be applied:

If H blank then H5 and G blank
If H blank then H2 and E blank
If H blank then H4 and I blank

If the three possible next states are now examined then there are a further 8 applicable rules:

If G blank then G5 and H blank
If G blank then G1 and D blank
If E blank then E7 and B blank
If E blank then E1 and D blank
If E blank then E8 and F blank
If E blank then E2 and H blank
If I blank then I 8 and F blank
If I blank then I 4 and H blank

A complete set of these rules would make it possible to solve the problem by a process of random search using the technique known as generate and test. This involves comparing each new state as it is generated with the goal state until a match is discovered. The search may be either breadth-first (in which case each layer of the decision tree is generated in its entirety before the next layer is generated) or depth-first (in which case each limb of the tree is generated in turn up to some preset limit).

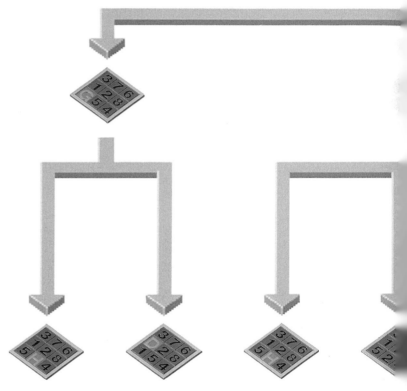

Goal

'known' — the problem will be solved if we can find how to get to it. This is not the case in game-playing, where the machine must look ahead and evaluate all the possible states of the board that can be foreseen in order to choose the one which is both attainable (despite an opponent's best efforts to the contrary) and most advantageous. In chess, for example, even check-mate itself is not a single, unique board state, but any one of an almost infinite variety of board states in which an opponent's king cannot be extracted from check. The fact that a problem-solving program already knows what it is looking for before it starts, so to speak, means that it is not necessary to generate a complete tree and then go through the process of evaluating all the nodes at the final level, backing up the values,

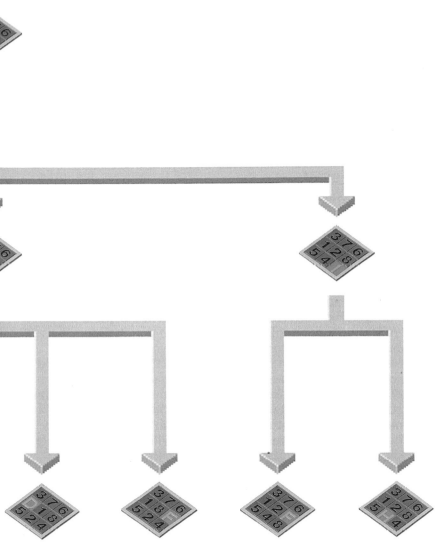

and so on. Instead, as each new node is generated the state which it represents can be compared with a description of the goal state to see whether they match. In other words, the tasks of generating the tree and searching it for possible solutions can proceed step by step in parallel with one another.

In the case of both game-playing and problem-solving it can be said that the production rules *implicitly* represent all the states that exist within the 'search space' – that is to say, if all the rules were applied to every relevant node the result would be a gigantic decision tree incorporating every possible state change. The difference between the two can be summarized as follows. In game-playing it is necessary to generate a complete decision tree –

Once an effective set of heuristics has been devised, the basic generate and test technique can be refined to follow a procedure known as 'hill-climbing'. The search is no longer conducted by following one branch of the tree out to some preset limit and then, if no solution has been found, going back and generating a new branch, and another and another until a solution is discovered. Instead the machine generates all the successor nodes on the next level of the decision tree and then applies its heuristics to determine which should be selected for further expansion. The result is that the search traces a sort of zigzag path through the search space, rather like a dog following the line where the scent seems strongest (see below).

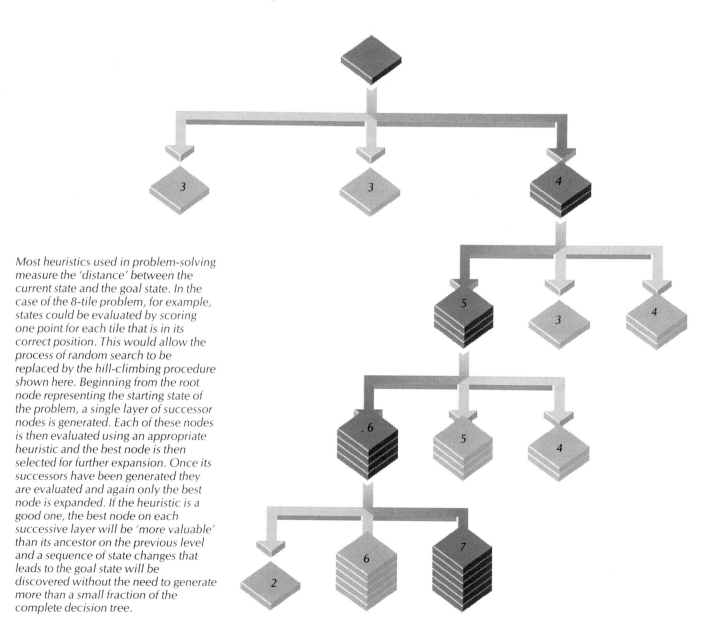

Most heuristics used in problem-solving measure the 'distance' between the current state and the goal state. In the case of the 8-tile problem, for example, states could be evaluated by scoring one point for each tile that is in its correct position. This would allow the process of random search to be replaced by the hill-climbing procedure shown here. Beginning from the root node representing the starting state of the problem, a single layer of successor nodes is generated. Each of these nodes is then evaluated using an appropriate heuristic and the best node is then selected for further expansion. Once its successors have been generated they are evaluated and again only the best node is expanded. If the heuristic is a good one, the best node on each successive layer will be 'more valuable' than its ancestor on the previous level and a sequence of state changes that leads to the goal state will be discovered without the need to generate more than a small fraction of the complete decision tree.

Naturally, success is by no means guaranteed. For heuristics, by their very nature, can never be foolproof. What seems like a promising sequence of state changes may lead, not to a solution, but to an *impasse* of one sort or another. It is, for example, quite common to arrive at a 'local maximum', a node from which there is no way to go but down, or a 'plateau', a region of the search space where all nodes have the same value. In order to escape from these situations it will be necessary either to backtrack and take a different turning at some earlier level in the tree or to experiment by generating a sequence of several nodes and only then pausing to apply the heuristics and discover whether the deadlock has been broken; this operation may have to be repeated several times, just as a dog which has lost the scent will cast about in ever-widening circles in the hope of picking it up again.

BEST-FIRST SEARCHES

Depth-first searches are not, however, the only possibility. There are circumstances in which a breadth-first strategy may be more advantageous. Indeed, as we have already seen, this is usually the method favoured in game-playing, where the entire decision tree is generated to cover the entire search space within reach of the machine before the search process is begun. But a pure breadth-first strategy is extremely demanding in terms of the amount of memory space required and in most cases the choice will fall upon a mixed strategy known as 'best-first' (see next page). This is essentially a variation of the hill-climbing procedure, the difference being that as each new set of nodes is generated they are compared not only with one another, but also with nodes that were generated but not expanded (i.e. their successors were not generated) at previous levels. Thus, if the search seems to be heading away from a solution rather than towards one, it is always possible to backtrack and try an alternative route.

If a best-first search is to be fully effective it is also necessary to evaluate each node by combining *two* functions. The first, as in hill-climbing, is a heuristic which provides an estimate of the distance still to be covered before a solution is reached. But the second is quite simply a record of the number of steps that have already been taken in order to reach the node concerned, i.e. the total number of ancestor nodes which precede it. Thus the two functions, in combination, provide an estimate of the total 'cost', in terms of state changes, of the path that leads from starting state to goal state via a given node. This procedure was first described by Hart in 1968 and is known as the A* algorithm and can be set out as a series of step-by-step instructions that can be relatively easily translated into a computer program.

AND/OR GRAPHS

So far all the techniques we have examined follow the same strictly linear format: the structures which represent the progress of a search are such that every time the machine extends the search it must

The basic hill-climbing procedure can be further developed if the value of each newly generated state is compared not just to the value of the other states which share a common ancestor on the preceding level, but to the value of all the known states generated at previous levels. This will allow the search to proceed according to a technique known as best-first. The first stage of the search (top) follows the hill-climbing method, but the heuristic now gives the lowest value to the best node and the highest value to the worst.

Thus, when the three successors of the single root node are generated and it is determined that their values are, reading from left to right, 8, 7 and 6, it is the rightmost that is selected for expansion, generating a further three successor nodes that are worth 8, 10 and 12. Since none of these values is as good as the 7 of the centre node on the level above, the right-hand branch of the tree is abandoned at the next stage (centre) and the successors of the central node are generated. When evaluated, these three nodes score 10, 9 and 8. There are now three nodes, all apparently of equal promise, since each has been evaluated at 8. If, however, we now add in the 'cost' of reaching each of these nodes, counting 1 point for each state change required, it becomes clear that the best node is the so far unexpanded one on the left-hand branch of the tree, since it scores 9 (8 + 1) as against the 10 (8 + 2) of its rivals. This branch, previously the least promising, is therefore now expanded (bottom), generating a further three nodes which must now be evaluated, bearing in mind that a cost of 2 points will be incurred in reaching any of them.

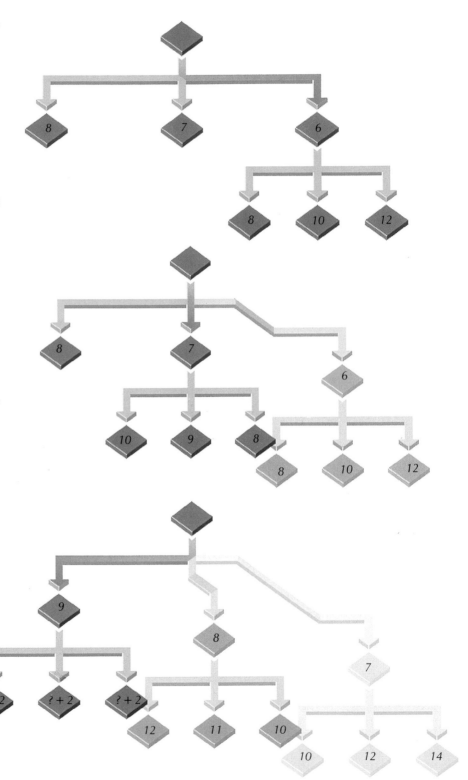

make a choice and select one node for expansion. For this reason, the structures are called 'OR trees' (or 'OR graphs'). But there are many problems where it would be helpful to dispense with this sort of step-by-step progression and substitute a procedure which allowed for the fact that a solution can often be reached only indirectly or that the solution of the main problem may best be reached via the solution of one or more subsidiary problems.

Suppose, for example, we find ourselves stranded late at night and far from home. We face a choice between a long cold walk *or* finding a taxi. But suppose that, in addition, we discover that we have come out with very little money. Now our dilemma is increased: either we walk home *or* we borrow some money *and* find a taxi. In other words, assuming that we are reluctant to choose the walking option, we now have two problems, both of which must be solved. Simply finding a taxi would be pointless because we have no money to pay the fare, and obtaining the money will not help us unless we can also find a taxi.

This sort of problem can best be represented by a structure called an AND-OR graph. Now, while some of the lines linking successor nodes to their ancestors still represent simple OR choices, others are linked by arcs that represent AND combinations and show that if further nodes are generated on either path, success will depend upon a goal state being discovered further along the other path as well (see below).

The search techniques for AND-OR graphs must take account of the fact that when two paths through the search space are linked by an AND arc the total cost of arriving at a solution will always be made up of the sum of two values. In the case of our problem of finding a way to get home, we must add the 'cost' of borrowing the money to the 'cost' of finding a taxi before we can make a fair comparison with the 'cost' of walking home. In order to deal with this point, the values attached to nodes radiating from an AND arc are added together, and the cost of travelling from the arc to the nodes is also

An AND-OR graph can be used to represent the problem faced by someone stranded late at night with no money. One of the branches leading to a solution (walking home) is a simple OR branch; but the other two branches are linked by an arc in order to show that the alternative solution (going home in a taxi) is dependent on both obtaining some money AND finding a taxi.

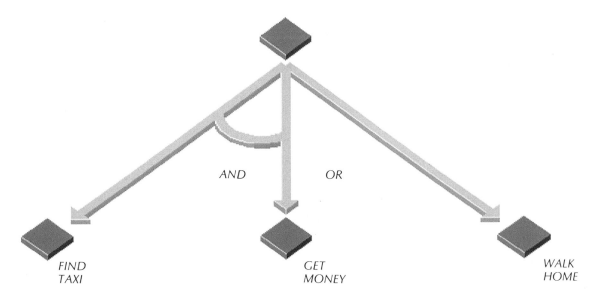

FIND
TAXI

AND   OR

GET
MONEY

WALK
HOME

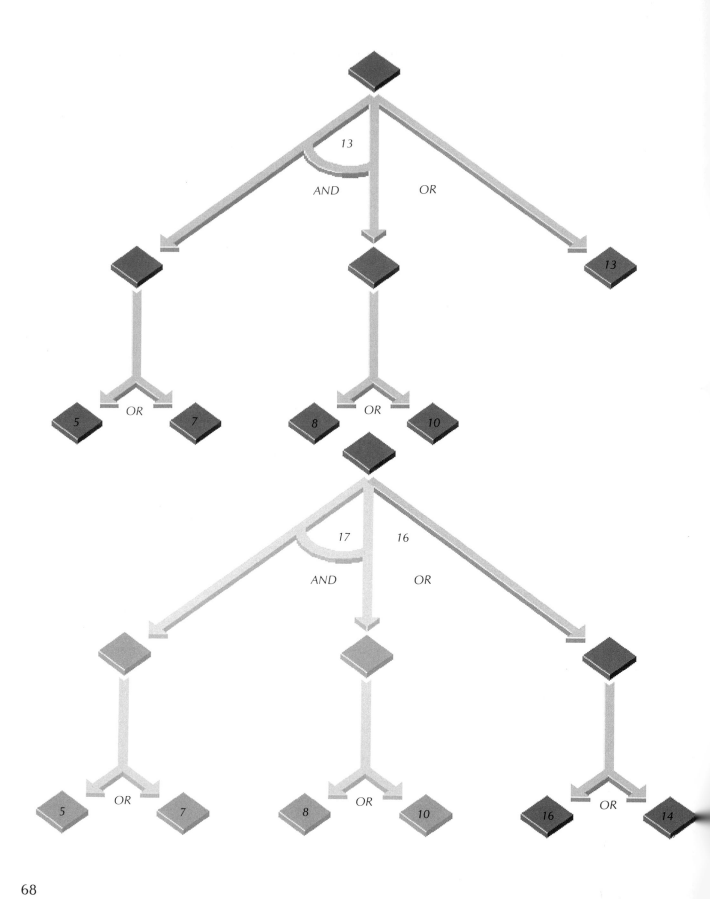

added, before the grand total is backed up to the arc itself. The machine can then determine in which direction to expand the search by comparing these backed up values with similar ones at other arcs, or with the values attached to nodes that have no ANDs in their ancestry (see left).

Another factor which must be considered is the need to make sure that time is not wasted expanding one branch of the search if it is linked by an AND arc to another branch which has come to a dead end and been shown to be unsolvable. Finally, it is always possible that an OR branch in one area of the search space will lead back to a state that already exists on an AND branch in another area. This means that the shortest route is not always the 'cheapest' — a roundabout path that includes no ANDs may be less costly than a direct one which involves finding solutions along a subsidiary AND branch. For this reason, some programs evaluate nodes only in terms of the distance which remains to be covered, ignoring the costs so far incurred.

BI-DIRECTIONAL REASONING AND MEANS-ENDS ANALYSIS

Now we must turn to yet another possible search strategy, known as bi-directional reasoning. In its simplest form, this consists of two breadth-first searches conducted simultaneously, one working forwards from the starting state and the other working backwards from the goal state. If new levels of the two decision trees are generated alternately, and the newly generated nodes on each tree compared with each other, then as soon as a match is found the shortest possible route between starting state and goal state will have been discovered.

Bi-directional reasoning is often used to solve what are known as robot task problems. Typically, these involve calculating the most economical sequence of moves required to perform some simple task such as restacking a pile of coloured blocks in a different order (see next page). It was also the basis of one of the direct descendants of the GPS, a program called STRIPS. Devised by R. E. Fikes and Nils Nilssen of the Stanford Research Institute, STRIPS guided a mobile robot called SHAKEY which was required to navigate its way around a series of 'rooms', making its way through connecting doorways and avoiding various obstacles.

Bi-directional reasoning is not, however, without its difficulties. If, for example, there are several starting states *and* several goal states, there will always be a risk that the forward search and the backward search will pass each other like ships in the night. If this occurs, then, at best, time will have been wasted finding not one solution but two. For a problem of any size, moreover, the breadth-first strategy, even when pursued in both directions at once, may generate decision trees that are unmanageably large. In the GPS and its derivatives, therefore, the use of bi-directional reasoning was coupled with another technique, 'means-ends analysis', which allows the distance between current state and goal state to be reduced by stages. In other words, rather than being treated as a whole, the problem is broken down into a series of smaller sub-

Opposite: When evaluating the nodes on an AND-OR graph it is necessary to take account not only of the fact that, when two branches are linked by an AND arc, the values of the terminal nodes must be combined, but also of the costs involved in traversing both branches. In the case of the top illustration, the best node (assuming that it is the one with the lowest value) might appear to be the one at the bottom left, with a value of 5, certainly it appears far more promising than the one on the far right which has a value of 13. If, however, the 5 is added to the value, 8, of the best node on the other branch of the AND arc and the combined total of 13 is backed up to the arc (centre) it becomes apparent that both branches of the OR choice at the root node have the same value. To resolve the question, a problem-solving program might expand the rightmost branch of the tree (bottom illustration), generating two new nodes, of which the best is valued at 14 (right). But before concluding that the score of 13 at the AND arc represents the best available score, it is necessary to add in the cost of traversing both branches: this involves 4 state changes, bringing the backed-up score at the arc to 17 — a higher, and therefore worse, value than the alternative figure of 14 plus only 2 state changes.

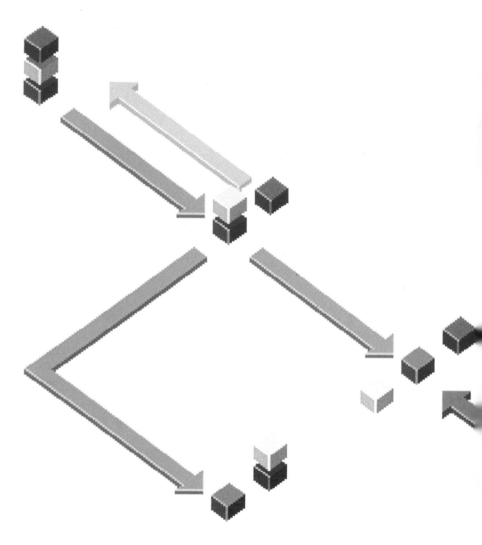

Bi-directional reasoning is here used to solve a simple robot task problem. The starting state of the problem is shown at the top left, where three coloured blocks are stacked in the order red-on-yellow-on-blue. The goal state is the situation at the bottom right, where the blocks have been restacked in the order red-on-blue-on-yellow. The first stage in the forwards reasoning process involves taking the red block off the top of the stack and putting it on the ground or, of course, back on top of the stack which would simply restore the problem to its starting state. The first stage in the backwards reasoning process is also clear: if the red block is to be on top of the stack in the goal state then the last state change must involve picking it up off the ground for if at this point it was not previously on the ground the only other place it could have been was on top of the stack.

Returning now to the forwards reasoning end, there are only two possible steps that might advance the problem towards a solution: the yellow block must be picked up and either placed on the ground or stacked on top of the red block. Similarly, if we switch back to the backwards reasoning end, only two of the states that might precede the one where the red block is on the ground and the blue one is stacked on the yellow need be considered: the state where all three blocks are on the ground and the state where the blue is on the red. But the first of these states, the one with all three blocks on the ground, is identical to a state we have already reached from the forwards reasoning end. It has therefore been established that the most economical route from starting state to goal state involves just four state changes: take the red block off the top of the stack and put it on the ground; take the yellow block off the blue block and place it on the ground; pick up the blue block and stack it on the yellow one; pick up the red block and stack it on the blue one.

problems, each of which can be tackled separately. This has the effect of restricting the size of the search space; for instead of a single decision tree radiating outwards from a single root node, there will now be a series of trees each terminating in a node which represents both a solution of one sub-problem and the root node from which the search for a solution to the next sub-problem will commence (see page 73). Seen in these terms, means-ends analysis is no more than a technical term for the strategy we adopt when we decide that a difficult problem will be simplified if we tackle it one step at a time.

But the success of the strategy depends crucially upon the problem-solver being able to determine whether the solution to a sub-problem will indeed bring the problem as a whole nearer to a solution or whether, on the contrary, it represents no more than a sideways or, worse still, a backwards move in the overall search space. To put it slightly differently, there is still a need for some heuristic yardstick that can be used to measure the distance between the current state of the problem and the goal state (or the starting state, in the case of backwards reasoning).

The algorithm employed in means-ends analysis is rather different from those we have discussed so far. It starts by defining a set of 'operators' appropriate to the problem that is being considered; these represent the *means* – the various actions that can be taken in order to transform one state into another. For each operator there will be one or more production rules. The left-hand side of a rule consists of a list of preconditions – in other words it catalogues the criteria which must be met by a state description before the operator can be applied to it – while the right-hand side describes the result, this represents the *ends* – the way(s) in which the state of the problem will have been changed as a consequence of applying the operator.

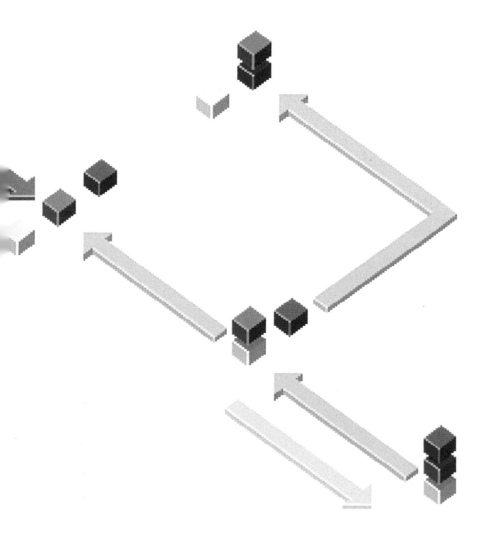

MEANS-ENDS ANALYSIS

Let us suppose that we are faced with the problem of how best to arrange a journey from our home in Amsterdam to an hotel in Brussels. We shall limit the *means*, i.e. the operators, to four: AIR, RAIL, BUS and TAXI.

There is a single rule for AIR which has two preconditions: in order to apply the rule we must already be at Schipol airport and we must have a valid ticket. The *end* of AIR (the result of applying the rule) is that we arrive at Brussels airport.

RAIL again has one rule with two preconditions: we must be present at the station at Amsterdam and have the money to buy a ticket. The end of RAIL is that we arrive at the railway station in Brussels.

There are three rules for BUS: The first has the precondition that we should be at home and have a little cash, and either money for a railway ticket or a valid airline ticket; the end is that we arrive at Amsterdam station. The second has the precondition that we are already at Amsterdam station (the terminal for airport buses) with a little cash and an airline ticket in our pocket, and the end is that we arrive at Schipol airport. The third has the precondition that we must be at either Brussels airport or Brussels station, still with a little cash, and the end is that we arrive at the hotel – the goal state.

TAXI also has three rules: The preconditions of the first are that we should be at home with a lot of cash and an airline ticket; the end is that we arrive at Schipol airport. The second has the precondition that we are at home with a lot of cash, enough for both taxi and railway ticket; the end is that we arrive at Amsterdam station. The third has the precondition that we are already in Brussels, at either the airport or the station, with a lot of cash remaining, and the end is that we are delivered to the hotel – again, the goal state.

The operation of the algorithm in its most basic form is extremely simple. Beginning at the starting state, home, we may apply one of two operators, BUS and TAXI (the choice depending upon whether we can meet the 'lot of cash' precondition that is attached to TAXI) and, as a result, will arrive at either Amsterdam station – where we may choose to apply either RAIL or BUS depending on which preconditions we can meet – or Schipol airport – where, assuming we have a ticket, we can apply AIR – and so on.

In the case of the example shown the task of measuring the distance between current state and goal state is, clearly, very straightforward. Unfortunately, however, there are many categories of problem where it is far from obvious how progress towards a solution might be measured. To take a very simple instance, you cannot measure progress through a maze in terms of the distance between your current position and the exit, for it is in the nature of mazes that you may have to go 'backwards' in order to go 'forwards'.

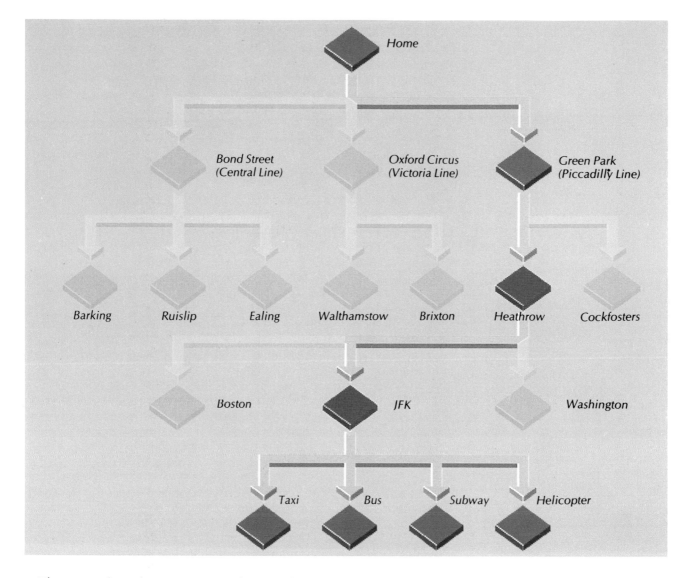

The example is, however, unrealistic in that, if we were planning a real journey the major decision would be whether we should go by plane or train, and we would make this choice before we turned to the subsidiary issue of whether we should take buses or taxis to and from the terminals at either end of the journey. Means-ends analysis can be elaborated to work in a similar fashion, to solve the most important parts of a problem first and then bridge the comparatively minor gaps that remain.

The key factor is, of course, the need to determine which parts of a problem are of primary importance and which are secondary and can, therefore, be temporarily set aside. This requires the use of heuristics which will enable the machine to select the operators with results that will significantly reduce the distance between the current state and the goal state or, if backwards reasoning is being used, the current state and the starting state. When such an operator is identified it may be applied, even if its preconditions do not exactly match the current state, or its results do not match the goal state.

In effect the result will be a 'bridge', standing in isolation in the middle of the search space, which, if the right choice of operator has been made, represents a solution to the main part of the problem. The gaps on either side of the bridge represent the sub-problems that still have to be solved, this can now be done by searching for operators with preconditions and results which match the states on either side of the gap. If the problem is a large one there may be several such 'bridges' with further gaps between them, and the process of linking the bridges to each other may involve the creation of several smaller bridges and a search for further operators which will close the remaining gaps.

THE LIMITS OF MECHANICAL PROBLEM-SOLVING

There is no disputing the fact that means-ends analysis, and the other search strategies we have been discussing, are extraordinarily ingenious and elegant logical devices. It is also clear that, in some respects at least, they are closely related to our own problem-solving methods. But before we conclude that artificial intelligence can confidently look forward to the day when machines will be able to cope with real-life problems, it will be salutary to remind ourselves of a number of points.

The first and perhaps most telling is that, so far at least, it has proved impossible to extend these techniques to cope with the kind of situations which arise in the real world. This is in part due to inadequacies in other areas of artificial intelligence – before industrial robots can even begin to solve problems in the home or on the factory floor, for example, they will need vision systems that allow them to see where they are going and what they are doing. But there is a further difficulty. In the field of problem-solving, as elsewhere, artificial intelligence researchers have generally started by reducing tasks to what were perceived to be their logical essentials. The assumption was that if ways could be found of dealing with the central issues then it would be comparatively easy to extend the methods to cope with the 'messiness' that charac-terizes the real world. But the world beyond the laboratory walls is rather more complicated than had been supposed. Its contents are rarely arranged in the well-ordered fashion that typifies a chess board or a so-called 'block-world' made up of simple objects with well-defined geometrical forms (see Chapters 5 and 7).

So, once artificial intelligence ventured beyond the contrived simplicity of the laboratory, it was confronted with a 'combinatorial explosion' quite as dramatic as that faced by the chess-player who tries to look half a dozen moves ahead – and far less amenable to logic. In real-world problems the factors multiplied to form combi-nations that were simply beyond the capacity of existing algorithms. If, for example, a set of tools is tossed higgledy-piggedly into a box, then the task of picking up the screwdriver which happens to be at the bottom of the box can no longer be solved by the sort of methods we have been discussing. In effect, the state of the objects defies precise definition – and the number of possible states that might occur within the box is, to all intents and purposes, infinite.

The combinatorial explosion is a phenomenon that affects all branches of artificial intelligence and can be illustrated by the familiar problem of the travelling salesman who must make calls in a number of different towns, planning his journey in such a way that he travels the shortest possible distance. When there are only three calls to be made, the problem is fairly trivial, for there are only six possible routes. But double the number of calls to six and there will be 720 possible routes; double it again to twelve, and there will be 592,099,200! The combinatorial explosion, in short, is a consequence of the simple fact that the complexity of a problem increases exponentially each time a new factor is introduced. This means that the gap between laboratory problems and real-world problems is not a narrow crevasse which artificial intelligence can confidently expect to bridge in the fullness of time, but a yawning chasm which seems to bar the way to further progress along current lines of research almost indefinitely.

The second point to be made is that, in terms of the demands made upon our intelligence, actually finding the solution to a problem is frequently a comparatively straightforward task – the real difficulty lies in determining *how* to tackle the problem.

During our schooldays, for example, most of us will have been confronted with problems such as this:

> Train A leaves point X at 3.00 pm and travels at a steady 40 miles per hour towards point Y which is 100 miles away; at 3.30 pm train B leaves point Y and travels towards point X at a steady 20 miles per hour. When will the trains meet?

The problematical element is of course, in the way the question has been framed – as soon as it is recognised that the 'problem' is no more than a few simple 'sums' cunningly disguised, the solution is soon found. (For those who still find themselves flummoxed by conundrums of this kind, the calculation goes as follows. Between 3.00 and 3.30, train A will travel $40 \div 2$ (i.e. 20) miles. Thus, when train B departs, the two trains will be separated by $100 - 20$ (i.e. 80) miles and closing at a speed of 60 $(40 + 20)$ miles per hour. They will therefore meet 80 minutes later, at 4.50 pm.)

Similarly, the essence of a 'brain-teaser' is the need to find a method appropriate to the problem. Consider, for example, a puzzle concerning cannibals and missionaries. Three missionaries, Alan, David and Hugh, have been captured by cannibals. They are told that if they want the chance to convert their captors, they will first have to demonstrate their intelligence by solving the following problem. The cannibals have five wooden balls, two black and three white. The missionaries are told that they will be blindfolded and one ball will be placed on the head of each; then, with the blindfolds removed, each will be asked in turn to name the colour of the ball that is on his own head. If none of the three is able to answer correctly, then into the stewpot they will go.

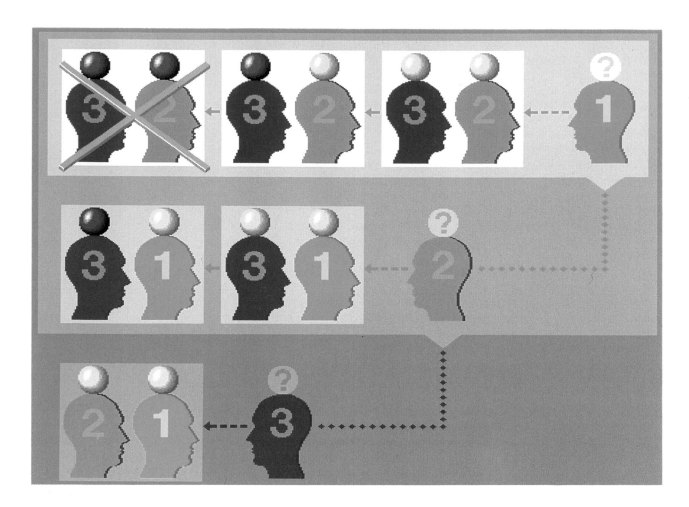

Obviously, if the cannibals put black balls on two of the missionaries' heads the third would have no difficulty in deducing that the ball on his on head must be white. But in this case, they put white balls on the heads of all three. Thus when Alan, the first to be asked, sees that both his colleagues have white balls on their heads he has no means of telling whether the ball on his own head is the third of the white ones or one of the two black ones: he has to say that he does not know the answer to the question. David faces the same problem and is forced to give the same answer. Yet Hugh, the last to be asked, is able to say with complete confidence that the ball on his own head is white. How could he have known?

The answer is not that he possessed some insight which his colleagues lacked, but that, provided he had faith in his colleagues' intelligence, he could deduce the colour of the ball on his own head on the basis of the 'don't know' answers given by Alan and David. The secret of Hugh's success lies in his use of 'nested thinking': in other words, he had to consider not only the problem as it actually appeared to him, but also the problem as it *might* have appeared to Alan and David (see above).

This example illustrates the point that once we see *how* to solve a problem we have, in many cases, overcome the major difficulty. But the problem-solving techniques used in artificial intelligence are concerned merely with implementing the sequence of 'mechanical' operations needed to find the solution to a problem once an appropriate method has been identified. It could be argued that if programs based upon these techniques behave intelligently, then the intelligence is that of the programmer, who not only selects the search strategy to be used, but also determines how the states of the problem should be represented, formulates the production rules and devises appropriate heuristics.

There is, moreover, another factor that seems to come into play once a human problem-solver has decided how a particular problem should be tackled. In many cases, people do not arrive at a solution by any process of explicit reasoning; rather they seem to rely upon what might be called the 'Aha factor'. A very good example is provided by the cryptic crossword puzzle, for only in the last resort will the experienced crossword addict try to 'work out' the answer to a clue. Much more often the answer seems to come to him almost out of the blue; one moment the clue is apparently meaningless, the next moment all has become clear.

Consider the following crossword clue: 'Thing I tar in order to make waterproof (9)'. The *aficionado* will immediately recognize that the phrase 'in order' is an indication that the solution is likely to be an anagram and a quick check will reveal that the otherwise senseless phrase 'thing I tar' contains the required number of letters. So, the answer is an anagram of 'thing I tar' which is a synonym for 'waterproof'. Up to this point the reasoning has been explicit and logical – though it should be noted that we have only got this far because we have appreciated the ambiguity of 'in order', a feat not easily duplicated by a program. If, as is likely, you have already spotted that the correct answer is 'raintight', you may like to pause and consider how this conclusion was reached?

If we had followed the sort of procedures used in artificial intelligence we would either have had to search through all the possible combinations of the letters *thingitar*, of which there are over 5,000, or run through all the words we know meaning 'waterproof' to see if any of them were made up of those nine letters. However, many readers will probably have found that the answer simply 'came to them'. Others may have made use of their knowledge of English spelling to do a few rapid experiments: 'Could it be a word ending in . . .*ing*? That doesn't seem to work. What about the common combination of consonants *thr*? Can't make any sense of that. Or *ght*? *aght*? No. *ight*? could be. *right*? *intaright*? *rightinat*? try *tight*? *Aha*, of course, it must be *raintight*!'

A good deal of our problem-solving seems to be done in this fashion. It is as if, by playing with the elements of a puzzle, we are able to jump this way and that through the search space, generating a series of possible solutions in rapid succession and quickly discarding those that lead nowhere. By comparison, even the most sophisticated search strategies used in artificial intelligence seem plodding and cumbersome.

Opposite: How the third missionary, Hugh, was able to save himself and his two colleagues. The top row shows the three combinations which the first missionary to be interrogated, Alan, might have seen. Hugh knows that he did not see one on the left (two black balls) because if that had been the case Alan would have known that the ball on his own head must be white. Hugh also realizes that David will have made the same calculation. But if, when David's turn came, and he saw one of the two combinations in the second row, then had he seen the one on the left (a white ball on Alan's head and a black one on Hugh's) he would have known that the ball on his head must be white for, had it been black, Alan would not have had to say 'Don't know'. Since David was not able to give an answer it is clear to Hugh that David must have seen the combination on the right of the middle row and that the ball on his own head is clearly a white one.

CHAPTER 5

USING LANGUAGE

However intelligence is defined, there can be little doubt that, beyond a certain point, its development is crucially dependent upon the ability to use and understand language. It is not just that 'dumb animals', or dumb machines for that matter, are unable to communicate anything but the simplest of messages and thus unable to tell us what they are thinking; but also that, lacking a language within which to frame their thoughts, it seems unlikely that they are capable of the sort of abstract thought that we associate with 'high' intelligence.

It is for this reason that we attribute our own rise to the 'top' of the biological pyramid to our mastery of language. If we had not learnt to use words it seems probable that we would have remained permanently stuck at the level of the great apes; a bit more advanced, perhaps, as tool-users or social hunters, but quite incapable of developing anything that would be recognizable as a civilization. Indeed, for biologists and anthropologists, the link between intelligence and language-use is something of a chicken-and-egg issue. Did *Homo sapiens*, alone among the animal kingdom, develop language because we were the most intelligent species? Or did we become more intelligent than other animals because some evolutionary fluke equipped us with rudimentary vocal chords and thus gave us an opportunity which was denied to other creatures?

The latter proposition is strongly argued by some of the researchers who have been teaching gorillas and chimpanzees to use sign languages, and who claim that the animals, once equipped with a means of communication, can develop language skills akin to our own, albeit of a very primitive nature. Others find the evidence unconvincing and believe that the language gap between human beings and other species will remain forever unbridgeable.

What is not in doubt is that unless intelligent machines are able to communicate easily and freely with human beings, and vice versa, their usefulness will be extremely restricted. For this reason alone, language-use has been a central concern of artificial intelligence from the earliest days.

COMPUTER LANGUAGES AND NATURAL LANGUAGE

Ultimately, of course, all mathematical or logical operations taking place inside a computer are conducted in machine code – i.e. strings of binary 0s and 1s. But it became clear very early on that if communication between man and machine was restricted to machine code the computer would never realize its full potential. Writing a program in machine code is a long and painstaking task and one requiring detailed and specialist knowledge of the computer's internal circuitry, for every central processing unit (or microprocessor chip) is designed to accept one particular form of the code – in technical terms, one 'instruction set'. So almost as soon as people had begun to write programs they also began to seek ways of simplifying the process by encoding instructions in abbreviated form and equipping the machine with specialized programming which would enable it to translate those instructions into machine code automatically.

The first efforts in this direction concentrated on what are known as assembly languages – essentially, these consist of coded abbreviations which can be substituted for the machine-code sequences that represent standard instructions such as 'MOVE', 'ADD', 'STORE' and so on. The programmer types in a sequence of such coded instructions and the computer then 'assembles' its own program by substituting the machine-code equivalents on a one-for-one basis. In the early days, assembly of the program was often a separate operation, the assembly program simply generating a tape which the operator then input into the computer when he wanted to run the program.

Assembly languages certainly speeded things up, and it was easier to remember that 'Multiply' was, say, /M rather than 00111001, but they hardly amount to 'languages' in the accepted sense of the word; they offer little more than a simplified vocabulary and a minimal grammatical structure. It is left up to the programmer to work out the sequence in which the elementary operations each symbol represents should be performed, and this means that every single step has to be spelled out right down to the smallest detail. In order to get the machine to add together two numbers, a programmer will have to give it the instruction to 'FETCH' the first number, not forgetting to specify the address where that number is stored in memory, then do the same for the second number, followed by an instruction to 'ADD' the two together and then an instruction to 'STORE' the resulting figure at another specified address. Assembly languages are, however, still widely used. In the hands of a skilled programmer, they can produce programs that are far more economical, in the sense that they contain only the essential instructions and therefore run more quickly, than those written in 'high-level' languages.

It was only in the mid-1950s that these high-level languages, the ones which we now generally think of as computer languages, began to appear. The first to enjoy widespread success was FORTRAN (standing for FORmula TRANslation) which was devised by a team of IBM programmers led by John Backus between 1954 and 1956. Others, such as ALGOL, BASIC, COBOL, PASCAL, etc., soon followed. Today the range of languages, and the variety of 'dialects' within languages, is so great that it sometimes seems as if the computer scientists have created their own Tower of Babel.

The point about a high-level language is that each instruction may represent a whole series of elementary operations at the machine-code level. This means that, in order to understand a high-level language, a computer must be equipped with a specialized program, called a compiler, which translates a single instruction into what is, essentially, a small machine-code program that the computer can then implement. From the computer user's point of view, the advantage of high-level languages is not only that they free him from the need to follow the computer's operations at the detailed, step-by-step level of machine code, but also that they are designed to bear a superficial resemblance to human speech.

Existing high-level languages are, however, still very far removed from the sort of language we use in our everyday life; indeed they are totally unintelligible to the vast majority of the population who are unfamiliar with computers. Even a language like BASIC, which was specifically designed to be used by beginners, had to be shaped with the requirements of a machine, rather than those of a user, in mind. The use of words like PEEK or POKE, for example, which instruct the computer to perform specified operations, represents little more than a token gesture to the lay user. For artificial intelligence, clearly, the goal must be machines which can understand and communicate in 'natural language'. Such machines would have to be able to understand questions or follow instructions phrased in ordinary, colloquial speech – 'What happens to the net profit if that cost increase we were discussing last week comes through?', 'Stack the big parcels over there and put the little ones in this box here' – and respond in terms which would be comprehensible to the average, untrained human worker.

SURFACE STRUCTURES AND DEEP STRUCTURES

It was fortunate that, just as the prospect of devising natural-language programs began to look like a serious possibility, our whole understanding of what constitutes a language was revolutionized and given a new mathematical rigour. This was very largely the result of the work of one man, the American mathematician Naom Chomsky.

Before 1957, when Chomsky's seminal work, *Syntactic Structures*, first appeared, linguistics was concerned with the analysis of grammatical structures only in so far as this contributed to the task of classifying languages, comparing them and establishing their relationships, if any. The analysis was of a traditional kind: sentences were parsed in order to determine the parts of speech used and their grammatical relationships. The grammar of a language was both a set of rules which prescribed how the words of a language such as Latin, French or English *should* be put together in order to form 'correct' sentences, or, in the case of 'primitive' languages, a description of the grammatical structures employed by native speakers.

Chomsky, however, saw a grammar as a set of rules of a rather different kind, something much closer to the laws which scientists formulate in order to describe the workings of nature. He also suggested that, beneath the differing 'surface structures' (the words which we actually speak or write), there lay 'deep structures' that were based on rules common to languages that had different surface structures. Furthermore, he showed that these deep structures could be expressed in mathematical or logical terms. For artificial intelligence, searching for ways in which a logical machine could master language, Chomsky's ideas might have been heaven-sent. Not only did they allow the whole issue to be approached with a rigour and formal precision that had hitherto been lacking, but the fact that they were expressed in mathematical terms meant that they could readily be translated into programmable form.

Chomsky's grammatical models were in fact very closely related to the sort of abstract, or hypothetical, machines that we discussed in Chapter 2. In essence, he saw a grammar as a set of rules that, if implemented 'mechanically', could 'generate' all the possible *grammatical* sentences in a language and, what was equally important, would *not* generate any of the *ungrammatical* ones.

This approach allowed Chomsky to tackle an issue central to the nature of grammar: how can we account for the creativity that is involved in using a language? Any language will, of course, have a finite number of words in its vocabulary; and grammarians must assume, if their labours are not to be deemed futile from the start, that any grammar will contain a finite number of rules. But, clearly, some of those rules can be applied more than once in the same sentence. We can, for example, start with the sentence: 'I am having lunch with a man who publishes books' and enlarge it by adding another phrase using the same construction, '. . . and who lives in London', and another '. . . and who has three children', and so on without breaking any grammatical rules. Admittedly the sentence will soon become unmanageably long, but the point is that there is no clear rule that says when we have to stop. And this means that a finite number of rules, applied to a finite number of words, can generate an infinite number of sentences.

In fact, even in everyday speech, each of us will construct some sentences which are *new*, which have never been constructed before in the entire history of the language. How then do we, who construct the sentences, and our listeners or readers who understand them, both recognize that they are grammatical? And, when we do inadvertently construct an ungrammatical sentence, how does our audience *know* that it is faulty? In the case of a new sentence such judgements must, clearly, be based upon reference to a set of rules which all the users of a language have tacitly agreed upon.

But people who know no formal grammar, who have never learnt the rules governing surface structures, are able to make such judgements just as effectively as those who do know the rules. Indeed, we have all probably had the experience of hearing or reading a sentence which we immediately recognized to be ungrammatical without being able to put our finger on the mistake. If we could understand the nature of the unspoken rules we rely upon in making these judgements, we would have gone a long way towards solving the problems that are involved in constructing a language-using machine.

Before examining the explanations which Chomsky offered, however, we must pause to clear up one potential source of misunderstanding. When Chomsky talks of a grammar as a set of rules for *generating* sentences, he uses the word in an abstract and rather specialized sense. He does not suppose that language users

The decision tree below represents a finite state grammar that will generate sentences using just ten items of vocabulary: four articles (that, this, those and these) which can precede four subjects (man, woman, men and women), one verb (ran) and one object (races). Starting from the root node representing 'sentence', the hypothetical acceptor mechanism examines each word as it is fed in to see whether it is listed in one of the nodes representing a legitimate 'next state' on the tree. Thus, if the article 'these' is fed in the machine will accept it, moving to the state represented by the 'those/ these' node, in which state it can then accept either 'men' or 'women' but not 'man' or 'woman'. Eight sentences can in fact be generated by this grammar.

The decision tree to the right highlights some of the problems that begin to arise once a finite state grammar is enlarged to deal with bigger vocabularies and more complex sentences. The tree has now been extended to allow for the possibility of adding the adjective 'strong' between article and subject; there are now two verbs, 'runs' and 'run'; and the object, which may be either singular or plural ('race' or 'races'), can be preceded not only by 'the' but also by 'that/this' or 'these/those'.

consciously employ the rules to generate the sentences they utter, but rather that it is the existence of underlying rules which accounts for their competence. In other words, a grammar is an abstract formula that 'explains' our ability to construct grammatical, and for the most part *only* grammatical, sentences from any given vocabulary in the same sense that the traffic code 'explains' why we all drive on the same side of the road. We can always refer to the law that lays down the rules, but for the most part we obey it without pausing to consider why we do so. We have no difficulty at all, however, in recognizing when someone breaks it.

Thus, when we talk of a grammar generating sentences we are referring as much to the ability to understand what other people say, in the sense of being able to determine whether or not it is grammatical, as to the ability to construct the sentences we ourselves utter. In fact the hypothetical machines which Chomsky considered were all designed to 'accept' or 'fail' sentences fed into them, i.e. to determine whether or not they fell within the bounds of a given grammar. This is a point that may become clearer if we actually look at an example, so we will start by considering the first and simplest type of grammar discussed by Chomsky, what he called a 'finite state grammar'.

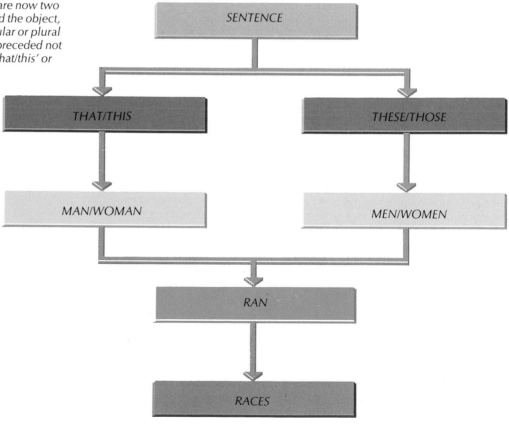

A machine designed to implement a grammar of this kind must accept or reject each word in the order in which it is fed in. Thus the machine will accept (or the grammar can generate) the sentence 'That man ran the race', but it will fail the ungrammatical sentence 'Those man ran the race', for having accepted the plural article, 'those', it must fail the singular noun, 'man', which comes next. Complications arise, however, when additional words are added, as in 'Those strong men ran the race'. For now the machine has to have some means of remembering that 'those' was plural while deciding whether or not to accept 'strong'. In technical terms, this means that the machine will require additional internal states, a point that becomes clearer when we consider the process of accepting a sentence in terms of the decision-tree model which will be familiar from earlier chapters (see left and below).

In practice the number of internal states required by a machine which was to handle even a very restricted version of natural language would soon become unmanageable. Moreover, as Chomsky was able to show, finite state grammars are, even in theory, insufficiently powerful to generate all the sentences of a language like English, which contains an indefinite number of so-called mirror-image sentences. These are sentences constructed in

At first glance this new structure appears satisfactory in that it will generate sentences such as 'These strong women run those races'. But further examination reveals a number of problems. In its present form the grammar would permit the acceptance of the ungrammatical sentence beginning 'These strong woman. . .'. If this was to be avoided there would have to be two 'strong' nodes, one between 'that/this' and 'man/woman' and another between 'those/these' and 'men/women'. Worse still is the fact that the loops in the structure which allow the articles 'that/this' to be incorporated between 'runs' and 'race', or the articles 'these/those' between 'run' and 'races', would also permit the acceptance of endless nonsense sentences of the form: 'This strong man runs that strong woman runs this man runs. . . .'. This confusion between subject and object could only be avoided by adding duplicate 'that/this' and 'these/those' nodes which would be incorporated alongside the 'the' node between the verb nodes and the object nodes.

This example clearly illustrates the point that in order to cope with even a very limited range of sentences a finite state grammar requires an acceptor mechanism with a virtually limitless range of internal states.

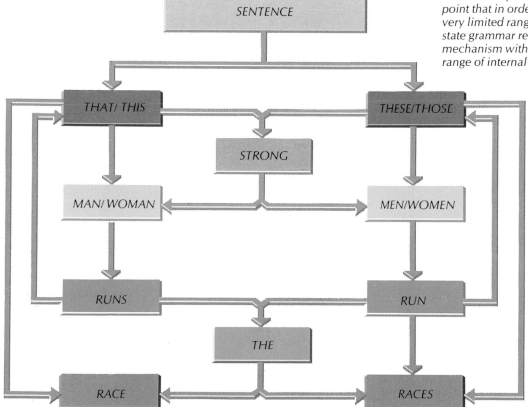

the form of a palindrome, where there are dependencies between the first element and the last, the second element and the next to last and so on. A simple example is, 'Coaches who believe that men who run races that are long need stamina are right' – 'are right' is dependent on 'coaches', 'need stamina' on 'men', and 'are long' on 'races'.

In order to cope with all possible sentences of this form, it would be necessary for a machine to have an infinite range of states. Given that a computer is, as we saw in Chapter 2, an example of a finite state machine, it might be thought that this requirement presented artificial intelligence with an insurmountable obstacle, that no computer however capacious its memory could ever be large enough to master natural language. In practice, however, the real problem with a finite state grammar is that a worthwhile vocabulary, coupled with even a fairly restricted set of grammatical options, will involve a machine in immensely long and complex search processes.

But the next kind of grammar which Chomsky considered, a 'context-free, phrase structure grammar', overcomes this problem in an extremely ingenious fashion. In order to generate a sentence using a phrase structure grammar it is necessary to have four sets of mathematical objects. First there is the vocabulary itself, usually described by the symbol V_t (for vocabulary of 'terminal' elements), and this can be as large or small as you please – in the case of people, of course, it consists of all the words they use or understand, in the case of a practical, working machine it may be convenient to restrict it to a few hundred, or even a few dozen, words. Next there is a vocabulary of 'auxiliary' elements, V_a, consisting of terms like *sentence, noun phrase, noun, verb phrase, verb*, etc., which are required in order to describe the grammatical elements themselves. Then there must be a set of production rules, P, and finally an element called S which, when fed into the machine, causes it to 'start'. S is usually included in the machine's vocabulary, V_t, i.e. the machine can be so constructed that it starts as soon as it receives any one of the words with which a sentence can legitimately begin.

The key to understanding the process lies in the nature of the production rules, P. These all take the form of substitution rules which determine the way in which a single object in V_a, such as *sentence*, may be replaced either by two or more smaller objects such as *noun phrase* and *verb*, or by objects from V_t. For example, a very simple specimen of the largest possible object, *sentence*, such as 'The man hit the ball', can be broken down into *noun phrase – verb – noun phrase*. Once the sentence has been broken down into its basic grammatical elements, these may be replaced by substituting elements from the vocabulary itself, V_t. The process of decomposing a sentence in this fashion can be represented by a decision tree, as before, or in a number of other ways (see opposite and pages 86–7).

The real ingenuity of a phrase structure grammar, however, lies in the fact that the memory of the hypothetical 'acceptor machine' can, notionally, be structured in the form of a 'push-down stack'.

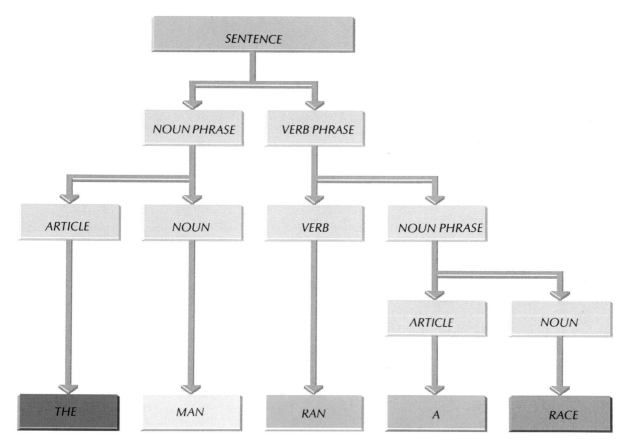

This can be visualized as something rather like the magazine of an automatic rifle – but storing objects from Va rather than rounds of ammunition. The essential feature of such a memory is that objects can only be added to or taken from the top of the stack, so that every time an object is added all those objects already in the store are pushed down one and every time an object is removed the one immediately beneath it rises to the top. But we do not need to actually describe how a push-down stack machine would work in any detail, or even decide whether such a thing could in practice be built. All we need is a precise description of what it will do, for this will enable us to write a computer program that will simulate its operation.

A machine with a push-down stack can, in principle, deal with all sentences that can occur in a language that is 'context-free'. Grammars that are 'context-sensitive', that take account, for example, of the need for verbs to agree with their subjects as in 'The man who runs the race' and 'The men who run the race', are more complex and will not be considered here. For our purposes the essential point is that the use of a push-down stack dramatically

This illustration and that on the next page show alternative ways of representing the structure of the sentence 'The man ran a race' in terms of a phrase structure grammar. The grey nodes on the decision tree all represent objects in the vocabulary of auxiliary elements (Va). The root node, representing the basic object 'sentence' is succeeded by two smaller objects, 'noun phrase' and 'verb phrase'. The 'noun phrase' node is in turn succeeded by 'article' and 'noun' which, in a final step, are succeeded by 'the' and 'man', objects from the vocabulary of terminal elements, Vt. In the same way, going down the right-hand side of the tree, 'verb phrase' is succeeded by 'verb' and 'noun phrase' and 'verb' is then succeeded by an object from Vt, 'ran', while noun phrase is again decomposed into 'article' and 'noun' which are replaced, respectively, with 'a' and 'race'.

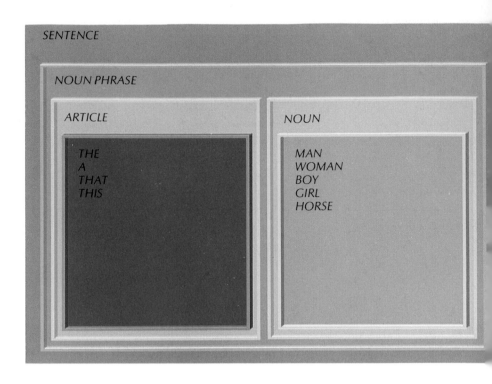

reduces the range of internal states required by the acceptor mechanism. A glance at the illustration on page 85, for example, shows that in order to determine whether or not the sentence 'The man ran a race' was grammatical, the acceptor required fourteen internal states – each represented by one of the nodes of the tree – for it could not accept the sentence until it had generated the final node, 'race'. A requirement for thirteen internal states obviously presents no problems, but had the number of objects in Vt and Va and the range of production rules been extended to cover even a very limited range of sentences, the tree would have contained thousands of nodes, most of them representing 'dead ends'.

Using a push-down stack, however, the acceptor does not have to 'remember' a list of known states, in fact all it has to consider is the state represented by the object currently on top of the stack. For as each new state is generated it will either be accepted (and can therefore be 'forgotten') or it will be placed upon the stack. The operation of the acceptor can be summarized as follows. It examines the current state, the object currently on top of the stack, and if it can be replaced by the next word in the sentence, then the word will be accepted and the corresponding object removed from the stack so that the one below it rises to the top. But if the object on top of the stack cannot be replaced by the input word, the acceptor replaces it by a string of objects from Va, inserting them into the stack one on top of another, and then starts again, examining the new object now at the top of the stack which will, of course, be the first object in the string. This process is best understood by following through a simple example such as that on pages 87–90.

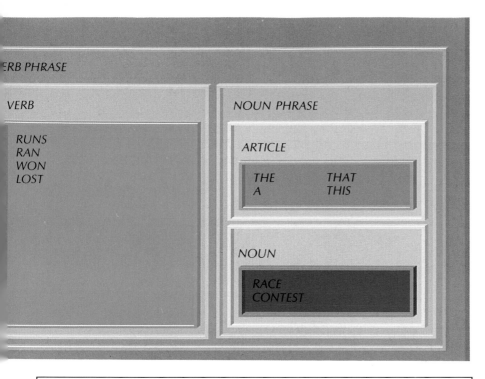

VERB PHRASE

VERB

RUNS
RAN
WON
LOST

NOUN PHRASE

ARTICLE

THE THAT
A   THIS

NOUN

RACE
CONTEST

THE OPERATION OF A PUSH-DOWN STACK

The advantages of a push-down stack are best understood by taking a simple example and following the operations of the acceptor mechanism step by step. For the sake of simplicity, we will limit ourselves to a very restricted language which can be defined, in terms of phrase structure grammar, as follows:

The first set of objects, Vt, consists of the following English words: man, woman, race, won, lost, strong, long, the, a.

The second set of objects, Va, contains seven elements:
Sentence – (S)
Noun phrase – (NP)
Verb phrase – (VP)
Noun – (N)
Verb - (V)
Adjective – (Ad)
Article – (A)

The production rules, P, are as follows:
(The symbol := should be read as 'can be replaced by'. Objects separated by the symbol/are alternatives; in all other cases a string of two or more objects must be kept intact and in the same order.)

1. (S):= (NP) (VP)
2. (NP):= (A) (N)
3. (NP):= (A) (Ad) (N)
4. (VP):= (V) (NP)
5. (N):= man/ woman/ race
6. (V):= won/lost
7. (Ad):= strong/long
8. (A):= the/ a

This illustration shows the same structure as that on the previous page, this time represented by a series of nested boxes. Each box is equivalent to one node on the decision tree and the boxes nested within it are equivalent to its successor nodes; thus the largest box, representing 'sentence' contains smaller 'noun phrase' and 'verb phrase' boxes, which in turn contain yet smaller boxes representing 'article', 'noun', and so forth. Now, however, the innermost boxes, the ones that contain the objects from Vt, each hold a number of alternatives. This means that instead of simply representing the breakdown of a single sentence, this illustration represents the structure of an entire grammar, albeit an extremely limited one, which can be used to generate a whole range of sentences such as 'That girl won the contest' or 'This horse ran this race'.

Yet another way of representing the same structure involves the use of nested brackets (in this case, for the sake of brevity, abbreviations have been used for the objects in Va and only one object from Vt has been included in each category): (S(NP(Art(the))(N(man))) (VP(V(ran))(NP(Art(a))(N(race)))))).

Finally, S, the starting symbol, may be either one of two elements from Vt, 'a' or 'the'.

The language we have defined contains a whole range of grammatical sentences – 'A strong man won the race', 'The strong woman lost a long race', and so forth. We shall now take just one of those sentences, 'The man won a long race', and imagine that it is fed, one word at a time, into a system made up of an acceptor mechanism and a push-down stack. In principle the operation of the acceptor is simplicity itself: as each word is fed in it compares it with the object currently on the top of the stack, and if the production rules show that the object can be replaced by the input word, then the word will be accepted, the object on top of the stack will be discarded and the next input can be fed in. But if the input cannot be accepted, the object on top of the stack will, if the production rules allow it, be replaced by other objects. When the stack has been emptied the entire sentence has been accepted; but if at any point none of the production rules are applicable to the object currently on top of the stack, the sentence will have failed. There are, however, some complications even in the case of this very simple language, as we shall see if we follow the process through one step at a time.

INPUTS	CONTENTS OF STACK	COMMENTS
the	(S)	When the process begins the stack is empty and the acceptor's first step, triggered by the input of one of the starting symbols, 'the', is to place the object (S) on the stack.
the	(NP) (VP)	Rule 1 has now been applied and the object (S) has been replaced in the only possible way, by substituting the string (NP) (VP).
the	(A) (2) (N) (2) (NP) (2) (VP)	With (NP) at the top of the stack the acceptor found that there were two applicable rules – Rule 2 and Rule 3. Since it had no means of knowing which of the two would be appropriate in this case, it could not simply discard and replace (NP), instead it has put the first possible replacement string, (A) (N), on top of (NP) and attached a (2) tag to all three objects to 'remind' itself that although it is

		currently applying Rule 2 it does have another option where they are concerned.
man	(N) (2) (NP) (2) (VP)	So far so good. The object at the top of the stack, (A), could be replaced by 'the' which has therefore been provisionally accepted and a new input, 'man' is now being considered.
won	(VP)	As it turned out, Rule 2 was the right one. For Rule 5 allows (N) to be replaced by 'man' which can therefore be accepted. Moreover, since the substitution of (A) (N) for (NP) under Rule 2 has turned out to be correct in this case, (NP) could be discarded from the stack and a new input 'won' can now be considered.
won	(V) (NP)	Rule 4 has been applied, replacing the object (VP) with the string (V) (NP).
a	(NP)	'won' has been accepted as a permissible substitute for (V) under Rule 6 and a second (NP) object has now come to the top of the stack.
a	(A) (2) (N) (2) (NP) (2)	As before, when confronted with (NP), the acceptor first tries to apply Rule 2.
long	(N) (2) (NP) (2)	'A' has been provisionally accepted and the corresponding object (A) has been removed from the stack, allowing (N) to rise to the top.
a	(A) (Ad) (N)	Since (N) cannot be replaced by either the input word 'long' or by any other object, the acceptor has switched from Rule 2 to Rule 3, removing (N) from the stack. (NP)

		has also been removed and replaced by the string (A) (Ad) (N) which is now the only possible substitute. Since Rule 2 has failed, the acceptor has also gone back to the previous input, 'a'.
long	(Ad) (N)	Input 'a' has been accepted and the object (Ad), now on top of the stack, is being compared with a new input, 'long'.
race	(N)	Rule 7 allows (Ad) to be replaced by 'long' which has therefore been accepted and the final input, 'race', is now being considered.
		'race' could replace (N) under Rule 6, so the input is accepted and (N) is removed from the stack. Since the stack is now empty and there are no further inputs the sentence has been accepted in its entirety.

The syntax, or grammatical structure, of most existing computer languages incorporates rules based on Chomsky's grammars which allow a computer to check the validity of the information or instructions that are fed into it. Let us suppose that the following line is added to a program written in BASIC:
500 IF (P = < 20) * (Q > 5) : GOTO 800
600 . . . .

(If variable P is less than 20 and variable Q is more than 5 the computer is instructed to go to line 800 in the program otherwise it should continue on to line 600)

This 'sentence' will be automatically checked, following the procedures we have been discussing, and added to the existing program. But if the programmer had inadvertently omitted the colon, and thus violated the grammar of BASIC, the sentence would fail to pass the check and the programmer would be confronted with the dreaded phrase: SYNTAX ERROR.

The production rules required to generate natural language are, of course, a great deal more elaborate than those used by the designers of computer languages like BASIC, which is why computer languages are so infuriatingly rigid and syntax errors so common. But, as artificial intelligence researchers soon discovered, the real problems with natural language are not syntactic but semantic, that is to say they arise not from the grammatical structure but from the fact that words have meanings which relate to objects in the real world.

THE MEANING OF WORDS

The third and last of Chomsky's grammatical models, 'transformational grammar', was designed to tackle at least some aspects of this problem. A transformational grammar is based upon the notion that a whole range of different sentences may be derived from a single underlying 'string' by the application of a set of transformational rules. For example, given the sentence 'The boy threw the ball', we may apply the passive transformation to get 'The ball was thrown by the boy', the interrogative transformation to get 'Did the boy throw the ball?' the negative transformation to get 'The boy did not throw the ball', all three at once to get 'Was the ball not thrown by the boy?', and so on. The point is that however much the grammatical elements may be shuffled by the application of transformational rules, the semantic relationships remain constant. Starting from the original sentence, the grammar will never generate sentences like 'The ball did not throw the boy' or 'Was the boy thrown by the ball?'.

But while they may prevent a machine from making nonsense of an existing sentence in the process of transforming it, the rules are, of course, no help at all when a machine has to decide whether or not a sentence 'means anything' to start with. For, syntactically speaking, there is absolutely nothing wrong with the sentence 'The ball threw the boy'; given the appropriate vocabulary, it can be generated by either a finite state grammar or a phrase structure grammar and application of the transformational rules will produce all the equally 'correct' sentences that can be derived from it.

In order to recognize that the sentence is nonsensical it is necessary to know something about boys, balls and throwing. The requisite knowledge can be formulated as a series of rules which might be applied by a machine. For example, given a vocabulary consisting of the nouns 'boy' and 'ball' and the verbs 'throw', 'catch', 'bounce' and 'hit', a program could be written that limited the way pairs of words could be brought together: it would allow 'boy throws', 'ball bounces' and both 'boy hits' and 'ball hits', but not 'boy bounces' or 'ball catches'.

However, little imagination is needed to see that if the vocabulary is expanded to include even a few hundred words, the number of rules required will rapidly become unmanageable. And if a machine was to have natural language abilities approaching those of a human being, it would have to take account of innumerable subtleties and ambiguities. It would, for example, have to have rules that forbade boys to be thrown by balls or balls to catch boys, but allowed boys to be thrown by questions or to be caught by other boys.

Despite such problems, researchers have continued to look for ways of tackling the issue of semantics. One of the best known approaches was that developed in the late 1960s by Terry Winograd, then working at the Massachusetts Institute of Technology. Winograd's program, SHRDLU, was designed to manipulate a block world made up of boxes, blocks and pyramids, but it was the semantic problems which this task involved that were the primary

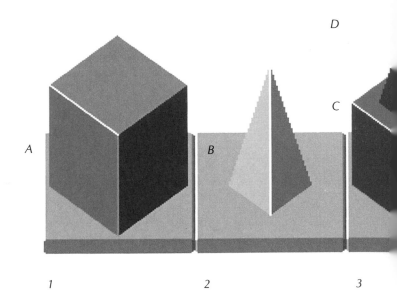

concern of his research. He started from the premise that a dialogue between a person and a machine cannot take place unless both participants share some basic knowledge of what they are talking *about*. This is, clearly, a requirement that applies with equal force to conversations between two human beings. Those of us who are not engineers, for example, cannot make an intelligent response to a remark such as 'The movements of a bell-crank can always be represented in terms of the operations of a four-bar chain'.

Winograd's approach was based on the idea that confusions of meaning could be avoided if the subject matter of the conversation was strictly limited, and if the machine had direct knowledge of it rather than having to rely on definitions supplied by the programmer. In fact, SHRDLU's block world existed only as an abstract model, in the form of another program inside the computer, and the machine's knowledge of it was therefore as complete as that of the human being who observed it on the display screen – by definition, the screen could show only what the computer 'knew'. The block world, in other words, consisted of a database in the computer's memory which listed both a description of each object – 'big blue box', for example, or 'small red pyramid' – and its current position which was recorded in terms of screen coordinates in exactly the same way as a point on a map can be recorded in terms of latitude and longitude.

Such a program has to be provided with some basic rules. It needs

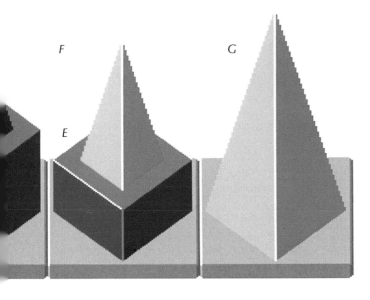

F

G

E

4   5

UNDERSTANDING A BLOCK WORLD

Let us suppose that we wish to devise a program that will allow a computer to discuss the contents of this block world with a human operator and to control a robot arm that will manipulate the various objects it contains.

The first step is to label the seven objects, A–G, and to number the five squares upon which they can be placed. We can now construct a database that describes the existing situation:

OBJECT	TYPE	SIZE	COLOUR	CURRENT POSITION	ON TOP OF OBJECT	UNDER OBJECT
A	Block	Big	Blue	1	—	—
B	Pyramid	Small	Yellow	2	—	—
C	Block	Big	Red	3	—	D
D	Pyramid	Small	Red	3	C	—
E	Block	Small	Red	4	—	F
F	Pyramid	Small	Yellow	4	E	—
G	Pyramid	Big	Yellow	5	—	—

Referring to this table, we can now define a number of mathematical sets. Seven of these will remain constant:

The set of all blocks: (ACE)
The set of all pyramids: (BDFG)
The set of all big objects: (ACG)
The set of all small objects: (BDEF)
The set of all blue objects: (A)
The set of all yellow objects: (BFG)
The set of all red objects: (CDE)

In addition, there are a number of other sets whose constitution will vary as and when objects are moved and the contents of the database are updated. At present, for example, the set of all objects to the left of the big yellow pyramid is (ABCDEF) and the set of all objects underneath the small pyramids is (CE).

Assuming that we have defined the language in which the dialogue is to be conducted and programmed the computer to handle it, let us now suppose that we ask, 'Is the big blue block to the left of the big yellow pyramid?' Having accepted the sentence as a grammatical one, the computer will proceed to replace the adjectives and nouns with sets from its database. So 'big blue block' becomes (ACG) (A) (ACE) (the set of all big objects, the set of all blue objects and the set of all blocks) and, in the same way, 'big yellow pyramid' becomes (ACG) (BFG) (BDFG).

Each group of sets is now reduced to a single set by eliminating the objects that are not common to all three sets in the group. So (ACG) (A) (ACE) becomes (A) and (ACG) (BFG) (BDFG) becomes (G) and the question now reads: 'Is (A) to the left of (G)?'

Next, the computer determines that the set of objects to the left of (G) is (ABCDEF) and the question can be further simplied to read: 'Is (A) (ABCDEF)?' i.e. is the set (A) included in the set (ABCDEF) to which the answer is obviously yes.

Let us now take another example and suppose that we instruct the computer to 'Pick up the small yellow pyramid'. This translates as 'Pick up (BDEF) (BFG) (BDFG)' which can then be simplified to read 'Pick up (BF)'. The language will obviously have been designed to deal with this sort of situation, where the computer needs further information before it can determine which of the two objects, B and F, it should pick up. It will therefore ask a question such as: 'Which small yellow pyramid do you mean?'

If we reply 'The one on top of the red block', the computer can now reformulate the instruction as: 'Pick up (BF) (the set of all small yellow pyramids) on top of (CDE) (the set of all red objects) (ACE) (the set of all blocks)'. This can be simplified to read 'Pick up (BF) on top of (CE)'. Next, referring to its database, the computer determines that the set of objects on top of objects in the set (CE) is (DF). As a result it can now further simplify the instruction to, first, 'Pick up (BF) (DF)', and, finally, 'Pick up (F)'.

to 'know', for example, that small objects can be put in big boxes but not small boxes or blocks, whatever their size; that pyramids can be put on blocks, but that blocks cannot be put on pyramids; and, rather more elaborately, that if told to pick up an object that was under another one it will first have to remove the one that is on top.

If the objects listed by such a database are numbered and categorized, and their positions catalogued the computer has a complete record of the current state of its block world. If, in addition, it is equipped with a suitable phrase structure grammar it can respond to questions such as: 'Where is the small blue box?' or 'Is the yellow pyramid on top of the green box?' with sentences such as 'The small blue box is to the left of the big red block' or 'Do you mean the big yellow pyramid or the small yellow pyramid?' It can also obey commands such as 'Pick up the small brown pyramid and put it in the big blue box' and record the consequent changes in its database. The example on pages 93–4 shows a typical dialogue sequence and the parsing process that the machine must follow in order to understand the question and determine the answer.

Unfortunately, the block-world approach, although illuminating in many respects, has turned out to be something of a dead-end. It has not taken artificial intelligence very far along the road towards the development of more utilitarian machines – robots which could work alongside human beings on the factory floor, for example. There are several reasons for this. As we have already seen, real-life problems tend to pose combinatorial complexities which defeat existing problem-solving algorithms. Moreover, as we shall show in subsequent chapters, artificial vision systems are only just beginning to be able to cope with real-world situations, in which objects are rarely arranged in the orderly fashion which characterizes a block world.

But as far as natural language is concerned, the difficulty with methods used by programs like SHRDLU is that they enable machines to present an illusion of understanding 'what they are talking about' without attacking the fundamental problems. For example, the rule that objects may be put 'in' boxes but must be put 'on' blocks is, as far as the computer is concerned, entirely arbitrary; it is not something that the machine knows in the same sense as a person who knows that one is hollow and the other solid.

This is precisely the point that John Searle was making when he attacked language-using programs for their failure to capture the property of intentionality (see Chapter 2). Ultimately, our knowledge of what a word means can always be traced back to the bedrock of first-hand experience. We do not have to refer to a rulebook in order to decide that the sentence 'The ball throws the boy' is meaningless because we have seen and felt balls and, as a result of that experience, we know that they are simply not the sort of things that can throw boys or anything else. A rule that 'balls do not throw things' is not, in the last resort, an adequate substitute for this sort of first-hand knowledge.

Ultimately, machines may not be able to understand what commonplace words like 'ball' and 'boy', or 'nut', 'bolt' and 'spanner' mean in the same sense as we do unless and until they can learn about the world at first hand. And this will, in turn, depend upon the development of artificial vision systems and other robot senses as well as learning mechanisms which will enable machines to construct their own internal representations of their environment. It should be added that even though the rule-based approach to semantics seems unlikely to break out of narrow, artificially restricted block worlds into the untidy, ill-defined world in which people live their everyday lives, it has enjoyed considerable success in areas which, in our terms, seem to require far more sophistication. This is a development we shall be looking at in the next chapter.

Before we leave the subject of natural language, however, we must come back to the question of syntax. For while Chomsky's ideas have, as we have seen, proved invaluable to artificial intelligence, they raise issues which are fundamental to any discussion of the nature of our own language-using skills and, therefore, to the relationship between natural intelligence and artificial intelligence.

Chomsky believes, as we have said, that phrase structure grammars (and transformational grammars, which are essentially phrase structure grammars with an additional layer of elaboration) model 'deep structures' which are not only the basis of all known languages, but of any possible language. These structures are, in other words, a reflection of some underlying set of rules that are 'built-in' to the mind of every language-user. This need not imply that the rules are explicit or that we are conscious of applying them; our brains, after all, perform myriad functions without our being aware of the fact – from regulating the heartbeat to translating a decision to turn on the television into movements of the arm muscles.

But if we 'know' and follow these rules, even without being aware of the fact, then it must follow either that we have learnt them or that they are innate – that is, a part of our genetic inheritance. The traditional view of language, before the publication of Chomsky's revolutionary ideas, was that children learnt to use language in the same way as they learnt to walk, to ride a bicycle or to do arithmetic: partly through a process of imitating their elders and partly as a result of formal instruction. Indeed, the great French anthropologist Jean Piaget and his followers carefully documented the way in which children's language skills developed and were able to divide the process up into a number of distinct stages which seemed to occur in step with the acquisition of other skills.

While the grammar of a language was viewed simply as a series of rules governing the surface structure it was still possible to suppose that a child might learn to talk during the few short months that separate the inarticulate baby from the infant whose utterances may still be short and subject to correction, but who is perfectly capable of making himself understood. But it seems very unlikely indeed that an eighteen-month-old child could master the sort of rules which, if Chomsky is right, are required to generate even the simplest of sentences. Yet it is undeniable that once a child begins to talk, he progresses very rapidly indeed from imitating single words or phrases such as 'Mamma' or 'I want' to constructing sentences which are 'original' and which, even if they do contain some mistakes, nevertheless demonstrate a mastery of grammar. It is also difficult to account for the fact that children still acquire a comprehensive grasp of the principles of grammar even if the adults around them speak in a careless or slipshod fashion.

Chomsky himself argues that the notion that language-use is an acquired skill cannot be sustained and that knowledge of deep structures must be innate, already programmed into our brains at birth. Or rather, to put his case more accurately, that our brains are programmed to develop language-using skills in rather the same way as our bodies are programmed to grow, to develop characteristic features such as big feet or curly hair, to change at puberty, and so forth.

In the 1970s, the debate between those who believed that the capacity to use language must be the result of this sort of preprogramming, led by Chomsky, and Piaget and his disciples, who continued to argue that it was acquired through learning, turned into a bitter controversy. In 1976 the two principals, each supported by a formidable team of experts, met at a chateau in France in order to debate the issue. The result was inconclusive; the arguments on both sides were thoroughly aired, but no converts were made.

Yet the question is of enormous importance to artificial intelligence – indeed, artificial intelligence may offer the only practical means of resolving it one way or the other. For if we assume, for the sake of argument, that Chomsky is wrong and that grammatical rules are learnt inductively, then at some point in the future it might be possible to build a machine which learnt to use language without relying upon its programmers to furnish it with a prepackaged set of rules. If this could be done (and we shall be examining machines that are capable of this sort of learning in subsequent chapters), it would certainly be a lengthy process. For the learning could only be the result of experience, of interaction with human language-users, and there is no reason to suppose that machines would learn any faster than people. Thus, it might well take ten or fifteen years to bring the machine's skills up to the level of those of the average teenager. On the other hand, it would only be necessary to do it once, with one machine. For once the language-using program existed it could be duplicated just like any other piece of software.

We might also conjecture that, if any such endeavour were to be successful, the machine would have to be able to make the crucial connection between words, symbols which represent reality, and reality itself. It would, in other words, have to possess intentionality, and its acquisition of *both* syntactic *and* semantic skills would proceed in parallel.

If Chomsky is right, however, artificial intelligence will have to pursue its investigation of the deep structures of grammar. In doing so it may help to lay bare the origins of human language. But the problem of semantics will remain unsolved.

CHAPTER 6

STRUCTURING KNOWLEDGE

There is, as we pointed out in Chapter 1, an important distinction to be made between knowledge and intelligence. But it should also be clear that although a machine may store knowledge without necessarily possessing intelligence, an intelligent machine that possessed no knowledge of any kind would be a rank impossibility. Thinking, no matter whether done by machines or people, pre-supposes that there is something to think *about*. The question of how, to what extent, and in what sense, machines can be imbued with knowledge is thus fundamental to all aspects of artificial intelligence.

People acquire knowledge in two ways: at first hand, through the medium of their senses, and at second hand, by listening to or reading about the knowledge accumulated by others. Knowledge acquired at first hand is, by definition, learnt by induction. A child, for example, quickly learns as a result of simple observation and, perhaps, painful experience, that objects left unsupported will fall to the ground, and comes to accept this as a fact of life. Only much later will he fit this piece of information into a deductive framework and learn that it is a consequence of gravity, which accounts not only for crockery falling off the table but also for the orbits of the planets.

As we shall see in subsequent chapters, many difficulties remain to be overcome before machines can be equipped to learn about the world inductively, from their own first-hand experience. In this chapter we are concerned with the ways in which existing human knowledge may be packaged so that machines can reason about it deductively.

But we must always remember that until machines are able to make the crucial connection between the abstract symbols that they manipulate and the 'real world' objects and events which those symbols represent, even second-hand knowledge stored inside a computer will remain qualitatively different from the same know-ledge stored inside a brain. To say this is simply to remind ourselves that there are fundamental differences between intentional systems, such as people, and unintentional ones, such as computers. The fact that, as we saw in Chapter 5, machines cannot know what words mean in the same sense as we do is just one example of the problems that arise from their lack of intentionality.

If knowledge amounted to no more than an accumulation of data, even a comparatively modest computer would have to be rated more highly than the most intelligent of human beings. For it is indisputable that, in terms of sheer capacity – the number of individual facts which can be stored and accurately retrieved – computer memories have far outstripped our own. Indeed, it is precisely because computers are able to store vast quantities of data that we find them so useful. Within microseconds they can tell a booking clerk whether there is a seat left in the smoking section on tomorrow's flight to Los Angeles, say, or give a sales manager details of a customer's credit status. But obtaining access to knowledge of this kind when stored in existing computer systems is rather like using an automated reference book – you may know that the answer to your question is in there somewhere, but you will only find it if you know how to get to that 'somewhere'. The enormous memory of the computer is only accessible because there is an human being operating the terminal, asking exactly the right questions in exactly the right way and in exactly the right order.

There is, in other words, a clear division of labour. The machine stores the data – it has the knowledge – but it is up to the human operator to determine which bits of that data are relevant in any given circumstances and to find his way to the appropriate location in the machine's memory – he provides the intelligence. Thus intelligence, in this context, could be described as the ability to analyse a problem and decide what you need to know in order to resolve it, coupled with the capacity to retrieve the relevant knowledge, and only the relevant knowledge, from memory.

Similarly, when we say that we ourselves are knowledgeable on some particular subject, we imply not only that we have a mental warehouse full of data but also that we can find our way around that warehouse without having to refer to a catalogue or a floorplan. If, for example, we are asked a simple question such as, 'Who were the stars of *Casablanca*?', we can probably produce the answer, 'Humphrey Bogart and Ingrid Bergman', almost instantaneously. Moreover, we would probably produce the same two names in response to a whole series of other, related, questions such as: 'Who said "Here's looking at you, kid" to whom?' or 'What two film stars do you associate with the tune "As Time Goes By"?'.

It would, of course, be perfectly possible to devise a computer system, called, say, MOVIEBUFF, that stored sufficient information to answer these questions, and similar ones about every classic movie ever made. But if MOVIEBUFF was to merit the title of an intelligent system it would have to be able to understand questions even when presented in non-standard format, and to respond rapidly without searching through its entire database and without the assistance of a human operator.

In order to design such a system it is necessary to try to figure out how we ourselves organize our knowledge – not only because this may be helpful to the designer, but also because the human being who asks the questions and the machine which provides the answers will only be able to communicate effectively if they 'think in the same way'. It is, therefore, not surprising that when artificial intelligence researchers addressed this issue they should have enlisted the help of psychologists and other specialists concerned with human, rather than machine, behaviour. Such collaboration has proved extremely fruitful – and not just for artificial intelligence. Indeed, over the past two decades cognitive psychology (the branch of the science concerned with the mechanisms of learning and memory), has wholeheartedly embraced what is known as the 'computer model' of the mind, and terms like 'database', 'information retrieval' and 'access time' have become as much a part of psychological jargon as of 'computerese'.

SCRIPT-USING PROGRAMS

One of the first examples of this cooperation between the two disciplines was the work of Roger Schank of the Yale Computer Laboratory and his psychologist colleague, R. P. Abelson. They were primarily concerned with finding a way of handling some of the semantic problems which are, as we saw in Chapter 5, so central to the whole question of natural language. In particular, they focussed on the ways in which human beings are able to pick up verbal clues in order to detect the context of a communication, thereby avoiding the semantic pitfalls into which language-using programs tumble so readily. Consider, for example, these two simple sentences:

David seized the steering wheel and drove off.
David seized the club and drove off.

Despite the fact that, in both cases, exactly the same words – 'drove off' – are used to describe David's action, we have no difficulty in recognizing that we are being asked to imagine two quite different sets of circumstances. In the first sentence David is clearly driving a car, in the second he is, equally clearly, hitting a golf ball. We are able to make these assumptions because we understand that the meaning of the phrase 'drove off' depends entirely upon the context in which it is used. If, for instance, the second sentence was extended to read, 'David seized the club and drove off the attacking wolves', then we would immediately envisage a different kind of club and a third, quite different, scenario.

In order to find a way in which a computer program might distinguish between a range of different meanings according to context, Schank and Abelson argued, it is necessary to analyse the mechanisms that underlie our own competence. This is, they suggested, attributable to the fact that we organize our vocabulary into a series of separate 'scripts'. Thus, when we encounter a sentence like those quoted above, we first look for the clues that betray the context – the words specific to one particular script – and then select that script in preference to the other possible alternatives. In the case of the first sentence, the appearance of 'steering wheel' immediately leads us to select a 'motor car script' and, if we read on, we will be prepared to encounter terms like 'clutch', 'kerb', 'overtake', etc. In the case of the second sentence, on the other hand, we would choose a 'golf course script' containing words like 'green', 'niblick' and 'birdie'.

Taking this model of human competence as a starting point, Schank and Abelson went on to develop a series of script-using programs which were able to understand simple stories – to 'understand', that is, in the sense that they could respond intelligently to questions about what had happened or who had done what to whom – or compose other stories incorporating the same basic elements as the original ones. For each story, or series of stories, a separate script was created in the program's database. As a script grew, its structure was elaborated so that instead of being merely a list of words which were associated with each other, it came to represent what were, it was claimed, a series of simple concepts.

If, for example, the 'golf course script' mentioned earlier was widened into a 'ball game script' and so came to include words like 'hit' and 'strike', as well as 'drive off', then the program could be told that all the terms implied the same basic action, hitting a ball with an implement in order to propel it from one place to another. The program would then be able to go well beyond the sort of question and answer sequences which might be mastered by a totally 'mechanical' system ('What did David do?', 'David seized the club and drove off'). To the question, 'What did David hit?', for example, the program might formulate the reply, 'The golf ball', and it might go on to respond to a further question, 'What was the result?', with the statement that 'The ball flew down the fairway'.

Inevitably, this brief outline does less than justice to the ingenuity of Roger Schank, and that of the other researchers who have built upon his work. But it has demonstrated that the techniques they have developed will allow a computer to conduct a dialogue in a manner that presents a convincing illusion of intelligence. It remains true that, until a computer can actually go out and play a game of golf, it will never 'know about golf' in the same sense as a human being who has played the game, or at least some other game involving bats and balls; but, equipped with a 'ball-game script', the machine might nevertheless hope to bluff its way through a conversation in the clubhouse!

ORGANIZING KNOWLEDGE

Although script-using programs have been developed with one particular application, natural language, in mind, they can also be seen as just one example of a whole range of techniques that artificial intelligence has devised for organizing, or structuring, human knowledge.

Indeed, Kenneth Colby has used rather similar methods to explore one of the more intriguing byways in artificial intelligence, the modelling of minds in which the inner perception of reality – the brain's database, as it were – has become distorted. His best-known program, PARRY, was designed to model the mental processes of an individual suffering from the kind of delusions that are generally classified under the heading of paranoia, in this case of someone who has become irrationally convinced that he is being pursued by the mafia. PARRY is, in fact, a script-using program with just one script. Asked any question, it will search for a word which links up with the mafia script, ignoring any clues that might point a less 'single-minded' program in other directions. If no connection is found, PARRY simply ignores the question and pursues its own obsessions. The program does not, of course, pretend to provide an answer to the really interesting question – why people develop such delusions. But it does reproduce, convincingly if only relatively superficially, the behaviour patterns of such unfortunates.

In order to store knowledge of any kind in a computer it is necessary to break it down into discrete chunks. For instance, to come back to our hypothetical MOVIEBUFF program, we might say that our knowledge of the movie *Casablanca* consisted of just eight such items that could be arranged under five headings:

Male stars: Humphrey Bogart, Leslie Howard, Claude Raines
Female star: Ingrid Bergman
Theme tune: 'As Time Goes By'
Most famous lines: 'Play it, Sam', 'Here's looking at you, kid',
   'Arrest the usual suspects'
Setting: Wartime North Africa

Now if we just catalogue all these facts in the database under the film's title, we can very easily arrange matters so that the computer will rapidly find the right answer to a question such as: 'Who starred in *Casablanca*?', for it will only have to find the entry for that film and then pick out the names listed under the 'star' categories. But if we require the program to be more flexible, to be capable, for example, of answering questions such as 'Which of Claude Raines' films is set in wartime North Africa?' with equal ease and rapidity, the number of 'headings' and cross-references will soon multiply in a formidable fashion. As a result the computer will either have to conduct very lengthy search processes or else will require the services of a human operator who can narrow down the searches by guiding it through a menu.

What is needed, clearly, is some system whereby the appearance of any single clue, such as a mention of Humphrey Bogart or 'As Time Goes By' or North Africa, will somehow cause the computer to 'pull out' not just the *Casablanca* file but all the other files that are related to it – it might, for example, have a 'Hollywood marriages' file which would record the fact that Bogart was married to Lauren Bacall, or a 'Movies about movies' file which would include *Play it again Sam*, the film in which Woody Allen paid homage to *Casablanca*.

Our own minds flit through the intricate chains of cross-references that are required to cope with this sort of task so easily that it is only when we try to replicate the structure of memory outside the brain that we realize just how complex it must be. In tackling the problem, artificial intelligence has adopted a single basic strategy, that of linking the individual chunks of knowledge by 'pointers' which not only indicate an association between two items but also express the nature of the relationship. LISP, the computer language favoured for most artificial intelligence applications, was designed to make it easy for programmers to deal with just this kind of problem. LISP, an abbreviation for List Processing Language, allows individual items of data – called 'atoms' – to be grouped

together in lists which can themselves be linked by pointers that
serve as cross-references to other lists. Set out in a LISP-like fashion,
the information about *Casablanca* might look like this:

```
(CASABLANCA (STARS (MALE
            (HUMPHREY BOGART (MARRIED TO — LAUREN BACALL))
            (CLAUDE RAINES)
            (LESLIE HOWARD))
            (FEMALE
            (INGRID BERGMAN)))
            (FAMOUS LINES
            (PLAY IT, SAM
            (FROM WHICH — TITLE OF WOODY ALLEN FILM
            (PLAY IT AGAIN SAM))))
            . . . . . . .
            (SETTING (TIME
            (SECOND WORLD WAR))
            (PLACE
            (NORTH AFRICA))))
```

Although this example is relatively trivial, it should make clear
the basic idea, which is that the information within each set of
brackets is a list which may be divided into sub-lists and sub-sub-
lists some of which may contain pointers, such as MARRIED TO and
FROM WHICH, that link them to other lists in the database. Using LISP,
or one of its many derivatives, programmers can play many
variations on this theme. In particular, the ways in which pointers
are used to link the various elements in a database can be varied to
produce programs that implement different models of memory. It
would, for example, be perfectly possible to employ the script-using
model and to treat MOVIEBUFF's *Casablanca* file as a script that is
'called' by the machine as soon as it encounters, say, 'Humphrey
Bogart' or 'North Africa', and that contains pointers linking it to
other, related scripts such as 'Woody Allen'.

Another way of organizing the same body of knowledge would
employ the tree structure examined in previous chapters. In this
case, each chunk of knowledge would be represented by a single
node and the rules for moving from one node to another would
express the relationship between them (see page 105). Thus it
would be possible to move from the Bogart node to the Bacall node
by applying a 'married to' rule or to the Bergman node by applying a
'starred with' rule, and if we moved back up the tree to the
'Casablanca' node, or sideways across it, to the 'Play it Sam' node,
we would find that other rules, leading to a 'Woody Allen' node,
had become applicable.

A third approach, first developed by P.H. Winston of MIT, is
based upon a rather different sort of structure known as a 'semantic
net'. The underlying idea is that if a number of small chunks of
knowledge are linked by pointers indicating their relationships the
resulting network will represent the 'meaning' of a larger, composite, chunk of knowledge. Thus, coming back to the MOVIEBUFF
example, we could link all the items in the 'Casablanca' file in order

to form a semantic net representing what the film 'means', in the sense that it sums up everything the machine needs to know about *Casablanca*, while being clearly distinguishable from the semantic nets for other movies (see page 106).

Yet another possible structure, first proposed by Marvin Minsky, Winston's colleague at MIT, is based on the use of what Minsky called 'frames', A frame can best be thought of as a rank of pigeon-holes or boxes in which a set of related facts can be stored. But, and this was the point that led Minsky to argue that frames offered a more flexible structure than semantic nets, each box may itself contain a series of smaller boxes, within which may be 'nested' yet smaller boxes.

Although any one of these techniques may be preferable to others for dealing with a particular kind of knowledge (semantic nets have, as we shall see, found particular favour in the field of artificial vision) they are all addressing essentially the same problem and are in many cases mutually interchangeable. Indeed, since most of the programs that have actually been written are super-imposed, as it were, on existing database systems, it could be said that they do not really determine how the computer stores knowledge, but how it *appears* to do so. The machine's performance may lead the human user to suppose that its database is organized in a particular fashion, but the reality may be very different. This is not to say that appearances are unimportant. As already indicated, it is absolutely essential that the user should feel that he understands the machine's 'thought processes' and that they should appear to be as nearly comparable to his own as possible.

If, for example, we asked MOVIEBUFF a question such as, 'Who was that star with the French sounding name who said: "Arrest the usual suspects"?', then we might feel some sympathy if it required some further prompting before coming up with the correct response: 'Claude Raines'. In such circumstances it would seem quite reasonable for the machine to ask, as another human being might, 'Can you remember the name of the film?' or 'Who were the other stars?'. But if its reaction was something like: 'No category listing for French-sounding names,' or simply 'Syntax error' we would quickly give up the effort to communicate with it.

A TURNING POINT FOR ARTIFICIAL INTELLIGENCE?

In the early 1970s, a number of artificial intelligence researchers, notably Edward Feigenbaum and Douglas Lennart of Stanford Research Institute and Marvin Minsky of MIT, began to reconsider the question of how best to organize and structure existing human knowledge in order to make it available to computers and, as a result of their work, the whole issue was to take on a fresh urgency. This reappraisal was a direct consequence of the fact that artificial intelligence seemed at that point to have run into something of a dead end. During the 1960s the 'artificial intelligentsia' (as the high priests of the new discipline had been dubbed) had proclaimed, with growing confidence and stridency, that the advent of the intelligent machine was at hand, and that of the super-intelligent

Opposite: The Casablanca *file, as it might be represented in the form of a knowledge tree. Note the way in which the structure would allow a machine to follow 'chains of thought' such as Casablanca – male stars – Humphrey Bogart – Lauren Bacall, or Casablanca – famous lines – Play it, Sam – Woody Allen – Casablanca. The pointers in this case are the rules that govern the transition from one node or state to its successors. Thus, having reached the 'Play it, Sam' state, the search can continue to the 'Woody Allen' state by applying a 'used quote' rule and then, by applying a 'paid homage to' rule, back to the 'Casablanca' state.*

This tree structure, unlike the ones shown in the following two illustrations, is a fairly literal representation of the way a database might actually be organized and, in its present form, makes it very clear how a machine would be able to find the answers to straightforward questions such as 'Who was the female star of Casablanca*?' But the structure would soon become confused and cease to be 'tree-like' if we added arrows indicating all the other possible links between nodes. For example, in order to show how a machine might cope with the question 'Which two film stars do you associate with the line "Here's looking at you, kid"?' it would be necessary to add arrows linking the 'Here's looking at you, kid' node to both the 'Humphrey Bogart' and the 'Ingrid Bergman' nodes, thus indicating that the program incorporated 'said by' and 'said to' rules which could lead it to make these transitions.*

machine just around the corner. But with the turn of the decade it had become increasingly apparent that such claims had been wildly optimistic. Artificial intelligence therefore faced a crisis on two fronts – one financial, the other conceptual.

On the financial front the threat came from the institutions, most crucially the US Department of Defense, which were responsible for funding research. They had been promised much and were now, with good reason, becoming sceptical about the value of their investment. In Britain, at that time the only country other than the US to have mounted a substantial research effort in artificial intelligence, the funding body, the Science Research Council, commissioned a distinguished mathematician, Sir James Lighthill, to investigate the current research programme and report upon future prospects. The result was a devastating critique which, in effect, dropped the British programme dead in its tracks.

It has become fashionable, in the light of subsequent developments, to dismiss the Lighthill Report as not merely over-pessimistic but also fundamentally misconceived. In our opinion, however, Lighthill accurately pinpointed the root of the problem that confronted artificial intelligence on the second, conceptual, front. If the Report is open to criticism, it is because Lighthill failed to foresee that, faced with the obstacles he identified, the artificial intelligentsia would regroup and counter-attack along a new axis, achieving a major breakthrough in the process.

The crux of Lighthill's argument was that while artificial intelligence had indeed achieved some impressive results in the laboratory, it would never succeed in reproducing them on the factory

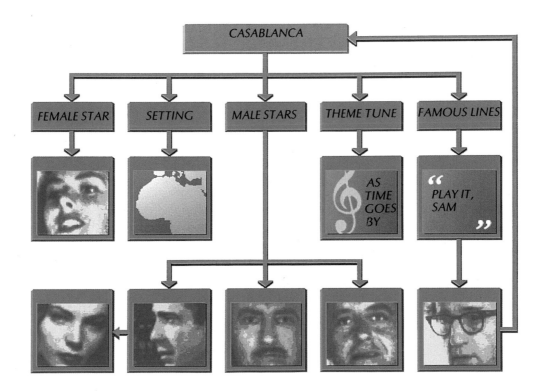

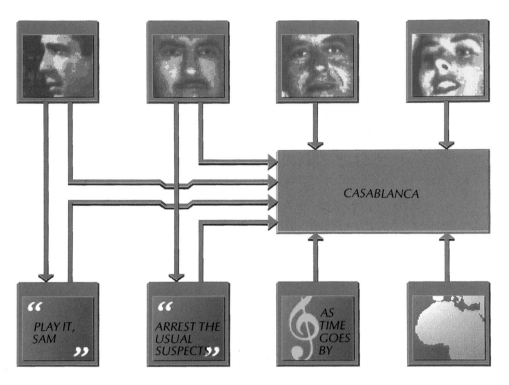

Here the Casablanca *file has been reorganized into a semantic net. Now all the states which, in combination, 'mean' Casablanca are linked directly to the main 'Casablanca' state. For this reason there is no state representing Lauren Bacall, who can be linked to the movie only by her marriage to Bogart. Note also that in order to reach the Humphrey Bogart state, for example, we no longer have to go through a 'male stars' state: instead we just follow a 'male star' pointer – or, more accurately, apply a 'male star' rule. However, the fact that the structure is not hierarchical like the knowledge tree in the previous illustration makes it far easier to include 'spoken by' pointers linking each of the 'famous lines' states directly to the star concerned. Semantic nets provide a useful means of representing knowledge bases where the emphasis is on grouping together data and indicating the ways in which they are associated, but their structure does not lend itself to representing chains of thought.*

floor, on the battlefield or in outer space. The researchers had, he suggested, made a fundamental error. They had assumed that once the problems had been analysed and solved at a highly simplified, theoretical level, it would be a comparatively easy matter to elaborate the techniques to the point at which they could be applied in the real world. The snag Lighthill pointed to was, of course, the combinatorial explosion – the exponential increase in complexity that occurs when real-world problems are substituted for carefully controlled laboratory experiments.

In fact, fully-paid-up members of the artificial intelligentsia like Feigenbaum were reasoning along very similar lines at much the same time, though their conclusions were naturally expressed in rather different terms. If artificial intelligence had made a mistake, they suggested, it was that too much energy had gone into the efforts to resolve basic, theoretical issues and not enough into practical research aimed at producing useful machines. Could it be, the argument continued, that the development of practical, workable products need not wait upon the resolution of fundamental issues? Thus, rather than continuing to besiege the citadel of theory, they proposed to bypass it and push ahead into what they hoped would be open country richly furnished with new research funds. The strategy succeeded.

Paradoxically, given that contemporary artificial intelligence had failed to devise systems capable of reasoning on the level of elementary human common sense, the target selected for the counter-attack was what might seem to be one of the strong points

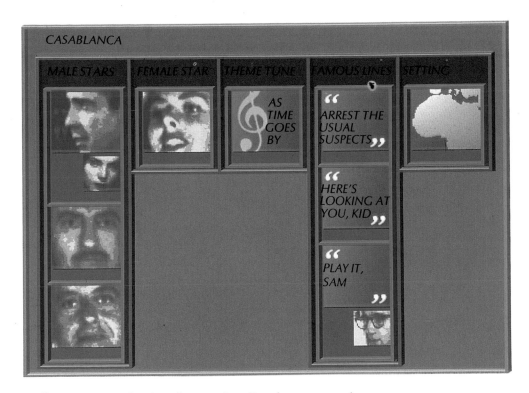

CASABLANCA

MALE STARS | FEMALE STAR | THEME TUNE | FAMOUS LINES | SETTING

AS TIME GOES BY

"ARREST THE USUAL SUSPECTS"

"HERE'S LOOKING AT YOU, KID"

"PLAY IT, SAM"

of human intelligence – professional expertise. But there was, of course, method behind such apparent madness. For the knowledge employed by an expert, unlike the sort of commonplace, casually acquired knowledge we rely upon in our everyday affairs, is likely to be formalized, codifiable and, above all, already fitted into a deductive framework. The reasoning processes employed by a doctor making a diagnosis, an engineer analysing a design or a lawyer preparing a brief are, in other words, much more nearly analogous to those of a computer running a program than the vague and ill-defined sort of reasoning we engage in when we think about more mundane matters.

PREPACKAGED EXPERTISE

Anyone who so much as glances at the science reports or the business pages of a newpaper is probably aware that 'expert systems' (sometimes called 'knowledge-based systems' or 'intelligent knowledge-based systems' – IKBS for short) are currently the focus of an intense interest that extends well beyond the world of computers and artificial intelligence. Expert systems are in fact the first product of artificial intelligence research to make a real impact in the marketplace, and as such they have given a welcome fillip to the whole field and a sharper commerical edge to much of the work being done in the laboratory.

The ancestor of all expert systems is generally reckoned to be a program called DENDRAL, developed at Stanford University in

A third possible way of structuring the Casablanca file, this time as a series of frames. Essentially, this is simply another, and for some purposes a clearer, way of representing the tree structure. Now the overall frame, representing Casablanca itself, contains smaller frames, each representing a state such as 'male stars', some of which, in turn, contain smaller frames representing states such as 'Humphrey Bogart', 'Claude Raines' and so forth. In this case, unlike that of the semantic net, it is possible to incorporate Lauren Bacall by adding a yet smaller frame within the Bogart one. Similarly, the 'Play it, Sam' frame includes a smaller, Woody Allen frame.

the mid-1960s in order to help chemists identify compounds on the basis of data obtained by spectrometric analysis. But it was only in the following decade, in the wake of the 'agonizing reappraisal' described above, that the expert system show really got on the road, with both Stanford University and Stanford Research Institute very much in the forefront. Today there are programs covering an impressive variety of 'knowledge domains' ranging from oil prospecting to tax law. Also available are a number of so-called 'shells' – programs which provide the bare bones of an expert system which the customer can flesh out by adding knowledge relevant to the domain with which he is specifically concerned.

The backbone of any expert system is, rather obviously, its 'knowledge base', the list of things it 'knows', and this may well take the form of one of the structures described earlier in this chapter. But an expert does not simply have a range of facts at his disposal, he also has a methodology, a way of reasoning about those facts, which allows him to infer further facts and to take appropriate action. Faced with a patient who complains of aches and pains, a sore throat and a high temperature, for example, a doctor might infer that the problem was a nasty bout of 'flu and recommend a few days in bed!

To the knowledge base, therefore, must be added what is known as an 'inference engine', a separate section of the program which operates upon the knowledge base, often employing techniques based upon those used in problem solving (see Chapter 4).

As expert systems have proliferated and the techniques for constructing them have been elaborated and refined, the field has become highly specialized, spawning a whole new sub-discipline called 'knowledge engineering' concerned with the problem of translating human expertise into a form in which it can be programmed into a computer. Rather than attempting to cover the whole complex subject we shall concentrate upon one particular technique known as 'logic programming' which provides a promising short cut between the human expert and the computer.

The branch of logic employed is a well-established mathematical language known as predicate calculus. Like any other language it has a rigorous syntactic structure of the kind described in Chapter 5. A 'sentence' in predicate calculus is called a 'well-formed formula' (wff) and is made up of simpler 'atomic formulae' which, in turn, consist of 'predicate symbols', 'variable symbols', 'function symbols' and 'constant symbols'. Brackets and commas are also used to indicate groupings of elements within an atomic formula and to separate the elements from each other.

The constant symbols can be thought of as the nouns in this grammar while the predicate symbols act as verbs, indicating the relationship between two constant symbols. Thus the sentence, 'John enjoys books' would translate into the language of predicate calculus as: ENJOYS (JOHN, BOOKS). In order to express generalities, variable symbols, representing a whole class of constant symbols, may be substituted for the constant symbols. In the case of the sentence, ENJOYS (X, Y), for example, there might be circumstances in which it would be appropriate to substitute 'John', 'Jane' or 'Joe' and 'books' or 'newspapers' for x and y respectively. Function symbols are used to represent compound objects, so that 'John's son Peter' would become PETER (SON, JOHN). Finally, the atomic formulae are linked together into wffs by the use of 'connectives'. Here we will limit these to four: v (which should be read as 'or'), ∧ ('and'), > ('implies') and − ('not'). A '−' can also be attached to a symbol to indicate a negative, as in '− ENJOYS (JOHN, BOOKS), which reads 'John does not enjoy books.'

The example on page 111 shows how this grammar might be used to translate a small piece of everyday expertise familiar to many car drivers into a set of wffs in predicate calculus. At this point we have created the knowledge base, which we might christen NOSTART. Now, in order to make use of it, we will require an inference engine. In our case this is a mechanism for manipulating production rules, very similar to those described in earlier chapters.

But before the inference engine can operate upon the knowledge base, the latter must be reformulated as a series of production rules with the following form. The left-hand side of each rule consists of a single wff in which the atomic formulae may be joined only by ∧ connectives – such wffs are known as 'clauses'. This means that existing wffs which contain other connectives must be transformed into clauses by means of standard logical operations (see next page). The clause on the left-hand side is linked to the right-hand side, which is itself a second wff, by the > connective. The wffs on the right-hand side take one of three forms: an 'action', a 'conclusion' or a 'suggestion'. The example goes on to show how NOSTART could be translated from its original form into a set of rules of this kind.

The inference engine is set into operation by the input of a wff which is, in effect, a statement of the problem. The first step is to find a rule with a left-hand side that matches this wff. Assuming that this is achieved, the next step depends upon the nature of the wff on the right-hand side of the rule. If it is an action then the answer to the problem has been found, at least so far as the system is concerned. But if it is a conclusion, then, somewhat confusingly, it represents an intermediate stage in the reasoning process and it will be necessary to search for another rule with a left-hand side that matches the conclusion. The third category of wffs on the right-hand side – suggestions – are, in effect, requests for additional input which might allow the system to identify the next applicable rule.

Naturally enough, few people would be happy to put their faith in such a system if it simply ground through the reasoning process until it reached an action and then left it to the user to either 'take it or leave it'. An expert system, just like its human counterpart, must be capable of justifying its recommendation of a particular action or, when it makes a suggestion, of explaining why it needs the additional information. The system is, therefore, capable of back-tracking along the sequence of rules that have been applied in order to 'explain itself' to the user. The example (see pages 111–12) showing a dialogue between NOSTART and a frustrated car owner, will help to clarify both the operations of the inference engine and the way in which the use of suggestions and backtracking allows the system to interact with the user.

TRANSLATING EXPERTISE INTO PREDICATE CALCULUS

In order to illustrate some of the principles used in designing expert systems we shall take a small (and necessarily simplified) piece of expertise drawn from a car driver's manual and construct a knowledge base called NOSTART. First we shall summarize the relevant points in plain language as follows:

If the car does not start and the engine does not turn over then the most likely cause is a flat battery.

See if you can start the car by using jumpleads. If the engine still fails to turn over this shows that the battery is probably OK and there are now three possibilities: either the starter is jammed or one of two components in the starter circuit is faulty – the ignition switch or the solenoid (the solenoid is the electrical relay that operates the starter when the ignition key is turned).

If the headlights are turned on and dim when the ignition key is turned the problem is not the ignition switch or the solenoid (the fact that the lights dim shows that the current is reaching the starter motor).

You can test the solenoid by pressing the button on top of it; if this causes the starter to operate the solenoid is not at fault.

These four statements could now be expressed in the language of predicate calculus as four well-formed formulae:

1. — start (car) ∧ — turnsover (engine) > flat (battery)
2. — turnsover (engine, jumpleads) > OK (battery) ∧ (jammed (starter) ∨ faulty (startercircuit))
3. dim (lights) > — (faulty (ignitionswitch) ∨ faulty (solenoid))
4. turnsover (engine, solenoid) > — faulty (solenoid)

CONSTRUCTING PRODUCTION RULES

We can now construct the following production rules based upon the four wffs above:
1. — start (car) ∧ — turnsover (engine) > flat (battery)
   (a conclusion)
2. flat (battery) > starts (engine, jumpleads)
   (a suggestion, i.e. the computer will suggest that the user see if the engine will start with jumpleads)
3. turnsover (engine, jumpleads) > is (flat, battery)
   (an action)
4. — turnsover (engine, jumpleads) > OK (battery)
   (a conclusion)
5. OK (battery) > jammed (starter)
   (a conclusion; note that since two conclusions cannot be linked by 'or' the predicate 'OK (battery)' leads both to this conclusion and to the one in the next rule – see below)
6. OK (battery) > faulty (startercircuit)
   (a conclusion)

7. jammed (starter) > dim (lights)
   (another suggestion, i.e. the system will ask 'Do the lights dim when the ignition key is turned?')
8. faulty (startercircuit) > turnsover (engine, solenoid)
   (another suggestion)
9. dim (lights) ∧ — turnsover (engine, solenoid) > is (jammed, starter)
   (an action)
10. — dim (lights) ∧ — turnsover (engine, solenoid) > is (faulty, solenoid)
    (an action)
11. — dim (lights) ∧ turnsover (engine, solenoid) > is (faulty, ignitionswitch)
    (an action)

REWRITING WFFs IN CLAUSAL FORM

The atomic formulae in the left-hand side of a production rule can only be linked by ∧ connectives. This may make it necessary to rewrite wffs containing ∨ connectives before incorporating them in the rules. This can usually be achieved by applying basic logical rules.

To illustrate the point let us reverse the second of the four wffs that are the basis of NOSTART so that it reads:

OK (battery) ∧ (jammed (starter) ∨ faulty (startercircuit)) > — turnsover (engine, jumpleads)

At the moment this wff has the form $x \wedge (y \vee z) > P$ and the distributive law in symbolic logic allows us to rewrite this statement as $(x \wedge y) \vee (x \wedge z) > P$ which can in turn be rewritten as two statements: $x \wedge y > P$ and $x \wedge z > P$. We can therefore rewrite the original wff as two clauses:

OK (battery ∧ jammed (starter) > — turnsover (engine, jumpleads)
OK (battery) ∧ faulty (startercircuit) > — turnsover (engine, jumpleads)

A DIALOGUE WITH NOSTART

USER: The car won't start. In fact the engine does not even turn over.
NOSTART: Try using jumpleads.
Comment: The system's translation database (see next page) has rendered the user's opening statement into '— start (car) ∧ — turnsover (engine)' which matches the left-hand side of rule 1. This led it to the conclusion on the right-hand side of rule 1 which matches the left-hand side of rule 2, leading to the suggestion 'turnsover (engine, jumpleads)' which it has then translated into the above reply.

USER: No luck. The engine doesn't turn over with jumpleads.

NOSTART: I see. Now I want you to try two tests and report the results. First, switch the headlights on and see if they dim when you turn the ignition key. Second, press the button on top of the solenoid and see if that makes the engine turn over.

Comment: When translated, as '— turnsover (engine, jumpleads)', the user's report matched the left-hand side of rule 4, leading to the conclusion 'OK (battery)' which matches the left-hand sides of both rule 5 and rule 6. The conclusion of rule 5 led the system to rule 7 and the suggestion 'dim (lights)' and the conclusion of rule 6 led to rule 8 and the suggestion 'turnsover (engine, solenoid)'.

USER: Why do you suggest the light test?

NOSTART: Since the battery seems to be OK one of the possibilities I must now consider is a jammed starter and this test will establish whether or not that is the problem.

Comment: The system has backtracked from the point the user queried, the suggestion at rule 7, to the left-hand side of rule 7, 'jammed (starter)' and then to rule 5 which states that the possibility of a jammed starter is one of the implications of finding that the battery was not flat.

USER: OK, I've done both tests. The lights did not dim when I turned the switch but the engine did turn over when I pressed the solenoid button.

NOSTART: The ignition switch is faulty.

Comment: The result of the two tests, when translated, matched the left-hand side of rule 11 leading to the action 'is (faulty, ignition switch)'.

USER: How do you figure that out?

NOSTART: Having established that the battery was OK, I then assumed that the problem was either a jammed starter or a fault in the starter circuit. If the lights had dimmed that would have indicated that it was a jammed starter. But given that they did not it has to be either a faulty solenoid or a faulty ignition switch. But if it had been a faulty solenoid the engine would not have turned over when you pressed the solenoid button. Therefore it must be a faulty ignition switch.

Comment: The system first backtracked to rule 4 to remind the user that it had already eliminated the battery. It then followed that conclusion forward to rules 9, 10 and 11, listing the various possibilities and explaining why all but one could be eliminated.

Expert systems would, of course, have little practical value if every potential user had to learn the language of predicate calculus in order to gain access to their expertise. The system will therefore have to incorporate a translation database that allows it to transform statements in natural language into wffs and to translate its own findings into a form which the user can understand. The creation of this database is the responsibility of the knowledge engineer who writes the program. He must not only ensure that the human expert's reasoning is reproduced accurately and in watertight form, he must also devise a standard form of words to represent each wff in the production rules.

The business of breaking down a body of expertise which may have been accumulated over a lifetime into a series of separate but interlinked chunks, and of translating each chunk into a wff, which may then have to be further transformed in order to make it into a clause, is clearly a demanding one. Moreover, the knowledge engineer's problems do not end there, for predicate calculus is not itself a programming language. So, before NOSTART could actually run on a computer, it would have to be reformulated yet again, this time using a high-level programming language such as LISP or PASCAL.

It was the possibility of short-circuiting this process and, at the same time, facilitating the task of actually eliciting human expertise and organising it into programmable form, that led to the development of a whole new class of computer languages. The best known of these logic programming languages, PROLOG, was devised by a team of researchers at the University of Marseilles in the mid-1970s and is now widely used in artificial intelligence laboratories. The advantage of PROLOG is that any program written in the language can be thought of as a list of clauses in the language of predicate calculus. In effect, therefore, a programmer using PROLOG is obliged, by the constraints of the language itself, to write his program in the form of a series of ready-made production rules. Another attraction of the language is that the use of nested brackets makes it very easy to represent the sort of tree structures that are used in problem solving.

There is one further factor that plays a large part in the reasoning of most human experts – uncertainty. Indeed, as anyone who has had cause to consult a lawyer or a surveyor will know, experts are rarely willing to commit themselves to an opinion that is completely clear-cut and unequivocal. Moreover, it is not uncommon to find that experts disagree among themselves about the significance that should be attached to a particular kind of evidence or the way in which a set of data should be interpreted.

There are a number of ways in which logical languages can be used to express ideas such as: 'Given the available data both x and y are possible, but x is more likely than y.' In predicate calculus, for example, it is possible to construct a wff in the form: 'Predicate (A) > Conclusion (B)', where B is the probability that the atomic formula Predicate A is a result of some cause, C. For example, the observation: 'Bill's late this evening. Probably a crisis has blown up in the office. But maybe the traffic's snarled up, or perhaps he's stopped off to have a drink with Frank', could be expressed in three production rules:

LATE (BILL) > DELAYED (OFFICE, 50%)
LATE (BILL) > DELAYED (TRAFFIC JAM, 25%)
LATE (BILL) > DELAYED (FRANK, 25%)

If Bill's presence is urgently required, this summary of the situation suggests that it would make sense to ring his office first and, if he is not there, then ring the bar where he and Frank usually meet. Similarly an expert system can be designed so that, if the application of its production rules leads it to two or more suggestions, such as RING (OFFICE, 50%) and RING (BAR, 25%), it will proffer them to the user in descending order of probability.

It is also possible for the programmer to so arrange matters that the system will allot its own probability ratings on the basis of data supplied to it. For example, told that weather records show that in seven years out of ten October has been a wet month when the preceding September was sunny it could conclude: SUNNY (SEPTEMBER) > RAINY (OCTOBER, 70%). But the use of words like 'sunny' and 'rainy' leads to another problem, how should they be defined? Do we just set some arbitrary limit and say that a month with more than 120 hours of sunshine is sunny and one with more than five inches of rainfall is rainy? Or is there some way in which a logical language could capture the subtler distinctions and gradations which we ourselves would employ?

It was in order to try to deal with this sort of question that Lofti Zadeh of Stanford University proposed the notion of 'fuzzy sets'. In traditional mathematics, of course, an object is either a member of a set or it is not: the set of whole numbers, for example, or the set of people who have seen the Taj Mahal, are well-defined entities. In fuzzy-set theory, however, a object can be assigned to a set with a variable 'degree of belonging'.

So, if we defined two sets, the set of rainy months and the set of sunny months, we could say that a December in which the rain poured down from the first day to the last and the sun never broke through at all could be assigned to the set of rainy months with a 'belonging multiplier' of 1. Equally, a glorious July during which not a cloud appeared in the sky could be assigned to the set of sunny months, again with a multiplier of 1. But an October in which there was a couple of inches of rain but also a welcome spell of autumn sunshine would be assigned to the set of rainy months with a multiplier of 0.3 and to the set of sunny months with a multiplier of 0.7. In the case of expert systems, the use of fuzzy sets makes it possible to express ideas with varying degrees of confidence. It allows the system to say, in effect: 'It is pretty certain that . . .' or 'It is unlikely, but not impossible, that. . .'.

A CAUTIONARY NOTE

What has been provided here is no more than a very brief outline, concentrating almost exclusively on one of the many possible approaches to the design of expert systems. We have barely begun to probe the enormous complexities of the problems involved, or to discuss the finer points of the knowledge engineer's art. But we have, we hope, said enough to show why this field of artificial intelligence is currently creating so much interest and excitement.

There are, however, some notes of caution which must be sounded. By no means all areas of human expertise are susceptible to this treatment. There are, for the moment at least, fairly strict limits to the size of an expert system – once a program is extended beyond a thousand rules its performance begins to deteriorate quite sharply in that the user may find himself sitting and waiting for quite appreciable periods while the computer searches through its knowledge base.

Expert systems are also limited to subject fields which are, as the jargon has it, 'well bounded'. In plain language, this means that while it is possible to deal with an area in which much specialized knowledge is involved, things become a great deal more difficult if human experts in the field also make extensive use of general knowledge and common sense.

A final, and perhaps more fundamental, problem is that the reasoning of expert systems is of a kind known as 'monotonic'. That is simply to say that the rules in the database must, by their very nature, be logically self-consistent, statements must be either true or not true. Yet human beings have very little difficulty in reasoning about a 'knowledge base' that contains gross inconsistencies and self-contradictions. To illustrate the point, consider the following three statements:

Birds fly
A penguin is a bird
A penguin does not fly

If confronted with any of these statements in isolation and asked whether it was true, most people would unhesitatingly reply 'yes'. But that does not mean that they are illogical, it simply means that they are accustomed to the idea that rules may still be valid for many purposes, even if it can be shown that there are exceptions to them.

It would of course be possible to take care of this problem in a expert system by changing the first statement to, 'All birds fly except penguins, ostriches, etc.' But what about these three statements?

Human beings do not want to die
Socrates was a human being
Socrates committed suicide

It would be nonsensical to try to take care of this inconsistency by modifying the first statement to, 'All human beings do not want to die except Socrates'. The version that is required to put matters right is clearly: 'Most human beings do not want to die but some do some of the time.' But how is the machine to know that the kind of modification that works in the case of first example does not work in the case of the second? Moreover, it is quite obvious that a rule such as 'Most human beings do not want to die, but some do some of the time' is worse than useless to an expert system.

These examples are, of course, trivial and over-simplified, but they may perhaps serve to show that those who claim that, with the arrival of the expert system, the key to artificial intelligence lies in our hands are being more than a little premature. The human brain still has quite a few tricks up its sleeve.

CHAPTER 7

THE MACHINERY OF VISION

In virtually everything that has been discussed so far it has been assumed that the inputs of data to an intelligent machine as well as its programs will be supplied by a human collaborator. In some cases this may make little difference; it is, for example, relatively unimportant that a chess-playing machine cannot actually see the board, since the board state can be fully and accurately described in symbolic terms. By the same token, since expert systems can only deal with the kind of knowledge that can be reduced to formal logical rules, the fact that they must rely upon their human users to describe a problem or to apply tests and report the results is largely irrelevant to their performance.

However, a great deal of our own intelligence, especially the elusive faculty of 'common sense', derives from our interaction with the world around us. Growing up – the process that transforms a helpless human infant into an intelligent adult capable of coping with his environment – involves the absorption of a continuous stream of data which the brain packages into the rough-and-ready set of rules and working hypotheses that we call 'experience'. And it is this experience that provides us with a basis upon which to evaluate, or make sense of, further data.

No matter whether we attribute this process to 'nature', arguing that the development is in some way preprogrammed into our brains, or subscribe to the idea that it is the product of 'nurture', believing that intelligence somehow 'bootstraps' itself into existence under the stimulus of experience, it clearly could not occur unless we were equipped to perceive our surroundings and observe the results of our own actions. It is, in short, inconceivable that human intelligence could exist in any recognizable form without the apparatus of the senses. Indeed, the whole concept of intentionality turns upon the idea that our thoughts are anchored to reality because the mental symbols which we manipulate represent real-world objects or events which we can see, hear, touch and smell.

These philosophical considerations alone constitute a powerful argument for trying to develop artificial equivalents of the senses, but there are also compelling practical reasons for doing so. It is, for example, very difficult to see how industrial robots can ever become genuinely versatile and adaptable workers unless they are able to see what they are doing and, perhaps, hear what human beings are saying. And if problem-solving machines are to deal with the sort of problems that are of real concern to most human beings, rather than being confined to brain-teasers of the kind discussed in Chapter 4, they will have to be able to see what the problem is for themselves, or at least have it explained to them in terms that the average human problem-solver can comprehend.

Ideally, of course, an intelligent machine would be equipped with the full range of human senses, together with senses such as radar, ultrasound or X-ray sensing which are inherently artificial. In terms of the equipment required to collect the raw data, such a machine is a perfectly practical proposition. There are already available a vast range of devices – known technically as transducers – such as TV cameras, microphones, strain and pressure gauges, even artificial 'sniffer' systems, which can capture information about the environment and encode it in a string of binary digits which can then be fed into a computer. Most existing robots also incorporate a number of sensors which are, roughly, equivalent to our own proprioceptive nervous system. This means that even though they cannot see their own arms or 'hands', they can sense the current position of their various joints and, if necessary, make corrections to ensure that those positions correspond with the ones that their program dictates.

But capturing the data is only the first step. The real problems – the ones with which artificial intelligence is primarily concerned – arise when we look for ways in which a machine might actually *understand* the data provided by its sensors. In discussing these problems and the methods by which they might be solved we shall concentrate very largely on a single sense, vision. There are a number of reasons for this. First, research into the practicalities of vision, together with work on automated reasoning, is currently the top priority in artificial intelligence laboratories. Secondly, many of the factors that have to be considered in designing an artificial vision system are equally relevant to the other senses. Thirdly, there are, as we shall try to show, good reasons for believing that vision may be the key to intelligence, in the sense that if a machine was to be capable of matching our own visual skills it would necessarily have to develop some counterpart to the internal, or mental, images which are the currency of so much of our own thinking. Finally, vision is the natural choice in a book which relies largely upon visual explanation. For the sake of completeness, however, we shall first briefly review the progress that has been made in producing artificial versions of the other senses.

THE OTHER SENSES

The least important sense is almost certainly that of smell, and perhaps for this reason work in the field has yet to reach the stage at which artificial intelligence would have anything to contribute. What do exist are a number of devices which can detect the presence in the atmosphere of a limited range of substances and, in some cases, differentiate them from each other by chemical or spectroscopic analysis.

In fact, our own sense of smell delivers very similar messages, which have relatively simple meanings – 'fire', 'sea', 'good food coming up', etc. – with the important difference that we are able to associate these messages with other sensations – the fear of fire, the sound of the sea, the sight of a plateful of roast beef, and so on. But we do not smell things 'in our heads' in the same way as, for example, we see things 'in our mind's eye'. It is, however, intriguing to speculate what might be the result if a machine were able to understand its surroundings in terms of smells in the same sense as a dog so obviously understands the world through its nose. If we could build such a machine, would we perhaps gain some insight into what it was like to live in a world of scents rather than a world of images?

Touch, again, can be disposed of rapidly since touch sensors are, as yet, capable of little discrimination. They can detect the presence of absence of an object and, in some cases, make simple distinctions, between soft objects which yield to pressure and hard ones which do not. But there is a long way to go before machines attain anything even approximating to the sensitivity of a fingertip or the manipulative skill needed to feel the shape of a complex object. Until that point is reached (or until vision systems are developed which allow a machine to see what it is touching) there is little scope for the application of intelligence.

The task of devising an artificial sense of hearing is of course inextricably bound up with the problems of natural language which we discussed in Chapter 6. The actual mechanics of hearing present few problems, however, for equipment that can encode and transmit speech as a stream of binary digits is the basis of all modern telephone systems, and an artificial counterpart of the cochlea (the spiral cavity of the inner ear in which sound waves are translated into nervous impulses) is relatively easily contrived.

The business of deciphering the encoded messages – recognizing the words that have been spoken – is more problematical. There are, it is true, systems at the prototype stage which can achieve this, but only under the most rigorously controlled conditions. The basic idea is that the combination of phonemes (the basic units of speech) which make up a word will, if analysed, yield a unique pattern of sound waves which can then be compared with sample patterns stored in memory in order to find the one that matches. The most obvious difficulty is that the pattern formed by the phonemes will vary from one individual to another according to their accent, pitch of voice, speech rhythms, and so on. This means that anyone who wishes to use such a system must first specify a carefully restricted vocabulary and then provide the machine with a spoken sample of each word. Subsequently the user will have to take care to stick to that vocabulary and to enunciate every word distinctly while avoiding the variations of tone and emphasis normally found in everyday speech.

When refined and fully developed such methods *may*, in the relatively near future, make it possible for executives to dictate their letters straight into a 'speech-driven word-processor'. But we should not imagine that such systems will be in any way intelligent. They may faithfully reproduce what they hear and spell all the words impeccably, but in no sense will they understand what is being said.

True understanding, moreover, depends not only on finding ways in which machines can parse sentences that are grammatically and phonetically faultless, it also depends on their being able to make educated guesses in order to fill in the blanks left by slipshod grammar or indistinct speech. It has become quite clear, as a result of many experiments in psychological laboratories, that we do not comprehend other people's speech as a cipher clerk decodes a secret message, taking each word independently and only looking for the meaning when we have completed the process. On the contrary, in the case of most routine conversation, either of the participants could probably complete many of the other's sentences long before he finished speaking. We achieve understanding depending as much upon our empathy with the speaker as upon our ability to interpret the sounds that reach our ears. This empathy frequently allows us to reconstruct what someone meant to say even if they have made a clumsy job of actually saying it; often, indeed, we are not aware that the speaker has omitted a word or left the sentence incomplete. Expecting a particular pattern of sounds, we automatically persuade ourselves that we have in fact heard it.

The script-using mechanisms described in Chapter 6 may be helpful here, in that they can resolve phonetical ambiguities by telling a machine whether one word is more likely to occur than another in any given context, but the suspicion remains that they provide a ingenious substitute for understanding while failing to capture its essence. Ultimately we come back to the issue of intentionality and the need for men and machines who are to communicate with each other to share a common understanding of 'what they are talking about'.

ENCODING VISION

Turning now to vision, we must start by looking at the way in which the raw data, in the form of a visual image, is actually captured and encoded in binary form. This is not because the mechanics of vision are, in themselves, particularly novel or more interesting than those of the other senses, but, because a grasp of the fundamental principles is essential to an understanding of subsequent chapters, and because it provides a basis upon which we may compare artificial systems with what is known of the natural one.

The vast majority of vision systems rely upon the use of a TV camera which performs the same basic function as our eyes — it translates patterns of light, focussed through a lens, into patterns of electrical impulses. In the eye, the incoming light is focussed on to the rods and cones of the retina; the light causes these specialized photosensitive cells to 'fire' (i.e. to discharge their electrical potential), and the resulting signals are passed, via a series of intermediary cells, down the optic nerve to the brain. Although matters are complicated by the fact that a certain amount of preprocessing takes place within the eye itself (a point we shall return to later), it is still true to say that the eye's essential role is to 'digitize' the image; a firing signal from one of the rods or cones represents a dot of light in one area of the visual field.

The artificial equivalent of the retina is a surface called a photocathode; this is scanned by a beam of electrons which causes a current to flow that is proportional to the intensity (and in the case of a colour camera, the colour) of the light, and this current can, in turn, be converted into a string of binary digits. The electron beam samples the image at regular intervals breaking the image down into

In order to generate a television picture the image is projected on to an electronically sensitive surface, called a photocathode, and the intensity (and in a colour system, the colour) of the light is sampled at regular intervals by a scanning electron beam. The beam travels along the lines of pixels from left to right, 'flying back' at the end of each line, just as the eye travels over a page of print. This process is repeated 25 times a second. Here the scan has reached the halfway stage; when the beam reaches the end of the last line of pixels, at the bottom right-hand corner, it will return and start a new scan at the top left-hand corner. For clarity's sake the matrix shown here contains only 192 pixels, but in reality most artificial vision systems deal with images made up of 512 lines, each containing 512

a series of dots or picture elements, known as 'pixels'. The image which appears on domestic TV sets in most countries is made up of 625 lines of pixels, but artificial vision systems are generally based on the use of a square matrix with 512 lines, each made up of 512 pixels.

One complete scan of the image thus involves taking just over a quarter of a million separate samples of the light ($512 \times 512 = 262,144$). In the simplest possible case, where a pixel is treated as being either white or black, one binary digit – a 0 or a 1 – can be used to encode a description of each pixel. But if the system is to represent grey tones intermediate between black and white it will be necessary to allot four or more binary digits to each pixel, in which case a single scan of the image will generate over a million bits of information, and the use of colour may require as many as 24 bits per pixel.

Given that an image will normally be scanned 25 times per second, it can be seen that any vision system must cope with massive amounts of data. The first step is for the information representing one complete scan of the image – called the pixel map or bit map – to be lodged in a specialized set of memory elements known as a 'framestore'. Some systems incorporate several frame stores, an elaboration which makes possible a variety of fancy computations; by comparing the content of successive frames, for example, moving objects can be identified and their speed measured. It is also interesting to note, in passing, that most of the more spectacular special effects seen on television are achieved by using framestores. A common example involves insetting one image within another, larger, one in order that the viewer may be able to see, say, both a long shot of a complete orchestra and, in one corner of the screen, a close-up of the soloist's hands.

Sticking for the present to a basic structure with just one framestore, a system that is to operate in real time – that is, to keep pace with events in the real world which is being observed – has just one twenty-fifth of a second in which to process the information in the framestore before it is replaced by a new batch of data representing the next frame. The aim must be to find some way in which the computer can extract the meaning of the information or, to put it slightly differently, recognize what is being seen. In other words the image, now encoded in a mass of binary digits, must be compared with a store of other images, similarly encoded, and the best match selected so that the computer can determine that the image represents, say, a cup and saucer, two spanners lying on a workbench, the Eiffel Tower or, perhaps, some object or objects that it has never seen before and is therefore unable to identify.

How is this to be achieved? The obvious assumption, and the one adopted by top-down artificial intelligence, is that the raw data representing the image itself must somehow be translated and, if possible, condensed, into another set of data representing a *description* of the image.

We refer to this step as 'obvious' for three reasons. First, because storing even a small set of pixel maps representing known images in framestores would require colossal amounts of memory – even more so if allowance was to be made for the fact that quite simple objects may present quite different appearances if seen from different angles or under different lighting conditions. Secondly, because the process of comparing a new image with a selection of known images, pixel for pixel, in order to find the one which matches would, if performed in the linear mode employed by a von Neumann computer, occupy the machine for minutes or even hours at a time. And, thirdly, because we find it very difficult to account for our own feats of recognition unless we assume that we extract some sort of formal description from the raw visual data. If if asked how we distinguish between a table and a desk, for example, we would probably say that while the former was supported by legs, the latter had tiers of drawers down either side; that there was space for two or more people to sit at a table but space for only one to sit at a desk; that a desk was likely to have a leather covering on the work surface, and so forth.

In order to describe the contents of an image we must first identify those features that are likely to be significant. In most cases, these will almost certainly be the lines which represent the edges of objects and the conjunctions of lines which represent their corners. An edge will, in turn, be represented by sharp contrasts between the tone or intensity of light in neighbouring pixels. So the first stage in processing the contents of a framestore almost always involves the

In order to find the edges in an image the computer must identify the points at which there is an abrupt change in tone or intensity. This is achieved by sweeping the image with a small block of nine pixels. If the process is to be effective, the blocks must overlap each other, and a complete scan of a 512 × 512 matrix will thus involve over a quarter of a million separate computations.

For the mathematically minded the algorithm employed compares the value of the central pixel, X, with those for the eight surrounding pixels, A to H. In the simplest possible example, where 1 represents a dark pixel and 0 represents a light one, if the result of the computation 8X minus A, B, C, D, E, F, G, H is greater than 0, then X must be a dark pixel with at least one light neighbour, but if the result of the computation is 0 then X is either a light pixel or a dark pixel with all dark neighbours.

application of an 'edge-finding algorithm' designed to locate the points at which such contrasts occur. In its simplest form this process involves 'sweeping' the entire pixel grid, examining one small area at a time, comparing the encoded descriptions of neighbouring pixels, and compiling a list of grid references, as it were, each of which will represent one tiny bit of an edge. In reality, of course, it is not the image itself which is examined but the contents of the framestore. However, the process is most easily thought of in visual terms as can be seen below.

When the computer has completed its catalogue of grid references, it will, in effect, have reduced the pixel map to a simple line drawing. Though it is again important to remember that what exists inside the computer is not a 'real' line drawing but simply a catalogue of points and vectors which represent the edges in very much the same way as a ship's course, plotted on a chart, can be represented in terms of points of latitude and longitude and compass bearings. In practice, given that any electronic system will be subject to a certain degree of random 'noise' or interference, the result may well be fairly messy, and at this stage it is therefore usual to apply algorithms which will clean up the image by eliminating rogue grid references which cannot be connected to others and filling in minor gaps as can be seen opposite.

Once the edges have been found, producing what is in effect a line drawing, it will almost always be necessary to clean up the resulting image in order both to eliminate fragmentary lines which are the product of distortions caused by noise in the system and to fill in gaps in those lines that represent significant features. Shown here are, first, a typical 'noisy' image and, second, the cleaned-up version.

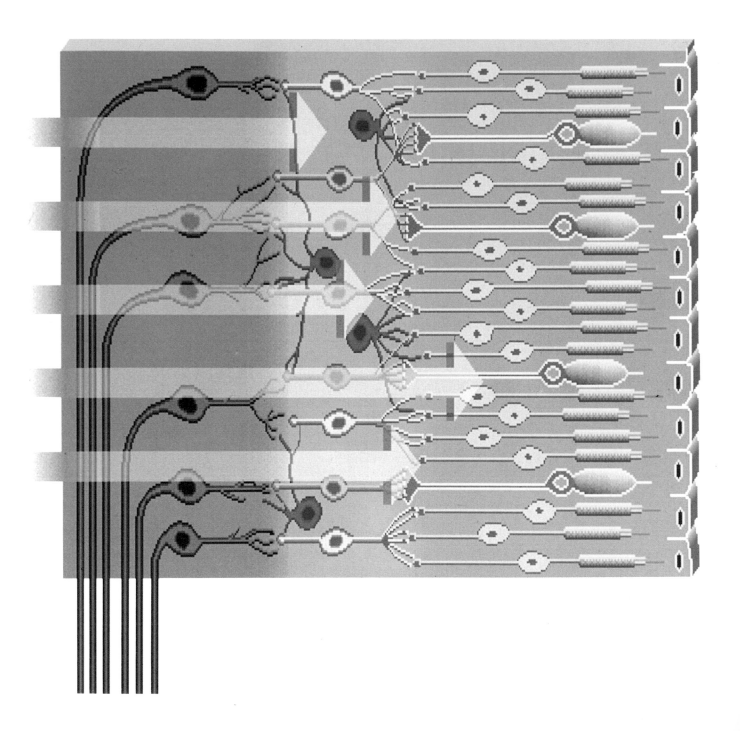

NATURAL VISION

There is a good deal of evidence to suggest that, in the preliminary stages at least, our own visual processing system works on similar principles. We mentioned earlier that some preprocessing of the signals from the light-receptive rods and cones takes place within the retina before they are transmitted to the brain – this must be so, if only because there are more light receptors in the retina than there are fibres in the optic nerve. In fact the signals from the rods and cones pass through a complex intermediate level containing two quite distinct classes of cells before reaching the ganglion cells which relay them to the brain.

Although our understanding of the role of these networks of cells is far from complete, there are good reasons for believing that one of their functions is to suppress random or accidental signals and hence clean up the retinal image. This is achieved by a mechanism known as reciprocal inhibition. Briefly, the rods and cones are interconnected in such a fashion that when one cell fires it stimulates its neighbours and their firing signals tend, in turn, to suppress the firing activity in the original cell. Thus, if a cell starts to fire 'by accident', its activity will cause its neighbours to try to switch it off again, and it will only continue to fire if the incoming light provides a stimulus sufficiently strong to overcome the inhibitory influence of its neighbours.

This same mechanism of reciprocal inhibition also enables the retina to achieve what is known as 'edge-enhancement' (see next page). By emphasizing contrasts in tone between neighbouring areas in the retinal image it allows the eye to pick out those features that are likely to be significant.

PARALLEL PROCESSORS

The mechanisms in the retina are, clearly, very different from the edge-finding algorithms described above. This is not the place to discuss the differences in detail, but one distinction which can be drawn between the natural system and artificial ones based upon the use of traditional von Neumann computers is both highly significant and directly relevant to artificial intelligence.

Computer edge-finding algorithms, as we have seen, involve the repeated application of relatively simple logical operations to each small section of the image in turn: the encoded information representing a small group of pixels is taken out of the framestore and placed in the registers of the central processor, the logical process is applied, the result is set aside for future reference, and the computer moves on to consider the next group of pixels. In the eye, by contrast, all the signals from the rods and cones are processed simultaneously – in parallel. The difference between parallel processors, of which the brain itself is the archetype, and serial or linear processors, epitomized by the von Neumann computer, is a fundamental issue, of importance to the whole of artificial intelligence, and we shall be returning to it in Chapter 9. For the moment, however, we shall simply concern ourselves with the practicality of

Cross-section of one tiny area of the retina of the human eye. The light is shown entering from the left of the picture and passing through three layers of cells before reaching the light-sensitive rods and cones on the right. The pattern of signals generated in the receptor cells (there are about 200 million rods and 10 million cones in a single retina) is then transmitted back (leftwards in terms of this illustration), via two intermediate layers of cells, to the ganglion cells the fibres of which form the optic nerve that carries the encoded description of the retinal image to the brain. The intermediate layers of cells preprocess and condense the raw data gathered by the rods and cones, and it seems reasonably clear that one of the effects of this preprocessing is to eliminate the effects of noise and to enhance the contrasts between areas of different intensity which are likely to represent edges and other significant features.

At first glance there is little to distinguish these two strips from each other: both seem to be made up of two halves, one a darker red than the other. If, however, the centre of the right strip is obscured by holding a finger in front of it, it will be seen that the colours on either side are in fact identical; the 'edge' in the centre has been created by shading a narrow strip on either side of it. This optical illusion, devised by Craik, Cornsweet and O'Brien, makes it clear that our own visual system automatically concentrates our attention on the contrasts, which are likely to represent the significant features in an image, even at the expense of conveying a false impression of the image as a whole.

using artificial parallel processors to speed up operations such as edge-finding which are, we surmise, dealt with in the eye the networks of cells in the retina.

There are already several such devices, known as array processors, in existence. One of the most advanced and best-known is the Cellular Logic Image Processor (or CLIP) designed and built by a team of researchers at University College London under the leadership of Professor Michael Duff. In fact CLIP machines are already being used in areas such as medical research where their ability to extract the significant features very rapidly from the often confused and murky images yielded by X-ray or microscopic techniques is extremely valuable.

The basic idea of a machine of this kind is that instead of being fed, one small chunk at a time, into a single processor, all the data representing a single scan of the image is input simultaneously into an array of processors, each of which deals with its own chunk. In the case of CLIP the arrangement is very simple: one processor (in

fact a specially designed logic chip) is allotted to each pixel, and each of the processors is linked to its immediate neighbours in the array so that it can exchange information with them.

If we now imagine the sequence of events that follows the input of the batch of data representing a single frame, we can form a general idea of how the machine operates. At the first stage in the cycle each processor receives and takes into store the information describing its own pixel. At the next stage it transmits this information to its neighbours and, in turn, receives a description of their pixels. It can then apply a number of different algorithms which involve comparing these inputs and, perhaps, modifying the description of its own pixel as a result. In some cases the process may terminate at this point (a simple algorithm that will find the edges in a black-and-white image is illustrated on page 129). But in other cases further exchanges of information may take place and this will cause information originating in one processor gradually to 'propagate' across the array.

Here we see how an image is, in effect, projected on to the CLIP array Bprocessor. Each of the cubes in the lattice represents a processing element, a custom-made silicon chip, which 'sees' just one pixel of the image in the background and is able both to communicate with and to receive signals from its four immediate neighbours.

The design of CLIP was to some extent based upon the structure of the retinal networks of the eye, and similarities will be extended in the next generation of machines now being built by Professor Duff and his colleagues. The idea is that individual processors should be given the freedom to vary their programs as a computation progresses. Instead of simply applying a single, predetermined set of instructions, each processor will be able to make decisions about what it should do next based on the results it and its neighbours have obtained so far. Such MIMD (Multiple Instruction, Multiple Data, as opposed to SIMD, or Single Instruction, Multiple Data) machines would clearly be capable of handling some of the more

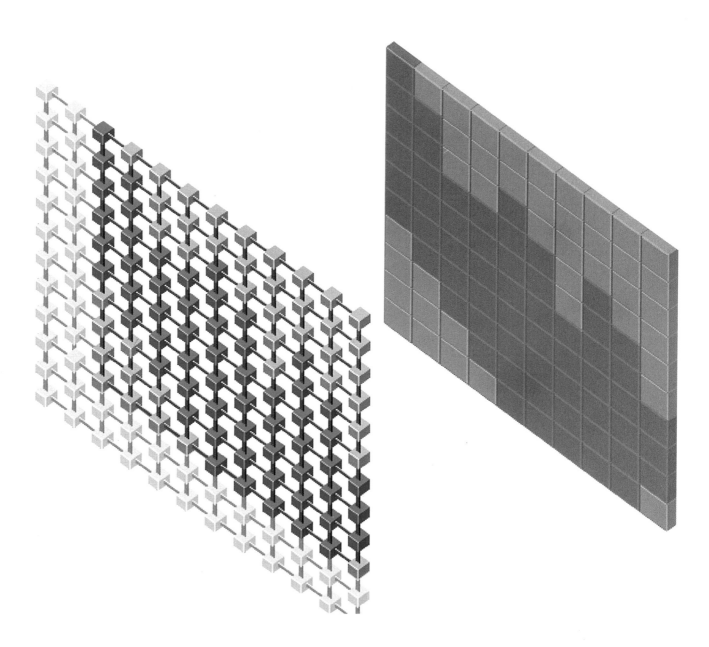

sophisticated tasks, such as feature identification, which will be discussed in Chapter 8.

Edge-finding is only the first stage in extracting the meaning from an image. Having reduced the pixel map to a line drawing, it is then necessary to find some way in which a machine might determine what the lines actually represent. At this point, however, current thinking about visual processing splits up into several divergent streams. We shall look at three possible approaches to the problem in Chapter 8, before returning in Chapter 9 to the subject of parallel processors and examining a very different way of tackling the whole question of artificial vision.

The result of applying a simple edge-finding algorithm to the image shown left. The processors that 'see' the pixels around the edges of the black image have set themselves to 1 and all other processors have set themselves to 0. Because all its processing elements operate in parallel, an array processor such as CLIP can achieve this result in just a few cycles of operation, a dramatic contrast to the long sequences of repetitive operations that a serial computer with a single central processor must go through.

Each processor has compared the value, X, of its own pixel (1 for black, 0 for white) with the values, A to D, for the four neighbouring pixels, setting X to 1 in the current cycle if, in the previous cycle, it was found that 4X minus A, B, C, D was greater than 0.

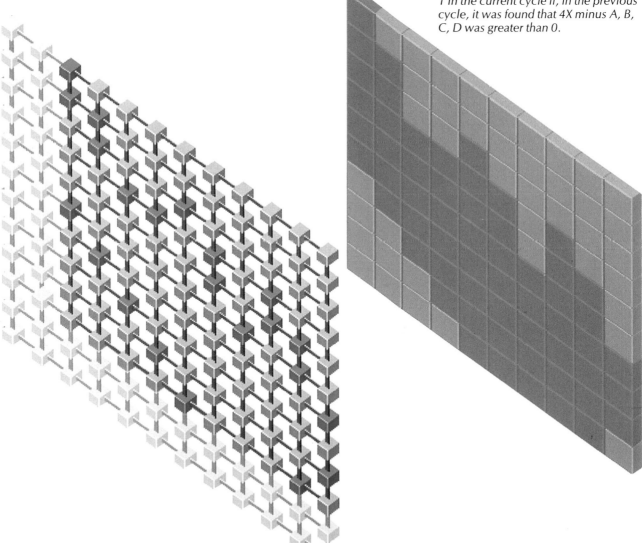

A typical application for the current generation of artificial vision systems. The robot is required to pick up the packages as they reach the end of the conveyor belt and stack them neatly in the box. A comparatively simple algorithm will allow the vision system to calculate the orientation of each package as it passes in front of the camera (top left), and this information is then passed to the robot enabling it to align its 'hand' appropriately before attempting to grasp the package.

CHAPTER 8

THE ANALYTICAL EYE

In all branches of artificial intelligence it is possible to draw a distinction between research which aims to elucidate the workings of the brain and, if possible, to replicate them, and the effort to design systems that can perform useful functions whether or not the way in which they achieve this bears any relationship to the way we perform similar tasks. In the case of vision, matters are complicated by the fact that four quite different approaches to the problem have emerged, each of which stands in a different relationship to these two objectives. We shall examine three of these approaches in this chapter, before moving on to discuss the fourth in Chapter 9.

TACKLING INDUSTRY'S CURRENT NEEDS

The first approach is straightforwardly utilitarian and is primarily concerned with the development of practical vision systems for use in industry. Indeed, since most of the equipment involved is designed to accomplish a very specific and restricted range of tasks, many would argue that it has little to do with artificial intelligence proper. However, pending the solution of the fundamental problems involved in designing general-purpose vision systems, those who are concerned with producing useful tools have had little choice but to tackle the job on an *ad hoc*, case by case basis.

Once the significant features of an image have been extracted (usually the edges, which can be found by applying the algorithms discussed in Chapter 7), there is a whole range of techniques which can be used to obtain the relatively simple information that might be useful to, say, an industrial robot.

Since a vision system will normally be used in conjunction with automated equipment that presents it with objects one at a time and in predetermined positions, the algorithms employed will only be required to analyse the geometrical properties of a single element. A typical application might involve using a vision system in conjunction with a 'pick and place machine' (a rather basic robot capable only of grasping an object and moving it to a new position).

In all, some 800 algorithms have been devised to serve a wide variety of purposes, but the simple example shown in the illustration opposite may serve to make the point that, for all their ingenuity, the algorithms are usually specific to one particular purpose and unashamedly 'artificial' i.e. although the task may be one that our own brains perform, it is inconceivable that they do so in the same way. In many cases, indeed, even the hardware itself may have been designed with one specific task in mind. This is because the sheer volume of information that has to be processed often means that the necessary speed is most easily achieved by hard-wiring the algorithm into a specially designed chip rather than using a general-purpose programmable computer.

Given one of these two images it is possible to determine whether it is a square or a circle by comparing the area, A, of the object (i.e. the total number of dark pixels) with the length of its periphery, P (i.e. the number of dark pixels that have white neighbours). In the case of a square the relationship is expressed by the equation $A = (\frac{P}{4})^2$, while in the case of a circle, schoolroom geometry tells us that dividing the circumference by π will give the diameter, halving the diameter gives the radius, R, and $A = \pi R^2$.

Such algorithms may provide a highly effective means of dealing with specific problems, but no one would suppose that they bear any relationship to what goes on inside our brains.

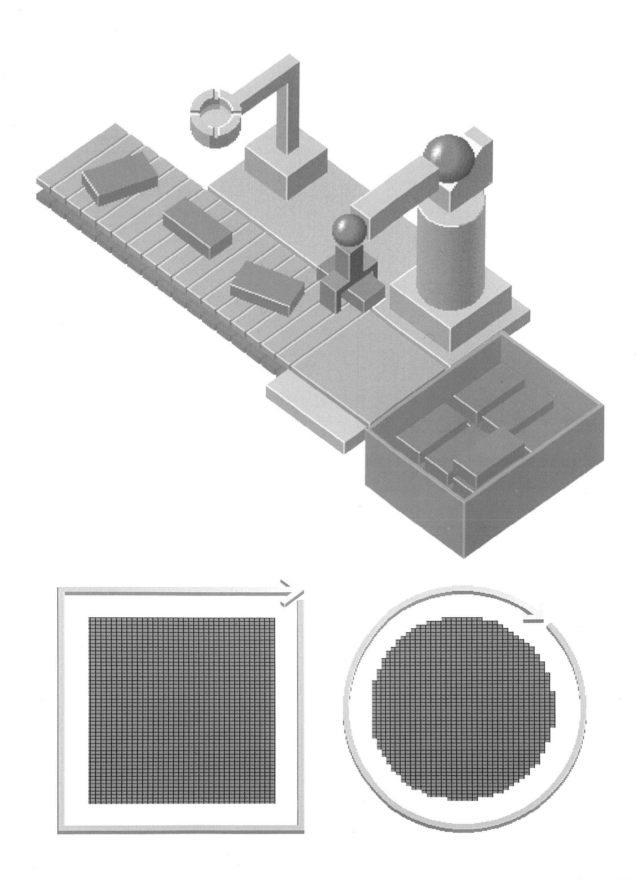

SCENE ANALYSIS

The second approach, sometimes called scene analysis, is a good deal more ambitious. Essentially, it represents the ideas about vision that have emerged from classical, top-down artificial intelligence. The earliest workers in the field, inspired in part by the needs of the American space program, set out to devise general-purpose vision systems which might, in principle, be used either to guide robot exploration vehicles around the surface of a strange planet or to provide a new generation of industrial robots with flexible and sophisticated visual senses. Thus, rather than considering specific problems, they sought to tackle the whole business of artificial vision from first principles. In most cases the starting point was the assumption that all three-dimensional objects can be thought of as composite shapes built up out of geometrical primitives — the cubes, pyramids, cones, etc. that are familiar from schoolroom geometry. If a way could be found of dealing with these basic elements, the argument went, it should be possible to elaborate the techniques in order to cope with more complex ones.

Virtually all the research that has been done along these lines has, therefore, centred on the use of 'block worlds' — small groups of simple objects which can be placed one on top of another, or so arranged that they appear to overlap or cast shadows across each other. Again, the first step is to find the edges; this done, it becomes possible to locate the corners, the points where two or more edges meet, and to label them. R.B. Roberts, working at MIT, showed how it was then possible to represent the relationships between the corners and the edges as a matrix (see opposite). Since each class of object produced a number of unique patterns on the matrix, depending upon the point of view from which it was being seen, the objects contained in any particular scene could be identified, and their orientations established, by referring to a catalogue of such patterns.

The use of additional rules also made it possible to deal with more complex scenes. If, for example, a T-junction is formed where two edges meet, then they must belong to two separate objects positioned one in front of another, and if this is so, allowance may have to be made for one corner of the more distant object being absent from the matrix (see page 134). Again, a ramp-like object will produce the same matrix pattern as a cube, but it can still be accurately identified if the orientation of each pair of opposing sides is checked to see whether or not they are parallel to each other (see page 134).

But the fact that these algorithms made massive computational demands when applied to complex scenes encouraged a search for simpler methods that might be more generally applicable. One of the most successful techniques was that devised by Adolfo Guzman at MIT and further developed by the late Max Clowes of the University of Sussex. The key perception was that combinations of edges can not only be used to locate the corners, they can also be treated as boundaries which enclose surfaces. If both corners and surfaces are labelled, then the relationships between them can again be represented in mathematical terms, this time as a graph

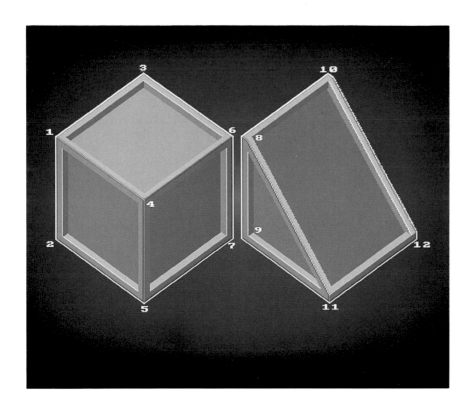

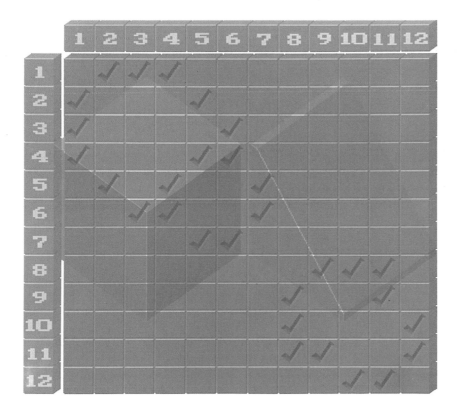

Having found the edges in this simple scene, it is possible to identify the corners and number them (top). The entire scene can now be represented in the form of a matrix (below). Although this would exist inside a computer only as a long string of binary digits, it is shown here in diagrammatic form. The twelve corners have been listed along both axes and the ticks indicate where two corners are linked by an edge – the vertical edge of the cube nearest the camera, for example, is represented by the ticks at the intersections of column 4 and row 5 and column 5 and row 4. As is clear from the illustration, the matrix patterns produced by the cube and the wedge are quite distinct from each other, and the fact that there are two separate groups of ticks clearly indicates that the scene contains two objects that do not overlap.

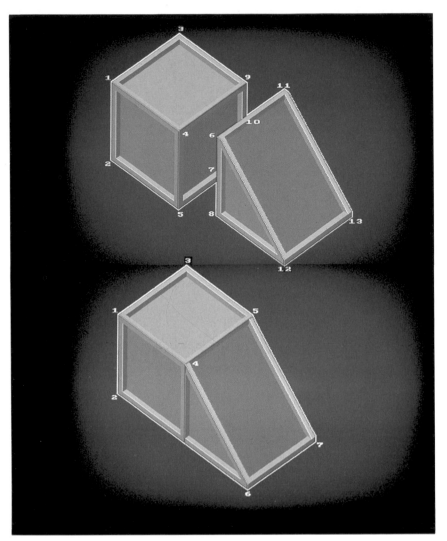

If the scene shown in the previous illustration is rearranged so the objects appear to overlap (top), one corner of the cube disappears and two new corners, 7 and 10, common to both objects are formed. A matrix would therefore show this as a single object with all 13 corners connected by edges. However, the presence of the two T-junctions which, in a simple block world like this one, invariably indicate an overlap, shows that there are in fact two separate objects.

If the wedge is placed alongside the cube (bottom), the corners and edges of the resulting composite object produce exactly the same matrix pattern as a simple cube. But the fact that edges 4–6 and 5–7 are not parallel with edge 1–2 betrays the fact that this is not a cube.

which will vary according to the class of the object (see opposite). Once more the way in which the edges meet will yield further clues as to the orientation of an object: in the case of a cube, for example, a star-shaped conjunction must represent the corner of a cube nearest to the camera, and an 'arrowhead' corner will always be closer than one at which two lines form an obtuse angle (see opposite).

The algorithms developed by Guzman and Clowes were successful as far as they went, but that was not far enough to deal with the composite shapes that are found in real-life scenes. If this approach was to be taken further, then it was necessary to find some way of representing the relationships between geometrical elements in more general terms. For example, it was necessary to take account of the fact that the apparent relationships between elements can change very dramatically with changes in viewpoint while in reality remaining constant, or, when considering broad categories of objects, that geometrical variations may be less significant than

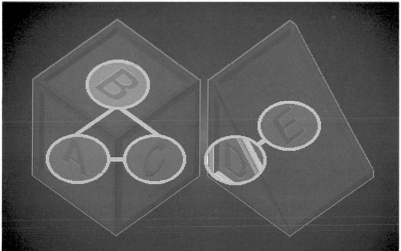

In a block world, whenever a group of three or more corners are found to be linked together by edges (i.e. corner 1 is joined to corner 2 which is joined to corner 3 which is joined to corner 1) it can be inferred that the edges represent the boundaries of a surface which can therefore be labelled (top).

Each surface can then be represented as a node on a graph and the nodes can be joined by links which represent the corners common to both (bottom). In the case of the 'cube' graph, for example, corners 1 and 4 are common to surface A and surface B, corners 4 and 6 are common to B and C, and corners 4 and 5 are common to A and C.

The graphs produced by different classes and combinations of objects will be quite distinct and, by referring to a database containing a representative selection of graphs, a machine can therefore determine both the contents of a scene and the way in which the objects are positioned relative to each other.

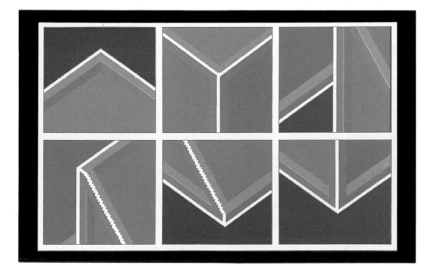

In a block world which contains only simple objects such as blocks, wedges, pyramids, etc., corners provide valuable clues. For example, an inverted V-shape (top left) must represent the far corner of an object while a star-shape (top centre) must be the nearest corner. A T-junction (top right) can only occur when one object overlaps another. The arrowhead (bottom right) must be further away from the camera than the star-shape, and other rules allow the corners of a wedge (bottom centre and right) to be distinguished from those of a cube or pyramid.

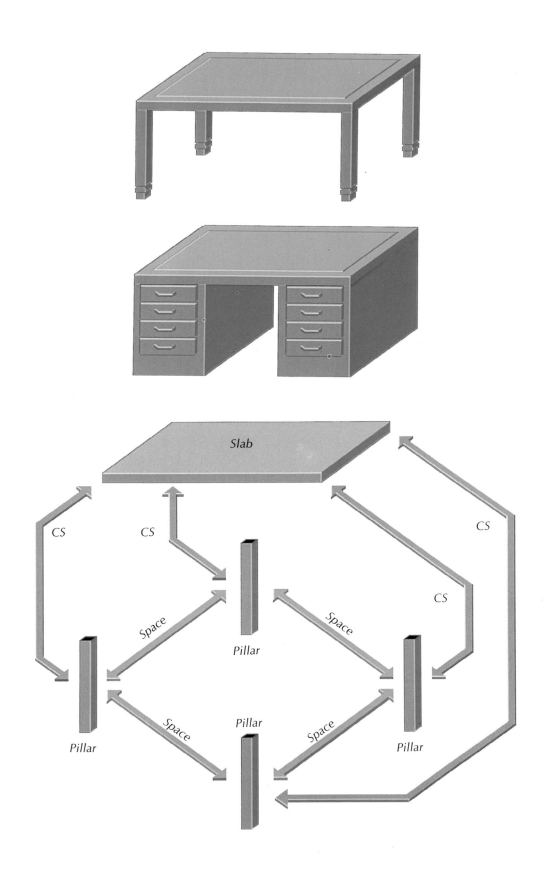

functional or other similarities. In other words, once the basic 'blocks' are assembled to form composite objects it becomes increasingly difficult to express their 'meaning' in purely geometrical terms. One possible answer to the problem was the concept of the semantic net developed by P.H. Winston of MIT in the mid-1970s. We looked, briefly, at Winston's ideas when discussing the techniques of knowledge representation in Chapter 6; applied to vision, they provide a way of representing the structure of a composite object by classifying *both* the basic elements *and* the way in which they are related to one another. To take a very simple example, semantic nets could be used to represent the idea that while a table consists of a slab supported by a pillar at each corner, a desk consists of a slab supported by boxes (the ranks of drawers) at each end.

There are, of course, complications arising from the fact that, seen from just one aspect, the structure of an object is seldom completely clear and unambiguous. Unless a table is viewed from below, for example, it will not be evident that all four pillars are actually connected to the slab and supporting it. In constructing a semantic net that could represent even a limited range of views of a single rather basic table it would, therefore, be necessary to build in a good deal of flexibility (see next page). But, at the same time, too much flexibility would result in a semantic net that embraced all sorts of arrangements of elements that were in some way table-like without actually being tables (see next page).

In practice, Winston suggested, a semantic net is best refined by using a learning process based upon trial and error. To illustrate how this might work, let us continue with the example of tables and

If we consider complex objects as composites made up of combinations of geometrical primitives, then the table and desk (top) could be defined as a 'slab' supported by a 'pillar' at each corner, and a 'slab' supported by a 'box' at each end. These two definitions can be translated into semantic nets (bottom), which not only catalogue the individual elements such as 'pillar' and 'slab' that go to make up a table or a desk but also express the relationships between elements – the structure of the net makes it clear, for example, that four 'pillars' and a 'slab' only constitute a 'table' if each of the 'pillars' is connected to the 'slab' by a 'corner support' (CS) pointer and separated from the other 'pillars' by a 'space' pointer.

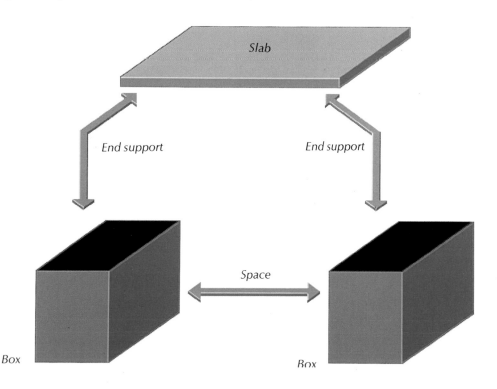

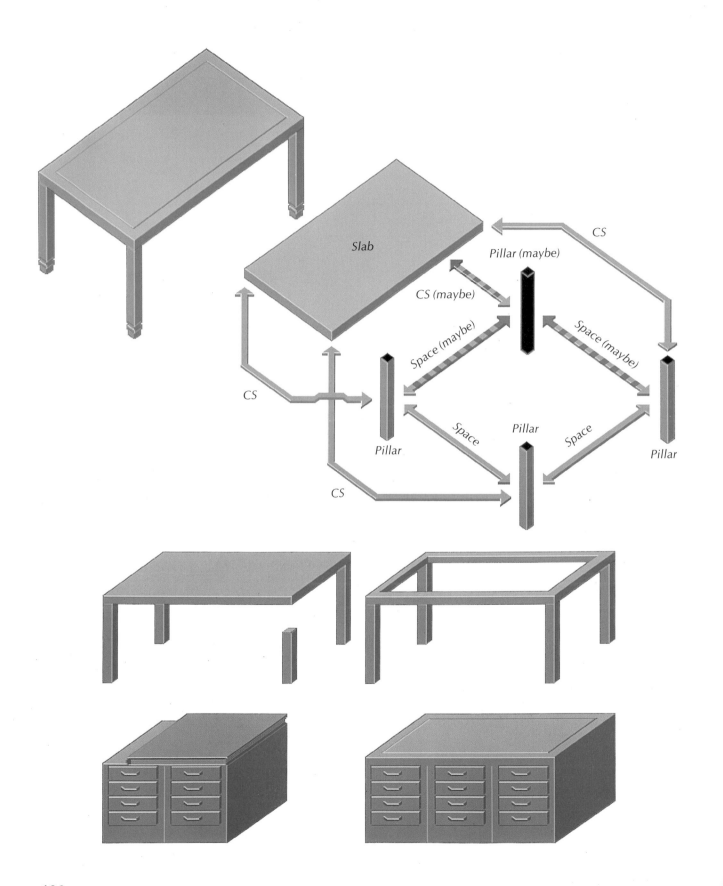

Slab

CS

Pillar (maybe)

CS (maybe)

Space (maybe)

Space (maybe)

CS

Pillar

Space

Pillar

Space

CS

Pillar

desks. We will assume that the computer has already been equipped with the programming required to distinguish between the three basic geometrical elements involved – 'slabs', 'pillars' and 'boxes' – and to identify the basic structural relationships – a space between two elements, the support of a corner of the 'slab' by a 'pillar' and the support of an end of the 'slab' by a 'box'. We will further assume that two crude semantic nets, one representing a slab supported by a pillar at each corner, meaning 'table', and the other representing a slab supported by a box at each end, meaning 'desk' have been provided by the programmer.

The machine will now be shown a series of images of tables and desks seen from different points of view as well as other images of non-tables and non-desks – objects or collections of visual elements which might meet some but not all the necessary criteria. In each case the machine will construct a semantic net representing what it sees and compare it with the representations already stored in memory in order to see whether a match can be established. The machine then reports its conclusions – 'table', 'desk' or, if it fails to find a match, 'neither' – to the programmer, who either confirms or rejects them.

If the computer is told that it has made a mistake, then a learning mechanism built into its program will modify the relevant semantic net in an appropriate fashion. If, for example, a genuine table has been rejected because one of the four pillars was not visible, one of the 'pillar' nodes and the 'corner support' and 'space' connections to the other nodes in the 'table' net will be qualified by the addition of a 'maybe' condition. Obviously, as the process continues, all the pillar nodes will become subject to such qualifications, and as a result a slab with no pillars at all would be recognized as a 'table'. To avoid this sort of mistake, more sophisticated learning algorithms will be required, enabling the structure of the net to be further elaborated so that it will match, say, any image in which three out of the four pillars are present, provided that at least two of them are supporting a corner of the slab.

In some respects at least it may seem that semantic nets mirror mechanisms which must operate within our own perceptual system. We are, after all, quite confident of our ability to distinguish a table from a desk – or a fork from a spoon, a Mercedes from a Jaguar, the face of a friend from any of the other faces we pass in the street. When we claim that we 'know' what these things, and tens of thousands of others besides, 'look like', are we not in effect saying that descriptions of them are filed away in our brains and that if we recognize something it is because we have flicked through the filing system, found a description that matches what we see and thus been able to attach a name to it?

Unfortunately, this conception of our visual memory very quickly runs into a number of difficulties. For example, it does not account for the fact that most people can, if they pause and consider for a moment or two, think of many things which they would feel confident of recognizing should they see them again, but which they are quite unable to describe clearly in any explicit fashion. If you doubt that this is so, then try describing to yourself a house that

In order to recognize the table in the top left picture the structure of the semantic net would have to be modified as shown below it. Now the presence of the fourth 'pillar' and its links to the other elements are subject to a 'maybe' condition, and this net would therefore match any image of a table in which either all four or three out of four 'pillars' were visible and could be seen to be supporting the corners of the 'slab'.

While the structure of semantic nets will have to incorporate a good deal of flexibility, in the shape of 'maybe' and 'perhaps' conditions, if they are to cope with even a limited range of representative images, too much flexibility will result in the erroneous recognition of 'non-tables' and 'non-desks' such as these.

you lived in many years ago, or one of the classrooms in your school, or try to compile from memory a detailed description of the shape of the car that you currently drive. The chances are that if you make a conscious effort to remember what any of those things look like, the first thing that will come into your mind is not a description but an image; and if you are able to frame a description in words, ask yourself whether those words are drawn directly from memory or whether they are in fact a description of an image that you see 'in your mind's eye'.

Admittedly, not everyone who makes this experiment will experience the same sensations, and the question of whether visual memories are 'encoded' in the brain as images or as descriptions of images is still a contentious and ultimately, perhaps, a meaningless one. But we hope that enough has been said to show that any parallels that might be drawn between the sort of knowledge that can be represented in a semantic net and the content of our own visual memory are likely to be superficial at best. Indeed, as we shall show, there is evidence to suggest that much of our own perceptual machinery operates in a fashion both more subtle and more elusive than the formal algorithms we have been discussing.

If, as we have suggested, this second approach has only a dubious and indirect relevance to the study of human vision, it must also be said that it has contributed very little to the design of practical artificial vision systems. The reasons for this failure are easily understood. For all the theoretical elegance of the algorithms that the researchers have devised, the fact is that most of the real-life problems to which they might be applied are more easily and cheaply solved by using one or more of the special-purpose algorithms discussed at the beginning of the chapter. It had of course been hoped that the arrival of general-purpose systems, whose designers had tackled the problem of vision by starting from the first principles of geometry, would change this situation by widening the range of applications. But this has not happened because, to put the matter in a nutshell, when the second approach tried to move beyond the contrived simplicity of the block world into the complexities of the real world it ran head-on into the implications of the combinatorial explosion.

It thus became clear that although the methods adopted might in theory provide a sound basis for artificial vision, in practice they were quite unworkable on the factory floor or in the warehouse, let alone in outer space. This setback was one of the factors that led to the development of the third approach which is generally associated with the work of David Marr, a brilliant young British neurophysiologist who went to head the artificial vision programme at MIT in the late 1970s. Marr died a tragically early death in 1982, but his ideas are still the focus of most of the work being done on artificial vision and therefore merit close examination.

LEARNING FROM NATURE

Marr was convinced that success could only be achieved by studying and learning from the natural system. In particular, he pointed to the experimental work done by neurophysiologists and psychologists which strongly suggests that the processing of visual information can be divided into a number of quite distinct stages which take place in different areas of the brain. He therefore laid down the principle that researchers who set out to tackle any aspect of vision must not only have sound computational theories – algorithms that can be shown to work – they must also be able to show that the function involved is one that would actually contribute to the competence of the brain and, if possible, have evidence of where and how it is accomplished.

A very good example of Marr's whole approach is provided by his own study of the networks of cells in the retina of the eye which, as we mentioned in Chapter 7, appear to preprocess the raw visual data before passing it on to the brain. One of the most puzzling features of our own visual skill is that we continue to see a white surface as white and a black one as black even when the former is in deep shadow and, therefore, reflecting less light than the latter, which is strongly illuminated. If our eyes functioned simply as receptors and measurement devices, like a photographer's light meter, this simply would not happen – the surface that reflected the most light would appear to be the 'lighter' of the two. The fact that we are able to distinguish between variations in the 'real' colour of surfaces and variations in illumination seems to be due to the fact that the former are normally abrupt whereas the latter are usually graduated. In other words, because we are able to detect the edges which are likely to denote a change in colour, we are able to compensate for differences in the intensity of illumination. The existence of some such ability would, amongst other things, account for the Craik-Cornsweet-O'Brien illusion (see page 126).

The actual processes involved in making such compensations are complex, and it is sufficient for present purposes to know that one of Marr's collaborators, Berthold Horn, succeeded in producing a computer program which can perform the task. For the real point is that Marr was subsequently able to show that there were features of the retinal networks that suggested that they might well have been 'designed', so to speak, to implement the algorithm upon which Horn's program was based.

However, Marr's most important and influential work was concerned with a later stage in visual processing, one that seems to take place in the visual cortex of the brain. Like most current thinking about the visual system, Marr's theories are based on the results of a series of famous experiments by the Nobel laureates David Hubel and Torsten Wiesel. By inserting minute probes into the visual cortex of monkeys, Hubel and Wiesel were able to measure the electrical activity of individual cells, as a result they discovered the existence of cells which seemed to function as feature recognition devices in that they responded only to the presence of very specific features in the visual field. What triggered these cells into firing was not simply the presence of one of three elementary features, which Hubel and Wiesel called 'edges', 'slits' and 'lines' (see next page) but also the orientation of that feature. There were, for instance, some cells which reacted only to vertical

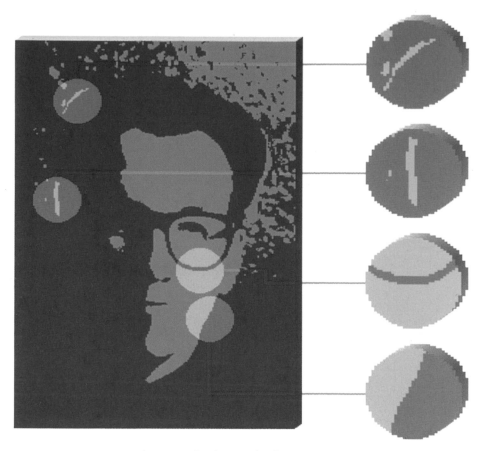

edges, and others which were triggered only by horizontal slits or lines that sloped downwards from left to right, and so on.

It also appeared that these cells were organized in structures, known as 'hypercolumns', each of which received information from one particular area of the visual field. In other words, the physical structure of the retina seemed to be mapped onto the structure of this area of the visual cortex, known technically as the 'striate cortex'. Moreover, microscopic examination shows that the hypercolumns, which run parallel to one another through the thin layer of 'grey matter' from the surface of the cortex to the 'white matter' beneath (see opposite), are composed of quite distinct layers, each of which seems to contain cells sensitive to one kind of feature in one particular orientation.

What this suggests is that the central area of the visual field (the area on which our attention is focussed when we look at something) is divided into a large number of separate sub-fields, each of which is monitored, as it were, by a single hypercolumn. And within that hypercolumn there are several different groups, or classes, of cells, each of which will react specifically to one kind of feature in one particular orientation. This summary is admittedly highly simplified, and should, properly speaking, be qualified with many ifs and buts, but it will, we hope, be sufficient for the purposes of this discussion.

It seems that having already postulated the existence of 'edge-

Here two 'slits', a 'line' and an 'edge' have been picked out of the image to show the sort of features that are believed to stimulate the feature-recognition cells in the hypercolumns of the striate cortex. Each group of cells is apparently 'aligned' to one particular kind of feature in one particular orientation, so the two 'slits' at the top of the illustration, for example, would elicit responses from different sets of cells.

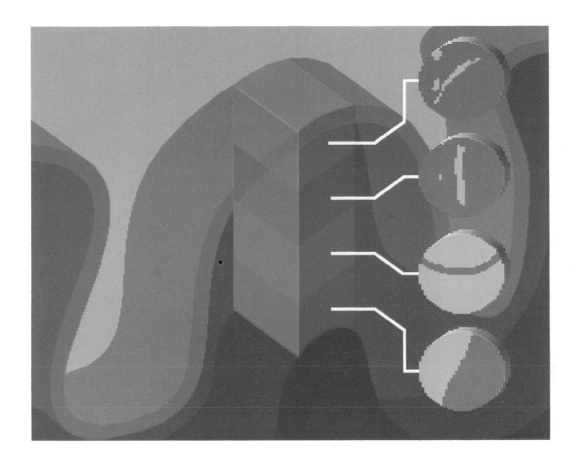

enhancement' mechanisms in the eye, we have now identified mechanisms in the brain which can plausibly be supposed to 'recognize' the presence and orientation of small segments of those edges, and segments of the 'slits' and 'lines' that are formed when two edges run parallel to each other. The position of each segment is also 'recognized', by virtue of the fact that each recognition signal originates within a hypercolumn assigned to one particular area. Thus, in principle at least, the information (i.e. the nerve impulses) generated within the ranks of hypercolumns could be thought of as representing a sort of line drawing, or sketch, of what is currently being seen. And it is indeed the crux of Marr's theory that such representations, which he called 'primal sketches', are generated within the visual cortex and that they provide the raw material for subsequent stages in the processing of visual information.

Following his own precept that analysis of brain function must go hand in hand with the development of computational theory, Marr was able to devise algorithms which enabled a computer to extract primal sketches from pixel maps lodged in a framestore. Such 'raw primal sketches' are, at first sight, extremely messy and confusing. But Marr was able to take things a stage further and design programs which, by concentrating on groups of elements and eliminating those that were isolated and unrelated to each other, could reveal the structures concealed within the apparent confusion (see next page).

The ranks of hypercolumns run transversely through the thin, wrinkled layer of grey matter which covers the surface of the cerebral hemispheres (the two dome-like structures which form the largest part of the human brain). The columns are stratified and it is thought that each layer is made up of cells aligned to one kind of feature in one particular orientation—the structure is of course far more complex than is suggested by this illustration, which is intended to convey only a general idea of the principles involved.

What is created is both an overall primal sketch of the entire scene and a series of smaller primal sketches, each representing one structure or group of structures within the image. Moreover, each structure, or, more accurately, the primal sketch which represents it, can be treated as a separate entity. Going back for a moment to the techniques discussed earlier in the chapter, we could think of the primal sketches which represent a single structure as being equivalent to the matrices that represent the cubes, wedges, etc. in a block world, while the overall primal sketch is equivalent to a semantic net in that it represents the way in which the individual structures relate to each other. The crucial difference is that a primal sketch is, literally, a representation of an image or part of an image, *not* a description of it. To put it another way, a primal sketch represents geometrical information, but the machine, or brain, which constructs it need know nothing of geometry.

Thus a primal sketch, whether of an entire image or one structure within that image, stored inside a computer can be said to represent the machine's knowledge of 'what something looks like'. (It is, of course, necessary to remember that primal sketches like those shown opposite are simply a 'print out' of information contained in computer memory, it is only for our own convenience that we need to think of a primal sketch as a 'picture'.) Naturally, if the primal sketches are to have 'meaning' (if, that is to say, the machine is to 'know' what they represent and be able to signal its recognition of new images which correspond to them) they must have 'labels' attached to them. Fortunately it is a comparatively easy task, in programming terms, to tell the machine that the individual elements in the sketch represent 'eyes' and a 'nose', or that the image as a whole represents a 'face' – nor is there anything artificial about such a process: children, after all, have to be taught how to name the objects they encounter.

In fact, the supposition is that our own labelling arrangements may be quite a bit more sophisticated than this. It may be, for example, that our knowledge of what, say, a giraffe looks like consists of both a primal sketch, a sort of pipecleaner model of a giraffe with the label 'giraffe' attached, plus a mental *aide memoire* to the effect that giraffes are large, and coloured yellow with large brown spots.

It is also believed that we have the ability to rotate a primal sketch in our minds, so to speak, and thus match it against the corresponding object even though it may appear in an unfamiliar position or orientation. If we are to account for our ability to distinguish between whole classes of objects which contain a wide range of variations, like dogs and cats, we must also assume that many of our primal sketches are highly generalized. This is a question we shall be returning to in Chapter 9. In the meantime it is worth noting that the primal sketch hypothesis does account for one rather intriguing point which was noted by Marr himself, namely the ease with which we recognize caricatures and cartoons, even when the subject's features are violently exaggerated or distorted. Might it be that a cartoonist's drawing is immediately recognizable because it is, in effect, a ready-made primal sketch containing all the

Primal sketches. If we imagine that the image in the top picture has been fed into a computer that is programmed to detect the edges and lines that are believed to stimulate the feature-detection cells in the striate cortex, then it would generate a crude primal sketch like that shown in the bottom left picture. Note that at this stage the sketch consists simply of hundreds of small and quite separate line segments, each representing the response of a single feature detector.

However, if the computer now examines the primal sketch and identifies the clusters and chains of features which seem to be associated and are therefore likely to represent coherent structures, it can construct the 'cleaned up' version shown in the bottom right picture. This image now represents a clear outline of the shape of the head and also contains a number of distinct shapes or structures to which labels such as 'glasses', 'eye' or 'hairline' could be attached.

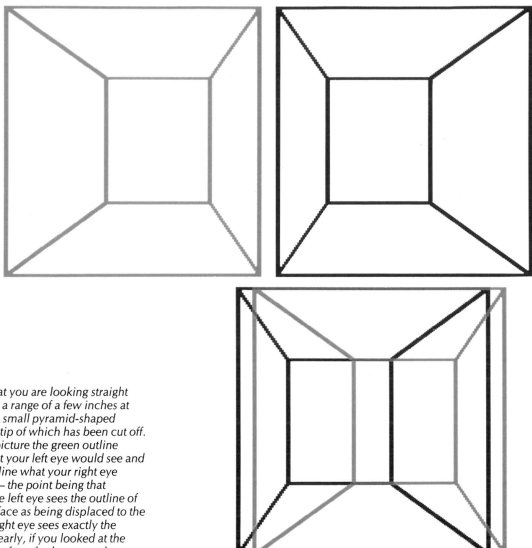

Imagine that you are looking straight down from a range of a few inches at the top of a small pyramid-shaped object, the tip of which has been cut off. In the top picture the green outline shows what your left eye would see and the red outline what your right eye would see – the point being that whereas the left eye sees the outline of the top surface as being displaced to the right, the right eye sees exactly the reverse. Clearly, if you looked at the same object from further away the displacement would be reduced – at a range of a few yards the disparity between the images seen by the two eyes would be very small indeed.

The bottom picture shows the two outlines superimposed upon each other, representing the conjunction of the two images that, were this a real object, would be fused by the visual system into a single, stereoscopic image. In fact, if you happen to own a pair of stereoscopic glasses with one red lens and one green lens, you will be able to see this illustration in 3-D and to verify that when the two images are fused the top surface 'comes nearer' as if it was actually projecting up out of the paper.

information our visual system actually needs and omitting only what is secondary and irrelevant?

Marr's other important contribution to the theory of vision concerned stereopsis, the perception of depth which is a consequence of binocular vision. It has long been known that our ability to judge how far away things are is due to the fact that although the visual fields of our two eyes overlap and both therefore see largely the same things at the same time, they see them from slightly different angles, and the closer something is the greater the difference between the two images (see opposite). But until the late 1960s it was generally assumed that the fusion of the two images to produce a single, stereoscopic, image took place at quite a late stage – in other words that the brain would recognize that the images from both the right eye and the left eye contained, say, a house and a car, before comparing the two images and coming to the realization that the car was closer than the house, or vice versa. This idea could, however, no longer be sustained after a famous series of experiments by the American psychologist Bela Julesz.

Julesz's subjects were asked to look at what are known as 'random dot stereograms', computer-generated images made up of random dots. If such a pattern is duplicated, and the two patterns are presented so that each eye sees only one of them, they will appear to the observer as a single, 'fused' image, just as someone looking through a pair of binoculars sees just one circular image and not two images side by side. The intriguing point is that if an area in one of the patterns is displaced so that each of the dots in that area is offset slightly in relation to the corresponding dot in the other pattern, that area will appear to be 'in front of' the surrounding pattern (see next page). Thus Julesz established that the visual system is capable of perceiving depth in patterns which contain none of the visual clues which, it had been previously supposed, the brain made use of in order to achieve stereopsis. The unavoidable conclusion was that the brain matched the two patterns one against the other, literally dot-for-dot.

In the simplest possible terms, this means that an artificial system which was to achieve a standard of stereopsis comparable to our own would have to be capable of matching the pixels in a pair of images pixel for pixel and then computing what the 'shift' between each pair of pixels implied about the distance of the objects in the field of vision. It would be difficult to imagine a more formidable task. Yet Marr, working in collaboration with Tomas Poggio, was able both to produce a workable algorithm and to show how it might be implemented by a hypothetical network of nerve cells.

In our opinion, of the three approaches to vision so far discussed, Marr's is far and away the most original, important and potentially valuable. Yet it must be said that although it has contributed a great deal to our understanding of the natural system, it has so far not resulted in any great advances in operational artificial vision systems. The reason is simple. When translated into programs which can run on an orthodox von Neumann computer, Marr's algorithms involve massive amounts of computation – the task of applying his stereopsis algorithm to a single 512×512 image, for example, may require the undivided attention of a mainframe computer for an hour or more.

A purist might say that such considerations are irrelevant, and argue that an algorithm, however impractical it may be when implemented on a computer, may nonetheless be an accurate model of brain functions. But for those who look forward to a day when true artificial vision becomes a practical proposition, as well as for the engineers and industrialists who are primarily interested in systems that can solve real problems in real time, the way forward would seem clear enough. Marr's ideas were largely based upon the study of a system, the brain, which employs parallel processing on a massive scale. It seems to follow that our best hope of matching, or at least approximating, the brain's performance is to design and build parallel computers.

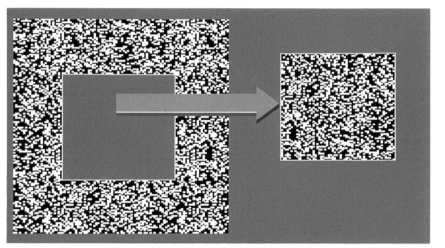

Constructing a random dot stereogram.

1. The first step is to generate a pattern of random dots and then to duplicate it.

2. Next, the right-hand pattern having been set aside, a square patch is cut out of the middle of the other pattern.

3. The hole in the pattern is now enlarged into a rectangle by removing an additional strip on its right-hand side and, at the same time, a corresponding 'space' is also created on the right-hand side of the patch that has been removed.

4. Now the patch is 'shifted' to the right, which leaves a blank space on the left-hand side (the pink area) which is filled in with more random dots.

5. The patch is now replaced in the hole.

6. If the second pattern is again placed beside the new 'shifted' version of it, the random dot stereogram is complete.

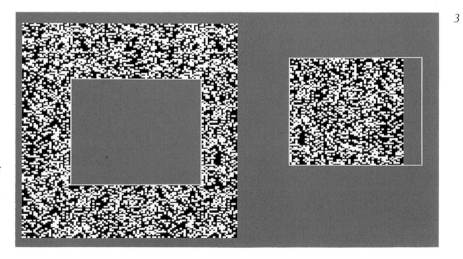

   Not everyone finds it easy to fuse these stereograms into a single image. But if you hold a card upright between the two patterns and then look at them at very close range, so that the card prevents the left eye from seeing the pattern on the right and vice versa, you should see a single, fused image in which the shape of the original square patch 'stands out' from the remainder of the pattern. The only possible explanation for this phenomenon is that the visual system recognizes the disparity in the position of each pair of 'shifted' dots and therefore 'sees' the patch as 'nearer' than its surroundings.

148

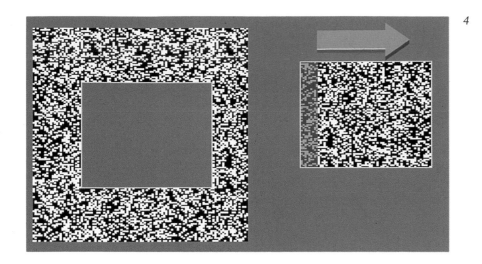

4

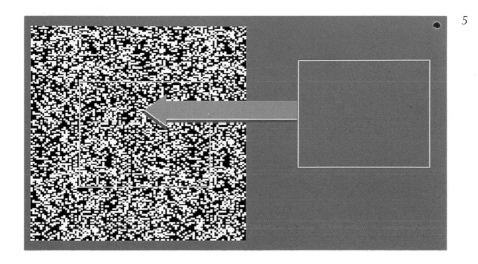

5

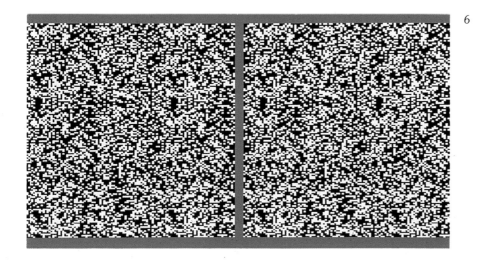

6

CHAPTER 9

NEW WAYS OF SEEING

The essence of a parallel computer is that it contains a number of separate processors and can therefore perform a whole series of logical operations simultaneously instead of being limited to the strictly serial, step-by-step mode of the traditional von Neumann design with its single central processor. The basic idea is thus a simple one. But the task of implementing it is far from simple and can be approached in many different ways. Indeed, the range of possible variations upon the theme of parallelism is seemingly limitless and a bewildering variety of alternative or 'non-von Neumann' architectures are currently proposed or actually under development. Some of these devices, like the array processors discussed in Chapter 7, contain large numbers of processing elements and mark a radical departure from traditional thinking, while others can be seen, more simply, as logical extensions of the single-processor design; some have been designed with specific applications in mind, others aspire to be general-purpose computers.

In the context of artificial intelligence, however, the most intriguing point about parallel computers is that they open up the possibility of exploring the bottom-up approach – that is, of modelling the mechanisms of the brain. We are, of course, a very long way from understanding these. But one thing at least is clear: the brain is, in the jargon of computer engineering, a 'massively parallel system' whose properties derive from the immensely complex interactions of millions of separate processing elements.

The fourth approach to vision, which will be discussed in this chapter and the one which follows, is therefore based on the premise that, if we want to build machines which can match our own visual skills, it may be necessary to examine brain mechanisms at a very fundamental level, and then try to design hardware which can reproduce their functions.

THE BUILDING BLOCKS OF THE BRAIN

We cannot begin to discuss the workings of the brain in any detail here, for it is a subject of immense complexity and even very basic factors are still undetermined or subject to controversy. What we can do, however, is to consider just one aspect of the brain, the one which is most relevant to the electronic engineer who sets out to model it: we can look at it as a mechanism made up of thousands of millions of elements, each of which has a *logical* function.

These elements are the nerve cells, or neurons, which are the basic building blocks of both the brain and the nervous system. There are many different kinds of neuron, but all share one basic characteristic which distinguishes them from other kinds of cell: they have the capacity to accumulate and discharge an electrical potential, a function which they perform only under certain clearly defined circumstances. The illustration below shows the structure of a typical, though highly simplified, neuron. Apart from the cell body, or *soma*, which contains the nucleus and the molecular machinery needed to manufacture the proteins that fuel the cell and maintain it in good working order, three features are significant from the present point of view.

There is, first of all, a single fibre, called the *axon*, along which the neuron's output flows when it 'fires', or discharges its electrical potential. Although the comparison is not strictly accurate, it will be convenient to think of the burst of pulses which travels along the axon when the neuron fires as analogous to an electrical current flowing through a wire. In other words, when a cell fires, it can be thought of as transmitting a signal rather similar to a single dot or dash in the Morse code.

Once it has left the cell body, the axon splits up into a large number of separate fibres, each of which terminates in a minute blob called a synaptic bouton, and each bouton is attached to the surface of another neuron (or, in the case of the 'motor neurons' which activate the muscles, to a 'motor endplate'). Thus, when a neuron fires the signal which it sends will be received by a large number of other neurons. But the neuron not only generates an output, a firing signal, it also receives inputs. For its own surface will also be covered with synaptic boutons which convey to it signals originating with other neurons. Although some of these receptors, or *synapses*, may be formed on the cell body, the

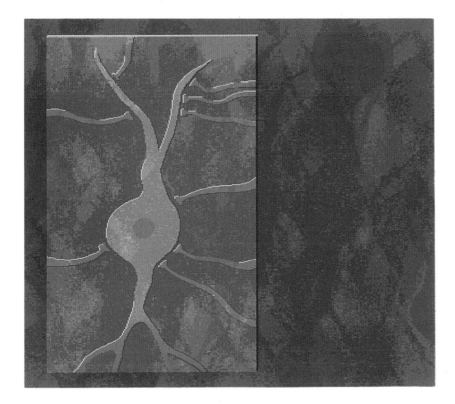

Although neurons come in many different shapes and sizes, all have certain essential features in common. The blob in the centre of this highly simplified illustration is the cell body, or soma. The two tentacle-like fibres at the top are the dendrites and the single fibre at the bottom is the axon along which the cell's electrical potential is discharged when it fires. Note that after leaving the cell body the axon splits up into a number of subsidiary fibres, each of which will carry the firing signal to another cell. Signals carried by the axonal fibres of other cells in the network are delivered at the synapses, of which just nine are shown here. In reality the entire surface of the cell would be covered in synaptic boutons since a typical neuron will receive signals from a thousand or more other cells.

majority are situated on the *dendrites*, tentacle-like processes which radiate from the central soma.

A neural net, a structure of interconnected neurons, thus consists of innumerable separate elements each of which can send a signal to one set of neighbours while also receiving signals from yet another set of neighbours. A crucial feature of any such system is that these complex interconnections will form a multiplicity of loops through which a neuron's output is fed back to its inputs via other, intermediate, cells. In some instances, indeed, the feedback is very direct, since an axon may have branches that form synapses upon the surface of the neuron from which it emanates, so that the cell will, in effect, signal to itself.

In examining the properties of a neural net it is important to note two factors. Firstly, the firing of a neuron can, for most purposes, be thought of as an all-or-nothing event. For the electrical potential which a cell can accumulate before it must be discharged is subject to a set limit or threshold, and once that threshold is exceeded the cell will fire. Moreover, once a neuron has fired there follows a period of a few microseconds – the 'absolute refractory period' – during which it cannot fire again. This means that the intensity of a firing signal is always the same, or, and here we come to the crux of the matter, that a neuron can be viewed as a logical element that will always be in one of only two possible states – either it is firing or it is not firing. We can therefore think of a cell that is firing as an element which is transmitting a 1 in the binary code and a cell that is not firing as an element which is transmitting a binary 0.

The second point is that the output of a cell – whether or not it is firing at any point in time – is a function of its inputs, the combination of the firing and non-firing signals it receives from other cells. However, the relationship between a neuron's inputs and its output is far from straightforward. To start with, while the firing signals generated by some neurons are excitatory (i.e. they increase the electrical potential of the receptor cells and thus bring them closer to their firing thresholds), the firing signals from other neurons are inhibitory (i.e. they decrease the electrical potential in the receptor cells and make it less likely that they will fire). Each neuron is thus rather like a member of a committee engaged in a non-stop series of votes for and against the proposition that the membership should fire when the next vote takes place. In each round of voting some neurons vote in favour of the motion (those that fire and have an excitatory effect), some vote against (those that fire and have an inhibitory effect) and some abstain (those that do not fire).

But the complications do not stop there. For, having collected the votes of all its neighbours, a neuron may then vary the significance which it attaches to each of them. Although the message that travels along the axon is analogous to a signal travelling along a wire, it travels, in this form, only as far as the synaptic bouton. There it triggers the release of infinitesimal amounts of chemicals called neurotransmitters; and it is these chemical messengers that convey the signal on the last lap of its journey, crossing a minute gap, called the synaptic cleft, which separates the synaptic bouton from the surface of the receptor cell. The precise ways in which neurotransmitters affect the electrical potential stored within a receptor cell are imperfectly understood, but it is significant that the degree of influence varies from one synapse to another. In other words, to return to our analogy, a cell may attach different weights to the votes of the other members of the committee.

To summarize: a neuron's output – whether it is in a firing or a non-firing state at any particular juncture – is determined by the behaviour of other neurons, and the influence exercised by each of these other neurons is a function of four variables. Firstly, a signal may either be present or absent. Secondly, if a signal is being received, its influence may be either excitatory or inhibitory. Thirdly, the extent of the signal's influence will be determined by the 'weight' of the synapse at which it is received. Finally, the neuron will only fire when the sum of all excitatory signals less the sum of all inhibitory signals exceeds a set threshold.

This may sound complicated. But if all the factors are known, it is a relatively straightforward job to produce a table which describes the way in which a neuron will react to every possible combination of signals (see page 155). The vital point, which is highlighted by the table, is that these factors effectively ensure that there are certain combinations of signals from other cells which will always cause a neuron to fire while also ensuring that no other possible combination of signals can result in a firing. In other words, we can say that the neuron *remembers* its function – it will always respond in the same way to any given combination of inputs.

In order to appreciate the significance of this point we must consider one final factor: that there are certain circumstances in which a neuron may change the level of its firing threshold and/or the values of its 'synaptic weights' so that the vote of a neighbouring neuron which was previously very influential suddenly becomes far less significant, or vice versa. As the table makes clear, any such changes will cause the cell to *learn* new patterns of behaviour – that is it will now fire in circumstances in which, previously, it did not fire. (It also true to say that such adjustments may cause the cell to fail to fire when previously it would have fired, but in practice this learning process is best thought of simply as widening the range of circumstances under which firing takes place.)

The mechanisms which cause these changes to take place are still imperfectly understood. But is is believed that they are initiated by a tiny minority of the synapses on the surface of the neuron which, it seems, exercise an overriding influence on its behaviour. When a firing signal is received at one of these 'dominant synapses' the neuron is apparently forced, willy-nilly, to do two things: firstly it must fire, and, secondly, it must adjust its threshold and its synaptic weights in such a fashion that it will in future fire whenever the combination of messages currently being received at the other synapses recurs. In effect, therefore, the arrival of a firing signal at a dominant synapse *teaches* the cell to recognize and respond to a combination of input signals which it formerly ignored. Thus, as well as being able to remember a function, a neuron is also capable of learning new functions.

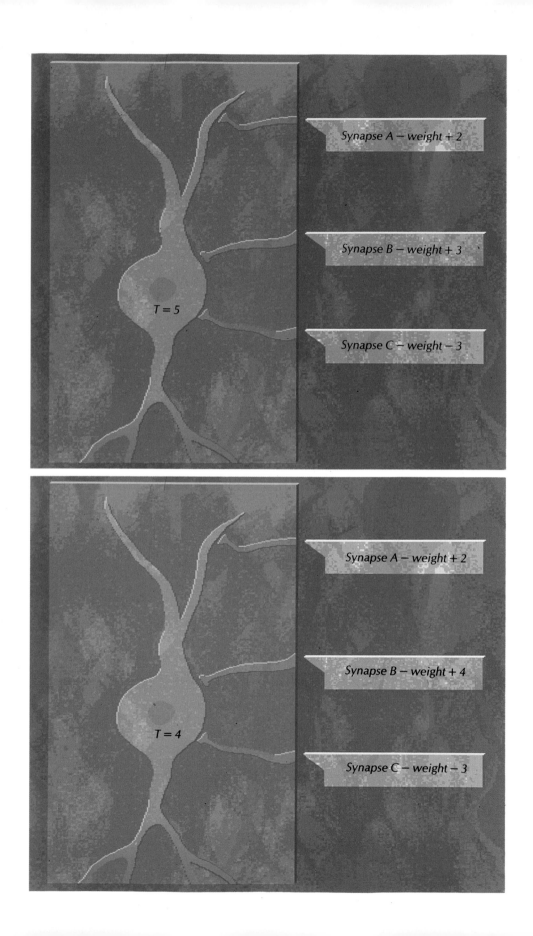

154

HOW A NEURON 'REMEMBERS' ITS FUNCTION AND 'LEARNS' NEW ONES

For simplicity's sake we shall consider a neuron with just three synapses through which it receives signals from three other cells, A, B and C. Let us suppose that the cell has a firing threshold of 5, i.e. it will fire whenever the number of 'votes' in favour of firing exceeds the number of votes against by that margin. We shall also suppose that the signals from cells A and B are excitatory while those from cell C are inhibitory. Thus, if the cell's synaptic weights are currently as shown in the first illustration, a firing signal from cell A will count as 2 votes in favour, a signal from cell B will count as 3 votes in favour and a signal from cell C will count as 3 votes against.

Given this information we can now draw up a table which shows how the cell will respond to each of the eight possible combinations of inputs. The first column simply shows which of the three cells (A, B and C) are firing, a 1 being used to denote a firing and a 0 to denote a non-firing. The second column shows the weights that are attached to the firing signals, and the third column shows the result, i.e. the majority for or against the cell itself firing.

SIGNALS RECEIVED	VALUE AFTER APPLYING SYNAPTIC WEIGHT	RESULT	SIGNALS RECEIVED	VALUE AFTER APPLYING SYNAPTIC WEIGHT	RESULT
A 0	0		A 1	+ 2	
B 0	0	0	B 0	0	+ 2
C 0	0		C 0	0	
A 0	0		A 1	+ 2	
B 0	0	− 3	B 0	0	− 1
C 1	− 3		C 1	− 3	
A 0	0		A 1	+ 2	
B 1	+ 3	+ 3	B 1	+ 3	+ 5 (Fire)
C 0	0		C 0	0	
A 0	0		A 1	+ 2	
B 1	+ 3	0	B 1	+ 3	+ 2
C 1	− 3		C 1	− 3	

Currently, as the table shows, the cell 'remembers' that it must fire if, and only if, A and B are firing and C is not firing. Now let us suppose that the cell receives a firing signal at a dominant synapse (not shown in the illustration) at a point when cell B is firing and cells A and C are not. The cell must now fire and it must also adjust its threshold and/or its synaptic weights so that it will in future fire whenever cell B is firing and cells A and C are not. This can be achieved by lowering the threshold to 4 and increasing B's synaptic weight to 4, as shown in the second illustration. As a result, the cell will now have 'learnt' a new function:

SIGNALS RECEIVED	VALUE AFTER APPLYING SYNAPTIC WEIGHT	RESULT	SIGNALS RECEIVED	VALUE AFTER APPLYING SYNAPTIC WEIGHT	RESULT
A 0	0		A 1	+ 2	
B 0	0	0	B 0	0	+ 2
C 0	0		C 0	0	
A 0	0		A 1	+ 2	
B 0	0	− 3	B 0	0	− 1
C 1	− 3		C 1	− 3	
A 0	0		A 1	+ 2	
B 1	+ 4	+ 4 (Fire)	B 1	+ 4	+ 6 (Fire)
C 0	0		C 0	0	
A 0	0		A 1	+ 2	
B 1	+ 4	+ 1	B 1	+ 4	+ 3
C 1	− 3		C 1	− 3	

ARTIFICIAL NEURAL NETS

Although it must be emphasized that our understanding of the workings of even the simplest neurons is still far from complete, the general outlines of their logical function have been clear ever since 1943, when W.S. McCulloch and W. Pitts of the University of Illinois published a seminal paper entitled: 'A Logical Calculus of the Ideas Immanent in Nervous Activity'. In the postwar years, the engineers and mathematicians who were developing the first computers were quick to note that striking parallels could be drawn between McCulloch and Pitts' model of the neuron and the valve circuits which formed the logical elements in the early computers, the crucial point being that a neuron could be thought of as a binary switch that could be turned on and off by different combinations of signals.

These similarities, and the intriguing possibilities that they seemed to open up were a major theme in the new science of cybernetics (see Chapter 2). Indeed the founder of cybernetics, Norbert Wiener, and others were able to exploit the parallels in order to make important contributions to our understanding of how the nervous system controls the limbs and regulates bodily functions such as heartbeat and respiration. These early successes encouraged the idea that it might soon be possible to launch a major bottom-up assault on the brain itself.

But although cyberneticians continued to analyse the behaviour of neural nets on paper, and were soon able to simulate it on computers, the attack had more or less petered out by the end of the 1960s. The obstacles it encountered were both practical and theoretical. On the practical front, the major problem was undoubtedly the fact that it proved impossible to devise an artificial equivalent of the neuron which was both reliable and easy to manufacture in quantity.

Efforts to construct working models of neural nets had been made on both sides of the Atlantic. In London, at University College, W.K. Taylor designed a machine which incorporated variable resistors (devices rather similar to dimmer switches) in order to mimic changes in synaptic weights, while in the United States Bernard Widrow tried to achieve the same effect by the use of an electro-chemical apparatus. In neither case were the results satisfactory. The British project involved roomfuls of complex switchgear and Widrow's Adaline machine turned out to be highly unreliable.

A different approach was adopted by Frank Rosenblatt of Cornell who produced a computer simulation of a neural net-type structure, called the Perceptron, which could be trained to recognize simple images such as the letters of the alphabet. But in 1969 Marvin Minsky and Seymour Papert of MIT published a book, *Perceptrons: the Principles of Computational Geometry*, which was, at the time, believed to expose weaknesses in Rosenblatt's ideas that were fundamental and irremediable. Essentially, Minsky and Papert showed that devices like the Perceptron – known as single-layer nets (see page 162) – could never compute some rather basic properties of an image, such as whether or not two elements were connected (see next page). Since such distinctions can be made by people, and can also be made by conventional computers using known algorithms, Minsky and Papert argued that those algorithms must model the brain's workings more accurately than a Perceptron. This was, in effect, a devastating attack on the whole concept of the bottom-up approach. It coincided, moreover, with a peak of optimism about the prospects for the alternative, top-down, approach, which had led many of the artificial intelligentsia to conclude that success was already within their grasp.

The result was that Rosenblatt's ideas were thought to have been discredited and interest in the bottom-up approach rapidly evaporated, especially where vision was concerned. Why bother, after all, to design and build new, complex and very probably unworkable machines when the digital computer was already tried, tested and, apparently, on the very brink of becoming intelligent?

With the benefit of hindsight we can see that this dismissal of the bottom-up approach was both foolish and unjustified. Certainly, the confidence which Minsky and Papert then felt about the inevitable superiority of the top-down approach to vision was soon to prove ill-founded, as we saw in Chapter 8. It is also fair to say that their attack on Rosenblatt's Perceptron was misconceived in at least two important respects. Firstly, the brain itself has some difficulty in sorting the spiral patterns upon which their critique was based, and people may only be able to resolve their own uncertainty about such images by following the lines round with a finger or a pencil. Secondly, Minsky and Papert totally ignored the fact that the networks of cells in the brain are vastly more elaborate than those simulated by the Perceptron and might reasonably be expected to have very different properties.

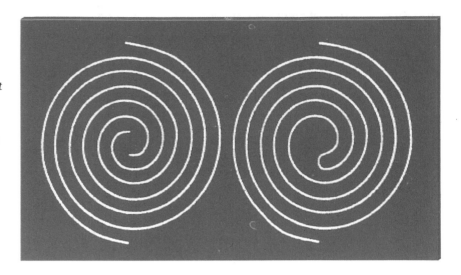

A SILICON NEURON

Although Minsky and Papert's attack on the Perceptron effectively
discouraged researchers from looking at neural nets as a possible
basis for computer architectures, there were a few individuals who
continued to pursue the idea of a bottom-up approach – see Chapter
11. Amongst them was Igor Aleksander, whose particular interests
lie in the field of artificial vision. The remainder of this chapter, and
the bulk of the one which follows, is concerned very largely with
the WISARD system which he and his colleagues have developed
over the past ten years. WISARD (the name is an acronym for Wilkie,
Stonham and Aleksander's Recognition Device) is not the only, or
necessarily the most important, project of its kind, and we shall be
looking at some of the other work in the field in Chapter 11. It is,
however, the largest artificial neural net so far constructed, and the
first such device actually to go on the market. It is also, for obvious
reasons, the project that the authors are best qualified to describe
and is therefore a convenient vehicle with which to explore the
possibilities inherent in the bottom-up approach to artificial intelligence.

The origins of WISARD go back some twenty years, to the mid-
1960s and the realization that advances in silicon chip technology,
then in its infancy, might one day result, quite fortuitously, in
'artificial neurons' becoming readily available off the shelf. For it
already seemed likely, even at that stage, that silicon memory chips
would one day replace the enormously cumbersome and costly
magnetic core storage devices which provided contemporary
computers with their random access memory capacity. So indeed it
proved, and as a result we have, over the past few years, seen the
memory capacity of even a workaday home computer grow from
16K (i.e. 16,000 bytes, or 128,000 binary digits) to 256K, 512K or
even 1000K with no corresponding increase in price.

A random access memory (RAM) element of the type we shall be
concerned with (known technically as a bit-organized RAM) can be

thought of as a row of electronic pigeon holes, each containing just one bit of information, either a 1 or a 0. The term 'random access' is used because, when such an element forms part of a computer's memory, all the pigeon holes are equally accessible, so that any kind of information, be it data or program instructions, can be put into storage and retrieved with equal ease and speed. Information is deposited in and retrieved from memory via two terminals, known respectively as data-in and output (see below). But if the computer's control unit is to keep track of what is stored where, so to speak, then each pigeon hole must have a label, a sort of telephone number which will allow it to be 'addressed' individually when it is required either to accept information into storage or to output the information which it contains. Each pigeon hole therefore has its own address, consisting of a string of binary digits. The larger the capacity of the RAM element, the longer the string. In the case of an 8-bit RAM (an element with just eight pigeon holes) like that shown in the illustration, for example, the addresses will consist of three digits, for there are just eight ways of combining three binary

Each of the boxes inside the blue casing represents one of the electronic pigeon holes in an 8-bit RAM element. Each box stores a single binary digit and has its own three-digit address. The red arrows entering the casing from the top represent the inputs at the three address terminals, the yellow arrow entering from the right represents the input to the data-in terminal and the green arrow on the left represents the element's output. To illustrate how the RAM operates, imagine that the digits 010 are fed in at the address terminals. This will cause the digit stored in the third box from the right to be output; in addition, if the write enable circuit is activated and a digit is fed in at the data-in terminal, that digit will be taken into storage at the same address.

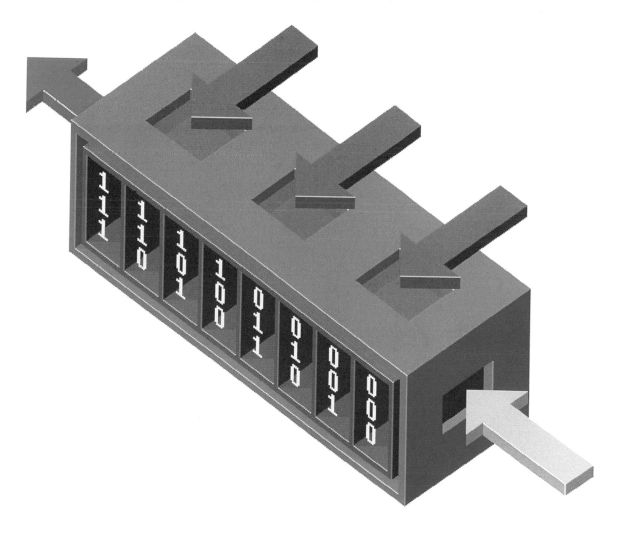

When in operation a RAM element is continually alternating between a read cycle, during which it will output the contents of any pigeon hole that is addressed, and a write cycle, during which new information can be written into a pigeon hole. This illustration represents the sequence of outputs and inputs which would occur when a pigeon hole containing a 1 is addressed. Initially, each time the system enters the read cycle the 1 is output (green arrows) but since the write enable circuit has not been activated nothing is written into memory during the write cycle. Next, the write enable circuit having been activated, a 0 is fed into the data-in terminal. The content of the pigeon hole immediately changes from 1 to 0 and the output changes to 0 in the next read cycle.

digits – 000, 001, 010, 011, 100, 101, 110 and 111. But if the size of the memory is doubled to 16 bits, each address will have to contain four digits, if it is doubled again, to 32 bits, then the addresses will contain five digits, and so on. In every case, one address terminal will be required for each digit and so the 8-bit RAM in the illustration has three such terminals.

In operation, the RAM alternates, many times per second, between a 'read cycle' and a 'write cycle'. When one of the pigeon holes is addressed its contents will automatically be transmitted via the RAM's output terminal in the next read cycle – without, it is important to note, being deleted from memory. In order to 'write' a new bit of information into memory it is necessary to operate a switch called the 'write enable'. When this has been done, then if a pigeon hole is addressed and a bit of information is simultaneously fed into the RAM via the data-in terminal, that digit will be taken into storage at the address indicated (see below).

All we now have to do in order to see how a RAM chip can be transformed into a 'silicon neuron' is to look at it in a new way, as a processor of information rather than simply a repository for it. The output terminal is clearly equivalent to the axon of a neuron, for when a RAM outputs a 1 it can be said to be 'firing' while a chip outputting a 0 is equivalent to a non-firing cell. The address terminals are the counterparts of the synapses that deliver the signals from other cells, for some combinations of signals at these terminals will cause the RAM to 'fire' while others will not. Finally, there is the data-in terminal, which, when activated by the write enable switch, fulfils the function of a dominant synapse in that it will alter the

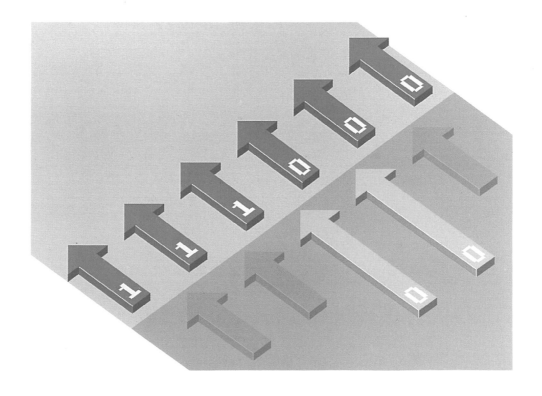

contents of a pigeon hole and so change the output produced by the RAM when that pigeon hole is addressed.

To illustrate the parallels between the two mechanisms, let us consider an 8-bit RAM element in which all the addresses have been set to store a 0, except address 010 which contains a 1. The result is that the RAM will, in effect, 'process' seven out of the eight possible inputs at the address terminal into a 0 output but will 'process' one input, 010, into a 1 output. It behaves, in other words, just like a neuron with three synapses on its surface which will fire only in response to one of eight possible combinations of firing and non-firing signals from other cells. Now let us suppose that we activate the write enable switch and deliver a 1 to the data-in terminal while simultaneously inputting the string 110 at the address terminals. The result will be that our artificial neuron 'learns' to fire in response to a second combination of signals; in fact, as the table shows, its behaviour is now equivalent to that of the hypothetical neuron we considered earlier (see page 155).

THE RAM AS A 'SILICON NEURON'

Suppose that six of the pigeon holes in an 8-bit RAM have been set to store a 0 while addresses 010 and 110 each contain a 1. The element's function, i.e. the output that it will produce in response to each of the eight possible patterns of input at the address terminals, can be set out in a table. If this is compared with the table shown on page 156 it will be seen that, if a 1 output is thought of as equivalent to a neuronal firing signal, then the RAM's function is identical, in logical terms, to that of the hypothetical neuron we considered earlier.

INPUT	OUTPUT	INPUT	OUTPUT
000	0	100	0
001	0	101	0
010	1	110	1
011	0	111	0

USING ARTIFICIAL NEURONS FOR PATTERN RECOGNITION

We have now established that a single RAM element is, in terms of logical function, equivalent to a neuron. (There are differences but these need not concern us here). Let us now consider how a network of RAM chips might be used in an artificial vision system. The input to any such system, as we saw in Chapter 7, consists of a series of long strings of binary digits, each string representing a single scan of the image. But, with many processors at our disposal, we can now look upon the input not as a string of digits which must be processed serially, in pipeline fashion, but as a pattern of digits which can be processed in a single operation. In fact, if we feed this pattern of digits into the address terminals of the RAM chips we will

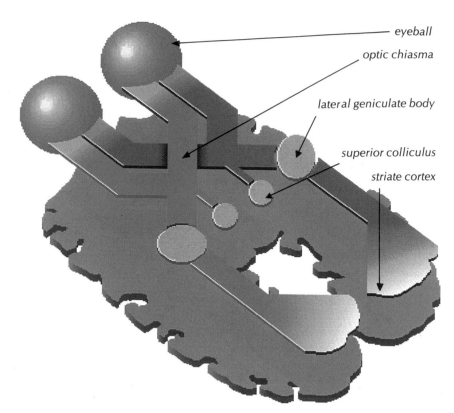

eyeball

optic chiasma

lateral geniculate body

superior colliculus

striate cortex

Top: The basic 8 × 8 grid. Each of the 64 pixels is either black (encoded as a binary 1) or white (encoded as a binary 0) and this blank grid would therefore be represented by a string of 64 0s.

Bottom: The washer image.

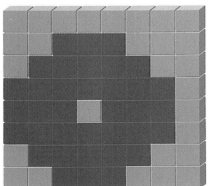

have an arrangement comparable to that which exists in our own visual system, where the axonal fibres which make up the optic nerve form synapses on the cells of the visual cortex, thus delivering the information captured by the eye to the processing centres in the brain (see above). In the cortex itself there are also a multiplicity of other synapses, allowing the brain cells to communicate with each other. But we shall start by considering what is known as a 'single layer net', a structure in which there are no interconnections between the elements, whose behaviour is, therefore, determined solely by the information that represents the image itself.

In order to make the explanation as simple as possible, let us suppose that we want to design a system that will recognize square images made up of just 64 pixels each of which is either black or white. The 8 × 8 pixel grid will, in other words, look rather like a blank crossword puzzle (see above left). Clearly, each pixel can be represented by a single digit, a 1 if it is black and a 0 if it is white, and a string of 64 digits will suffice to represent the entire image. It is, however, worth reminding ourselves that there are 2^{64}, or about ten million million million, possible ways of combining those digits, so distinguishing one particular pattern from all the possible patterns is by no means a trivial task.

Let us now imagine that we require the system to recognize the image shown in the illustration on the left which might represent, say, a washer. The most straightforward assumption would be that just one RAM with 64 address terminals is needed. If the digit representing each of the 64 pixels is fed into one of the terminals, then pressing a single 'teach button' that activates the write enable switch will in effect 'train' the RAM to fire whenever the same input pattern recurs.

There are, however, two objections to the use of a single large RAM element. Firstly, chips with the required capacity (2^{64} bits) are still beyond the wildest dreams of contemporary silicon technology and, secondly, such a system would have little practical value. For it would be capable of recognizing only the original, pristine pattern; and even if the washer is always presented in the same position on the grid (itself a rather restrictive demand) there is always the risk that noise will cause at least one of the white pixels to be misread as a 1, or one of the black pixels as a 0. We could, of course, guard against this possibility by teaching the system to respond to each of the further 64 patterns that could result from the distortion of a single pixel. But if we wanted to cover ourselves against the eventuality that two pixels might be distorted, we would have to consider a further 4096 patterns, and so on. Clearly, in this form the system is unworkable.

In fact, the roots of the problem are even more fundamental. For a system which simply recognized one size of washer in one predetermined position would be of little use to anyone. What is required is a machine which has a capacity for generalization and can recognize a washer – any old washer – even if it is not positioned with complete accuracy. Indeed, we could go further and say that we would like it to be capable of looking at other comparable images and judging whether, and to what extent, they were washer-like. For we ourselves perceive unfamiliar objects very largely in terms of their similarity to familiar ones – we might describe a zebra, for example, as looking like a horse with stripes or a leopard as a very large cat with spots, and so on.

The obvious way of dealing with the first problem, the impossibility of obtaining RAM chips with the required capacity, is to split the information derived from the image up into chunks and to allot each chunk to a separate RAM. And, if we do this, we will find that we have also solved the second problem, that of achieving a capacity for generalization. Suppose, for example, that we subdivide the image into eight sectors, each containing eight pixels. Now we need eight chips, but each need only have eight address terminals and, therefore, a capacity of 512 bits (note, incidentally, that the total memory now required has shrunk to a mere 4096 bits, a trivial amount in terms of contemporary hardware).

To see how the second problem has been solved, let us suppose that we train the system to recognize not just the single original pattern, but also the 64 variations of it that result from the distortion of a single pixel, that is 65 patterns in all. Each RAM will learn to recognize nine patterns, the one representing its own sector of the perfect image plus eight distorted versions of it. But all the RAMs will now fire in response to patterns with two, three, or even eight distorted pixels, *provided that* there is no more than one distortion in each sector of the image, and, as a little mathematics will confirm, there are over 43 million such patterns. Moreover, seven out of the eight RAMs will fire in response to an even larger number

Opposite: The pathways that carry information from the eyes to the visual cortex. The information leaves the eye in the form of nerve impulses travelling along the axons of the ganglion cells which form the third layer of cells in the retina (see page 124). Since the visual fields of the two eyes overlap (i.e. the left eye covers all but the extreme right-hand side of the right field and vice versa) while each hemisphere of the brain deals only with information from one side of the overall field, roughly half of the fibres in the optic nerves must cross over at the optic chiasma. Here blue has been used to represent fibres carrying information about the right half of the visual field and red to represent fibres carrying information about the left half; it can be seen that the left hemisphere processes information about what we see in the right half of the visual field and vice versa. However the axons of the ganglion cells do not lead directly to the processing areas in the visual cortex. Instead they terminate in an organ called the lateral geniculate body which serves as a sort of relay station, and it is axons of cells in this organ which actually form synapses in the hypercolumns of the striate cortex (see page 143). Note, too, the subsidiary branch of each optic nerve which forks off to the superior colliculus, the organ which controls the muscles that rotate the eyeball in its socket.

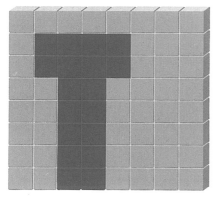

Top: The 64-pixel grid divided into 16 sectors each containing four pixels. Each sector is allotted to one 16-bit RAM and the input to each of the element's four address terminals represents one pixel.

Bottom: The bolt image.

of patterns. Thus, and this is the crucial point, the system will now recognize, with either total certainty or a very high degree of confidence, millions of patterns which it has not been trained to recognize – patterns which are like the original but not identical to it.

Since this process of subdividing the image has proved so successful, we might conclude that even better results will be obtained by carrying it further. If, for example, we used 16 RAMS, each with four address terminals (see left) and, therefore, a capacity of 16 bits, the total storage requirement would fall to 256 bits and a very high degree of generalization would be achieved. In fact, it can be shown that this is the optimum arrangement in the case of the 64-pixel image we have been considering. But in order to understand how the performance of the different configurations is measured we must consider not just one network of RAMS, but two separate networks, or discriminators as they are called, each of which can be trained to recognize a different image.

The point of having two or more discriminators in a single system is that it then becomes possible, by comparing their responses, to use the machine to distinguish between classes of objects, apples and oranges, say, or, more usefully, sets of components that are correctly assembled and those that are faulty. The best configuration for a discriminator is, therefore, not simply that which results in the *right* image being recognized with a high degree of confidence, it is also important that all other, *wrong*, images should be rejected with equal certainty.

To illustrate the point let us suppose that we want the system to distinguish between the washer image shown earlier and the image of a bolt (see left) and that we train the 'bolt discriminator' in the same fashion as we trained the 'washer discriminator', exposing it to the perfect image plus the 64 versions of it in which a single pixel is distorted. If we then test the system by showing it the two objects, we can express the results in terms of the number of RAMS which fire in each discriminator.

In the case of the system made up of eight 256-bit RAMS the responses will be in the ratio 8:3 (i.e. all eight elements in the washer discriminator, but only three of those in the bolt discriminator, will fire in response to the washer image and vice versa in the case of the bolt image). The responses of the discriminators containing sixteen 16-bit RAMS will be in the ratio 16:10. Initially it might seem that the first configuration is to be preferred because it seems to achieve greater certainty, for less than half the RAMS fire in response to the 'wrong' image whereas, in the case of the second configuration, well over half do so. But if we consider not the ratios themselves but the difference between the two figures – the size of the majority – it becomes clear that the second configuration will allow the system to make smaller and subtler distinctions. As a result, when dealing with objects that are very similar, or with images that contain a large number of distortions, it would still be likely to produce a majority of two or three in favour of the 'right' decision while the rival configuration would produce a majority of only one or, perhaps, a stalemate.

If, however, we continue the process of subdividing the input and using more and smaller RAM elements any further we begin to run into problems of a different kind. To understand what happens, we have only to carry the process to its logical conclusion and consider a discriminator made up of 64 RAMs, each with a capacity of just one bit. When such a system is trained in the way we have described, learning both the perfect pattern and the 64 versions in which one pixel has been distorted, the result will be that every element will have been taught to fire in response to both a black pixel *and* a white one and the system as a whole will recognize any and every pattern it is shown with one hundred percent certainty – i.e. two discriminators of this kind would each respond with 64 firings whatever the input. A system which falls prey to this sort of problem is said to have become saturated and will clearly be of no value.

The task of choosing the appropriate configuration for a system of this kind – known technically as the choice of *n*-tuple, *n* standing for the number of input digits allotted to each element – is one of the designer's most important tasks. For it is necessary to strike the right balance between generalization, which improves as the size of *n* decreases, and the risk of saturation, which is diminished as the size of *n* increases.

WHAT CAN A NEURAL NET DO?

The response produced by a single-layer net, consisting as it does of nothing more than a set of crude totals, representing the number of RAMs that are firing in each discriminator, might seem to have little relevance to tasks which require intelligence. In order to show that this is not so we shall now go on to demonstrate that such devices are in fact capable of performing tasks which approximate very closely to some of the functions that actually take place in the brain.

In Chapter 8 we described the mechanisms for identifying the orientations of 'edges', 'lines' and 'slots' which Hubel and Wiesel discovered in the hypercolumns of the visual cortex. So let us now consider how a neural net responds to simple patterns consisting of vertical and horizontal lines one pixel thick, as shown in the illustrations on the next page. Eight different lines of each variety can be drawn on an 8 × 8 grid and it is perfectly possible to train one discriminator on all the vertical lines and another on all the horizontal ones, producing, in effect, a machine that can distinguish between the two in a predictable fashion. In a system where each discriminator is made up of sixteen 16-bit RAMs any vertical line will cause all 16 RAMs in the vertical discriminator to fire, but only 12 out of the 16 in the horizontal discriminator, while in the case of horizontal lines, the ratio will be reversed.

But what happens if we present the machine with a series of lines that are neither vertical nor horizontal, such as those shown in the illustrations on the next page? As the caption explains, the sort of results are intriguingly similar to those that Hubel and Wiesel obtained when they exposed the 'feature detectors' in the brains of their experimental monkeys to the same sort of stimuli. For they found that although the detectors were 'aligned' to recognize

If one discriminator is trained to recognize all eight vertical lines one pixel thick that can be drawn on the grid and another to recognize all eight horizontal lines (top two pictures), their responses will be in the ratio 16:12, i.e. a vertical line will cause 16 firings in the vertical discriminator and 12 in the horizontal one. The high response to the 'wrong images' occurs because each RAM has been trained to recognize a four-pixel sector that is either half white and half black or entirely white and, since the eight black pixels in any such pattern are 'seen' by only four of the 16 RAMS, the other 12 are firing in response to the remaining white pixels in the image.

The 'decisions' which the system arrives at in response to the three images below, which represent lines that are neither vertical nor horizontal, become much clearer if we take the figure of 12 firings as a baseline – i.e. instead of saying that the discriminators' responses to the vertical and horizontal lines are in the ratio 16:12 we say that they are in the ratio 4:0. On this basis the response to the first line which almost forms a diagonal from the top right-hand corner of the grid to the bottom left-hand corner is − 2:− 2. The system is in effect saying: 'This line is equally unhorizontal and unvertical.' In the case of the second line the response is 3:− 2. This time the horizontal discriminator has decided that the pattern is similar, but not identical, to a horizontal line, while the vertical discriminator still feels it is quite unlike a vertical line. Finally, when it comes to the third line which produces a response of 0:2, the horizontal discriminator sees nothing very familiar but the vertical discriminator concludes that this line is at least half-vertical.

features with one orientation, they did not totally ignore features with a different orientation; rather their response varied according to how closely the orientation of a feature resembled their own particular alignment (see opposite).

If we now go on to look at what happens when we ask the machine to deal with vertical and horizontal edges we encounter a problem with an intriguing solution that has, perhaps, something more to tell us about the natural visual system. For if we train one discriminator on all the eight vertical edges that can occur on the grid and the other on all the horizontal edges we will find that, for the purposes of edge detection at least, the system is near saturation point. Each RAM has been trained to fire in response to either a square of four black pixels or a square of four white pixels and both discriminators will therefore respond with 16 firings to any edge which, like that in the illustration on page 168, falls on the borderline between the sectors allotted to different RAMS.

The root of the problem is easy to see: it lies in the symmetrical relationship between the connections of the RAMS' address terminals and the patterns on which they have been trained. And the solution is equally simple: instead of connecting the RAMS in an orderly fashion, we connect them entirely at random, as shown in the illustration on page 169. In order to verify that this does indeed improve matters we can calculate that the system would now respond to the two sample edges shown earlier as follows: both

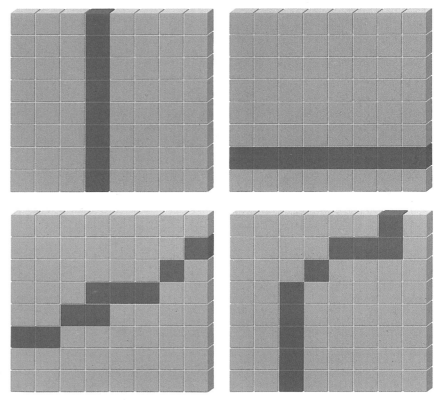

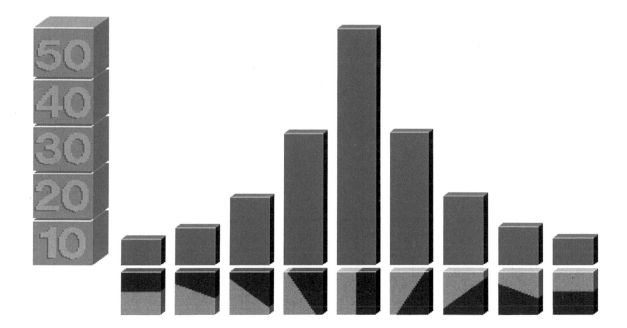

discriminators will of course respond with 16 firings to the edges on which they have been trained, but now the vertical discriminator only produces seven firings in response to the horizontal edge and the horizontal discriminator only produces eight firings in response to the vertical edge. This makes it clear that the decisions reached by the system are now quite unequivocal.

The real fascination of this discovery is that it strongly suggests that if we want to understand neural networks we may have to accept that systems connected at random will actually function better than systems with an orderly structure and that, at the microscopic level of neuronal connections, no two brains may be 'wired up' in the same way. Indeed, as we shall see in Chapter 10, once feedback is introduced – that is, once the elements of a single-layer net are interconnected to form a multi-layer one – we can, in practice, no longer analyse the network's performance in terms of the responses of individual RAMs and must, instead, consider the state of the system as a whole.

But before moving on to discuss this further level of complexity it is worth pausing to consider the capabilities of a single-layer net and to contrast its performance with that of an orthodox computer. The WISARD device, which is now commercially available as a pattern-recognition system, provides a very good case in point.

WISARD is vastly larger than the nets we have discussed so far, for it operates on images containing 262,144 pixels (a standard 512 × 512 grid) and each of its discriminators contains 32,768 RAMs, each with eight address terminals and, therefore, a total memory capacity

This bar graph shows the responses (i.e. the rate of firing) of a vertically-aligned edge detector in a monkey's visual cortex when exposed to a range of features in different orientations. It can be seen that while the vertical edge naturally produces a maximum response and a horizontal edge a very low one, the responses to edges that are intermediate between these two extremes gets stronger the more vertical they become. The cell's behaviour is in fact very similar to that of the vertical discriminator described in the previous illustration.

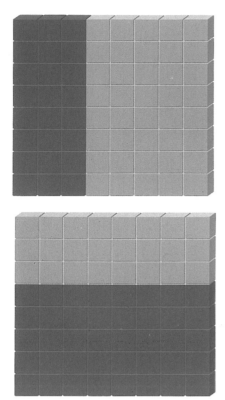

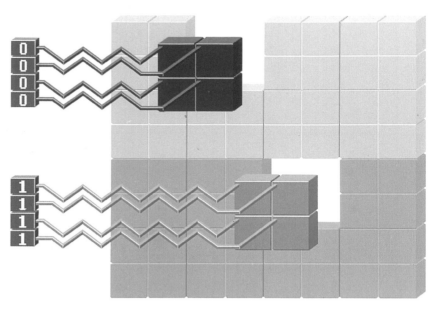

The illustration above right makes it clear why a system in which each RAM _is allotted a regularly-shaped block of pixels will rapidly become saturated if trained on patterns such as the edges shown in the margin. Four of the eight possible vertical edges and four of the eight possible horizontal edges fall on the boundaries between the blocks of four pixels; as a result, each_ RAM _will fire in response to either a block of four black pixels (address 1111) or a block of four white pixels (address 0000), and a discriminator that had been trained on all eight vertical edges would also recognize four of the eight horizontal edges with total certainty._

of some eight million bits. (This description is, in fact, somewhat oversimplified since the system can be reconfigured by the operator who may vary the _n_-tuple in order to optimize the system's performance for any given task.) The first thing to note is the sheer speed of operation. Each of the discriminators produces its response to a new image within one twenty-fifth of a second – over a quarter of a million bits of information are processed in a single cycle, a striking contrast to a traditional von Neumann computer which can process, at most, 32 bits in a single cycle.

The next point to be made is that a system of this size is capable of dealing with images of great complexity and can make remarkably subtle distinctions, indeed, in some respects it comes near to matching our own abilities – though it is of course very restricted in that it can deal with only a limited range of images at any one time.

WISARD's skills are perhaps most dramatically demonstrated by its ability to distinguish between individual human faces. If, for example, two discriminators are trained on, respectively, the faces of Jim and Joe, they will not only be able to recognize these two characters if and when they reappear, but if confronted with a third face, say that of Jane, they will be able to give an 'opinion' as to which of the first two she most closely resembles.

Moreover, and this is the vital point, the system is not trained on a single image of a face, a 'studio portrait' as it were, but on a 'live' image, the face as it might be seen on the television screen, moving, talking and changing expression. For in just the same way as the generalizing properties of a neural network allow it to cope with the distortions caused by noise, so they also enable it to generalize the variations that occur as the features move or the attitude of the head changes. As a result, having been trained on images which

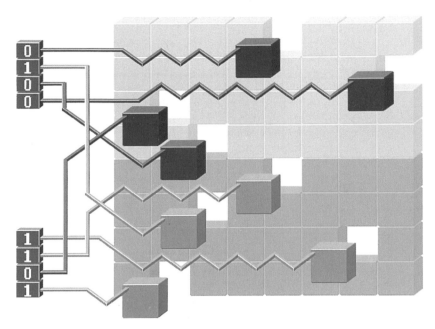

represent an individual seen in one attitude or with one expression
WISARD is able to recognize the same individual even when he
appears in a different attitude or with a changed expression.

This example is instructive because, if we pause and think about
what goes through our mind when we recognize a familiar face, we
will realize that we do not refer to a sort of checklist of characteristics such as colour of hair, shape of nose, size of mouth, etc. — the
sort of features that would have to be catalogued and defined in
order to devise a 'face-recognition' algorithm that might form the
basis for a computer program. Instead we simply 'know' that the
person on the other side of the room is our friend Peter as soon as
we enter; indeed it is quite likely that we will recognize Peter even if
he has his back to us, thanks to some indefinable characteristic of
his stance or gestures. It is probably only if we make an error and
mistakenly greet some total stranger who is very like Peter that we
will consciously recognize that Peter, unlike the person to whom
we are now offering embarrassed apologies, has, say, a noticeable
dimple in his chin or markedly prominent eyebrows.

In other words, although devices like WISARD are, as yet, capable
of modelling brain functions only at a very crude and highly
simplified level, we can already begin to sense that they might be
'like us' in some way that computers are not. This may sound a
somewhat vague and unscientific claim, but recent research by
Professor Fergus Campbell has provided some interesting evidence
which seems to support it.

Professor Campbell and his colleagues in the Department of
Psychology at Cambridge University have been studying the way in
which human beings will apparently recognize familiar objects
given even the most tenuous visual clues. Their subjects are asked

The solution to the problem in the previous illustration is to connect each RAM to a set of four pixels scattered at random over the grid. Here the connections of only two of the 16 RAMS are shown, but it can be seen that even a regularly shaped pattern on the grid will generate a unique and distinctive set of inputs to the address terminals.

to look at computer-generated random patterns which gradually increase in complexity and to say when they first 'see' some recognizable object in the pattern. (Their work throws an interesting light on the 'Rorschach blots' used by psychologists, for the results seem to show that we are all compelled to extract some 'meaning' even from patterns that are, objectively, meaningless.) The fascinating point is that if WISARD is trained on a series of images and is then exposed to patterns which gradually develop to more and more like those images it will achieve recognition at very much the same stage as a human being.

No less intriguingly, WISARD has proved that, when equipped with two cameras an inch or two apart, it too sees depth in the random dot stereograms which were described at the end of Chapter 8. To be more precise, it recognizes, just as we do, that random patterns in which the intervals separating matching 'pairs' of dots vary are different from each other. For once this distinction can be made it is a mere formality to add some simple mechanism that attaches the label 'nearer' to the pattern that causes higher rates of firing in one discriminator and the label 'further away' to the pattern which produces more firings in the other discriminator.

Finally, perhaps the most useful feature of WISARD from the practical point of view is that it can be programmed simply by 'showing it' the images or objects which it is required to recognize and pressing the teach buttons which train the discriminators. In practical terms, this means that the system can be adapted to any application that involves pattern-recognition, and that it can be switched rapidly from one task to another. In a recent experiment, for example, the machine, which had already demonstrated its ability to recognize individual faces as described above, was then trained to distinguish between two kinds of expression, a smile and a frown, which are common to all faces. As a result, having been exposed to a representative selection of smiles and frowns, it was able to tell anyone who appeared before the lens of the television camera whether they were smiling or frowning (see opposite).

In many ways, the training process is much more like teaching another human being than programming an orthodox computer. There are, for example, quite close parallels between training WISARD to recognize a set of images and turning the pages of a picture book while explaining to the child beside you, 'That's an elephant', 'This is a giraffe' and so on. Indeed, we shall show in Chapter 10 that a multi-layer net is capable of learning to match images and labels in just this fashion.

The essential point is that we need not concern ourselves with what is going on inside the machine – which RAMS are being set to recognize which groups of pixels, etc. – any more than we need to worry about what is going on in the neural networks of the child's brain. All we need to know is that learning is taking place. It is unnecessary, and perhaps very nearly impossible, to discover how and where, at the detailed level of the individual elements, knowledge is being stored; what matters is that the system as a whole will now know what a particular object, or a whole class of objects, looks like.

Opposite: In these two illustrations taken from WISARD's monitor screen the responses of the discriminators are displayed as bar graphs across the top of the screen, the longer the bar (coloured red) the higher the number of RAMS that are firing in the discriminator. In this experiment two pairs of discriminators were in use; one pair had been trained on smiling faces and frowning faces while the other pair had been trained on the faces of Igor Aleksander and his colleague Bruce Wilkie. As a result the system could distinguish between the two individuals and could also decide whether they were smiling or frowning. The information actually fed into the discriminators represented the highlighted areas of the pictures which have been outlined in red.

CHAPTER 10

THE IMAGES INSIDE THE MACHINE

A machine such as WISARD clearly represents no more than the first rung on the bottom-up ladder. There are, to start with, staggering disparities of scale between a net with a few tens of thousands of logical elements and even one small area of the brain, such as the visual cortex, which contains hundreds of millions of neurons. And that is only the beginning of the story; before engineers can even contemplate the design of really large-scale models of the brain, very much more will have to be discovered about both its organization and its operation. It is, for example, evident that there are many different kinds of neuron, but only in few cases have their specific roles been pinpointed. Similarly, on a larger scale, it is clear that networks of cells in different regions of the brain have different functions and interact in highly complex ways, but neurophysiologists have barely begun to unravel the intricacies involved.

However, we can take our investigation of the general nature of brain-like mechanisms at least one stage further. We can look at what happens when the elements in a single-layer net are interconnected in order to create a multi-layer network in which the artificial neurons, like their natural counterparts, respond not only to information input from the outside world, but also to each other.

ADDING FEEDBACK

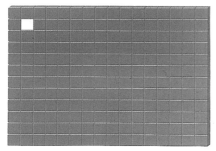

Image A

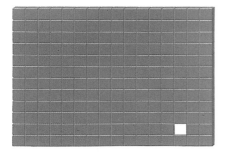

Image B

There is a very simple way of achieving this, which also has the advantage of making it relatively easy to keep track of the results. Instead of wiring up the output terminal of each RAM to the address terminals of other RAMs (the arrangement which would most closely recreate the physical structure of a real neural network), the output of each discriminator, that is the total number of RAMs that fire in response to one scan of the image, is displayed on a screen as a histogram, or bar graph. The information representing this image is then fed back into the address terminals of the RAMs, mixed up in a random fashion with the information that represents the next scan of the image (see opposite). As a result, each discriminator now 'sees' not only the image that is captured by the camera, but also its own response to that image together with the response of the other discriminator.

In order to understand the way in which the system now works it will be helpful to follow an experiment through from the training stage to its conclusion. The two images which will be used are black squares with a single white spot in either the top left-hand corner (image A) or a similar spot in the bottom right-hand corner (image B) (see left). These have been chosen because WISARD, in its original, single-layer, form, distinguishes between them with a very low

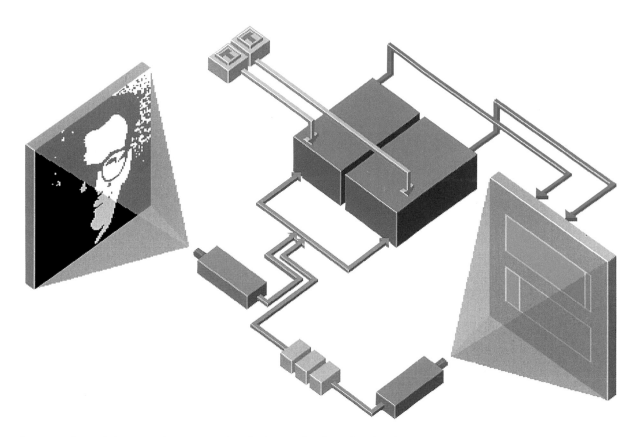

degree of confidence. The reason is obvious: the fact that both images consist very largely of plain black background means that even after training the vast majority of the RAMS in both discriminators are set to fire when they receive the pattern 1111 at their address terminals; consequently both discriminators will produce a high number of firings in response to either image.

Let us suppose that we first place image A before the camera and press the teach button for discriminator A. In the first cycle the discriminator will see image A alone and the RAMS will be set to fire in response to that pattern. As a result, in the second cycle, virtually all the RAMS will fire and, in the third cycle, the discriminator will see both image A and the histogram that represents its own RAMS firing in response to that image. If the teach button continues to be held down, the discriminator will therefore be trained to recognize the pattern formed by the combination of the two images.

Next we replace image A with image B and repeat the whole process, this time pressing the teach button for discriminator B. Now, the training operation having been completed, let us suppose that we again put image A before the camera. Initially, the response of both discriminators will be high, but that of A will be marginally higher and, as a result, its histogram will rise above that for B. Thus, when the information represented by the histograms is fed back, mixed in with the information representing image A, the combination of the two will form a pattern that boosts the confidence of discriminator A, but lowers that of discriminator B. As a result, in

In this illustration the blue boxes represent two discriminators. The input image on the screen to the left is being fed into their address terminals via the red wires and their data-In terminals are connected, by the yellow wires, to two teach buttons, one for each discriminator. Finally, the output of each discriminator, carried by the green wires, is displayed as a histogram on the screen to the right – the length of each green bar is proportional to the number of RAMS that are firing in the corresponding discriminator. The information representing the image of the histogram is then fed back into the address terminals of the discriminators, mixed up at random with the information representing the input image.

By allowing the discriminators to 'see', and therefore to respond to, their own outputs, this arrangement enables the system as a whole to distinguish between very similar patterns (see opposite) with a high degree of confidence.

the next cycle the combined pattern will seem even more familiar to A and even less familiar to B, and so on. With this feedback loop in operation, WISARD will, within a few cycles, distinguish the two patterns with 90% confidence, whereas it would previously have been able to muster no more than 20%.

The way the machine uses its own responses to resolve its initial uncertainty is very reminiscent of an experience familiar to most people. Anyone who knows a pair of brothers or sisters who were born as identical twins and who have grown up to look very similar, but not identical, in appearance, has probably been gripped by a feeling of momentary uncertainty upon meeting one of them in the street. But that uncertainty will soon have been replaced by a tentative hypothesis – 'I *think* it's Philip' – which will, equally rapidly, have turned into a postive identification – 'Yes, of course it's Philip.' In such cases, the surge of confidence which comes with the arrival of the feedback that confirms the initial hypothesis is often a vivid, almost physical, sensation.

There is, however, an important difference. For, in WISARD's case, confidence is being bolstered simply by the growing disparity between the number of RAMs that are firing in its two discriminators; but in our own case a much more selective feedback process is operating. It is as if, once the initial hypothesis has been formed, it serves as a trigger to the memory and allows us to recall the information that we need in order to confirm that the person we see is indeed Philip, not his twin brother. In other words, unlike WISARD at this stage of its development, we have access to a visual memory, a storehouse of mental images which can be recalled and inspected with 'the mind's eye' in order to check whether they match what we think we see.

REMEMBERING WHAT THINGS LOOK LIKE

The ability to form mental images, which not only serve as an aid to recognition but can also be recaptured at will, so allowing us to visualize what things look like even when we can no longer see them, is unquestionably one of the most fascinating and fundamental properties of the brain. For, quite apart from the phenomenon of visual memory, there is also a good deal of evidence to suggest that much of our thinking is conducted in the language of images rather than the language of words. It is very often the case, for example, that when we say we have 'seen' the anwer to a problem, we still have to struggle to articulate it clearly.

Happily, with the feedback arrangements we have described in place, WISARD provides a tool with which we can begin to explore the nature of mental, or 'internal', images and allows us to examine the way in which a machine can 'think about' such images.

The first step is to find some way in which an image may be represented within the machine – some means whereby WISARD may store and recall images rather than simply registering that they resemble or do not resemble the images on which it has been trained. We must transform the net into a visual memory.

By definition, before something can be remembered, it must first be learnt. So, going back for a moment to the natural system, we recollect that a neuron learns a new function when a firing signal is received at a dominant synapse. In the examples which we have considered so far the control of the RAMS' input terminals, the artificial equivalents of the dominant synapses, has been vested in the operator who, by pressing a single teach button, caused all the RAMS in a discriminator to store a 1 and to output it in response to a particular pattern of inputs at their address terminals. Now, in order to transform WISARD into a learning machine, the use of a teach button is abandoned, and control of the learning process is, in effect, decentralized. As a result, what WISARD learns becomes a reflection of what WISARD sees.

In order to understand this next stage in the machine's development we shall first of all consider the arrangement shown below. Here, one image, a small triangular block on a white ground, has been placed before the camera and is, therefore, being 'seen' by the address terminals of the RAMS. At the same time the data-in terminals have been connected up to a matrix which represents a second pattern of inputs, in effect a second image, this time of a large triangle, also on a plain background. If we wished to continue the analogy with the natural system we might imagine that each of the pixels in this matrix represents the input to a cell which will fire only if the pixel is a black one, and that each of these cells exercises a dominant influence over one of the elements in the net.

We could take the arrangement shown in the illustration one step further and connect the output terminals of the RAMS to another matrix. This would allow us to monitor the behaviour of the net and to see an image that actually represented its internal state. It is, however, important to realize that this representation would not necessarily be a literal one – in fact the image would only be recognizable if the connections between the output terminals and the matrix precisely mirrored those between the data-in matrix and the data-in terminals.

This new arrangement features just one discriminator (the blue box) and rather than being activated by a teach button, the data-in terminals have now been connected up to a matrix representing the image of a triangle. As a result, when the system is activated, those RAMS whose data-in terminals are connected to a black pixel on the matrix will be set to store a 1 while the others, being connected to white pixels, will be set to store a 0. But the addresses at which the digits are stored will be selected by the pattern of inputs at the address terminals, a pattern which represents the smaller triangle on the screen to the left. It follows that if the image of the small triangle is removed the network of RAMS will revert to a random state; if, however, the small triangle subsequently reappears, the pattern of firings and non-firings that represents the triangle on the matrix will be recreated and the net will move into a 'triangle state'.

If we now imagine, for simplicity's sake, that when this experiment commences all the RAMS in the net have been set to store a 0 at all their addresses, it becomes apparent that those RAMS with data-in terminals connected to the black pixels which form the triangle on the matrix will be set to store a 1, while all the other RAMS will continue to store a 0. It follows that the 'state' of the net as a whole will now represent the large triangle. But although it is the pattern formed by the large triangle that determines which RAMS are set to store a 1, it is of course the pattern formed by the small triangle that determines, for each of those RAMS, at which address that 1 shall be stored. It follows that, if the small triangle is removed, the RAMS will cease firing and the net will revert to a state in which all the RAMS output a 0.

Now let us suppose that the exercise is repeated, this time using images containing squares rather than triangles, and then repeated for a third time using circles. Imagine next that the data-in terminals are deactivated and that the triangle image is placed in front of the camera once more – how will the net respond? Clearly, only a certain number of RAMS will fire, for only some of them, those that were set to store a 1 when the triangle was presented at the data-in matrix, have been set to respond to the triangle image; but, as a consequence of their firing, and the failure of the other RAMS to fire, the state of the net (and the output which appears on a monitor screen) will represent a triangle. Furthermore, if we place the square or the circle before the camera we will find that the response of the net is to output the corresponding shape.

In some sense WISARD can now be said to remember what triangles, squares and circles look like: for it not only recognizes them, it signals its recognition by outputting the appropriate image. Moreover, we no longer need to allot a separate discriminator to each image, for what we now have is a net that, on being shown a triangle, will move into a 'state' that represents a triangle (and will, therefore, output the image of a triangle). Furthermore, if the triangle is replaced by a square the internal state (and the output) of the net will change to one that represents a square, and so on.

The fact that the machine produces an output that corresponds so literally to the input is, of course, a result of the way in which it is taught. It could, with equal ease, be taught to output a circle when it sees a square, or a triangle when it sees a circle. In fact, as explained earlier, the monitor screen on which the output can be displayed is no more than a convenience. Removing it would not alter the essential feature of the system, which is that it now has a range of internal states, each of which represents one of the inputs that it has learnt to recognize. But these internal representations are not of a literal kind, and their counterparts within the brain will not be discovered by the probing neurophysiologist. The internal states of any such system have 'meaning' only to the system itself.

THE LANGUAGE OF AUTOMATA

Any machine of this kind, that is one which has a set of internal, concealed states, falls into a category known to engineers as automata. The word automaton almost inevitably conjures up images of either sinister mechanical men out of the pages of science fiction or of the ingenious mechanical dolls of the eighteenth and nineteenth centuries which are also known as automata. But, to an engineer, an automaton is simply any machine or system which has a set of internal concealed states and whose next output, and/or next state, is determined not only by its last input but also by its current state.

To clarify the idea we can turn to an automaton with which most people will be familiar, the fruit machine. In order to operate the machine a player must first put a coin in the slot and then pull the lever, but for our purposes we will consider these two operations as a single input, called S for start. There are, clearly, two possible outputs, either the machine produces a jackpot (output J) or it does not (output N). Equally clearly, once the input has been provided, which of the two outputs follows will depend upon the internal state of the machine – if we could open it up and examine the mechanism we would, in principle at least, be able to discover whether or not it would produce a jackpot next time the lever was pulled. Since we are not privy to the secrets of those who manufacture fruit machines, we will assume, for the sake of simplicity, that it contains some simple mechanism which ensures that every tenth game will produce a jackpot. (In reality, of course, factors would be introduced in order to ensure that the behaviour of the machine had a degree of randomness.)

Such a device will have a range of ten internal states, which could be numbered, starting with state 1, the state which immediately follows a jackpot, and ending with state 10, the state in which a jackpot will be paid out to the next player. And the machine's behaviour can be fully defined by a set of rules, which take the following form: 'If in state X now and input S, then output? and change to state Y'. These rules can be set out in the form of a table which predicts what the machine will do under all possible circumstances. But the simplest and clearest way of decribing the machine's behaviour is to depict its *state structure* by means of what is known as a state diagram (see next page). Each state is represented by a node and the arrows that indicate transitions from one state to another are labelled with the input that will bring about that transition and the output that will accompany it.

The state structure of a fruit machine, and that of the many other automata, from thermostats to automatic gearboxes, which feature in our daily lives, is built into the hardware. But in the case of another familiar automaton, the computer, the state structure is determined by the software; in fact a computer program is simply a set of instructions that defines the state structure the computer requires in order to perform a specific task.

The brain, too, is an automaton – to make this statement is not necessarily to take a mechanistic view of human beings, it is simply to observe that the brain very clearly falls into the category of automata as we have defined it. But it is an automaton quite unlike those we have so far considered. There are some aspects of its state structure that may well be determined by the structure of the

THE STATE STRUCTURE OF AN AUTOMATON

The 'if. . . then. . .' rules which govern the behaviour of the fruit machine automaton described in the text can be set out in the form of a table which shows, for each combination of input and current state, what will be the output and the next state:

STATES	INPUT S
1	Output N, change to state 2
2	Output N, change to state 3
3	Output N, change to state 4
4	Output N, change to state 5
5	Output N, change to state 6
6	Output N, change to state 7
7	Output N, change to state 8
8	Output N, change to state 9
9	Output N, change to state 10
10	Output J, change to state 1

The same information is, however, much more clearly represented by a state diagram like that shown below. Each of the blue nodes represents one of the ten states and the arrows which indicate the transitions from one state to another are labelled to show both the input that triggers the change and the output associated with it.

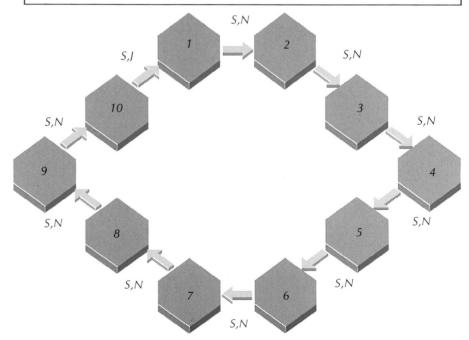

'hardware' – it is reasonable to suppose, for example, that control of autonomous functions such as respiration and of instinctive reactions is 'wired into' the brain at birth. The brain is also capable of developing its state structure as a result of processes comparable to the programming of a computer – learning multiplication tables by rote or learning how to do long division are obvious examples of this. But the brain has two further characteristics which seem to be absolutely fundamental to the property that we call 'intelligence'.

Firstly, new states are automatically created in order to represent new inputs – in other words we remember what we experience.

Secondly, links are established which cause new states to be associated with one another and with existing states. To see the process in operation we need only observe a child encountering an unfamiliar object for the first time and immediately asking both what it is called (i.e. what new state, representing the object's name, should be associated with the new state that represents its appearance?) and what it is for (i.e. how does it relate to the state structure that represents the child's current knowledge of the world?). What it is that impels the child to ask such questions is another matter and one that cannot be dealt with here, except to say that the desire to name what we see and to make sense of it appears to be a fundamental human trait. It may therefore be that curiosity, the compulsion to coordinate and refine the state structure of one's own brain, is an instinctual force.

It is these two properties which, together, provide the brain with the quality of intentionality. They ensure not just that words and images are cross-referenced in the memory, but that both are recognized to be no more than symbolic representations of objects or events that have an independent existence in the real world.

Apart from the fact that they seem to bootstrap themselves into existence, the state structures which develop within the neural networks of the brain have one further notable feature. This is that the structures themselves, the way in which the states are linked to one another, reflect the perceived relationship between the events which those states represent. It is this that allows us to build up what we call experience: a body of knowledge that is acquired inductively and which enables us to anticipate the way in which the world is likely to behave and to predict the consequences of our own actions.

In effect, the state structure of the brain-automaton can be seen both as a set of 'if . . . then . . .' rules which govern its own behaviour, and as a mirror image of a second set of 'if . . . then . . .' rules, the rules which appear to govern the behaviour of the outside world with which the brain interacts (see next page).

CREATING INTERNAL IMAGES

Returning now to the automaton with which we are currently concerned, WISARD, we see that at the conclusion of the experiment described above its state diagram contained four states: the 'triangle state', the 'square state' the 'circle state' and a 'random state' in which it will remain in the absence of any of the three known inputs (see page 181).

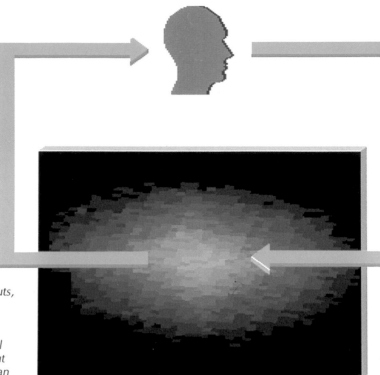

The relationship between the brain-automaton and the world. Our outputs, i.e. our actions and words, can be thought of as inputs into the world. Some of those inputs will have consequences, that is to say they will cause the world to produce an output which can, in turn, be thought of as an input to the brain-automaton.

The body of inductively acquired knowledge that we call 'experience' resembles the state structure of an automaton in that it consists of a set of rules of thumb that tell us that if, for example, we snap at a friend, then the world, in the shape of our friend, may enter an 'irritated state' and snap back. Similarly, were the situation reversed, we know that our own reaction, that is our output and next state, could well be determined as much by our present state as by our friend's behaviour – if we happened to be feeling tense we might well reply to a curt remark in kind, if we happened to be feeling relaxed we might well shrug it off.

Opposite above: A state diagram for WISARD after learning to recognize triangles, circles and squares. The input of any of the three known images will cause the net to move into the corresponding state, in which it will remain so long as the input continues – indicated by the arrows on the right of the illustration which lead back to the states from which they originate. But when the input is removed, the net moves back into a random state.

The outputs of the world – events and reactions – are the inputs to the brain

The outputs of the brain – words and actions – are the inputs to the world

The next step in its development is reasonably obvious. Rather than presenting the RAMS with two separate images, one at the address terminals and one at the data-in terminals, we can re-arrange matters to create the system shown in the next illustration (see opposite). Now the pattern on the input matrix represents the image that actually appears before the camera and, as a result, the appearance of a new image will cause the net to learn a new state, a state which represents that image. Thus, if the machine is shown a face, as in the illustration, the output image which appears on the monitor screen will be a representation of that face – it will in fact be 'WISARD's idea' of what that person looks like.

Just one further elaboration remains to be accomplished in order to transform WISARD into an automaton which begins to share some of the brain-like properties outlined above. The pattern that represents the output image must be fed back into the net's address terminals, mixed up, as before, with the pattern that represents the camera image. Now, if we suppose that the system has previously learnt what something, say the face of John Smith, looks like, the reappearance of John will not only cause the net to move into a state which represents his face, it will also generate an inner image of John which will be circulated over and over again in the feedback loop.

There is, therefore, a very real sense in which we can say that as soon as the machine 'sees' John it will start to 'think about' John. In fact, if we look at its state structure (see page 183), we not only see that input J (John's face) leads from the random state to state J, but

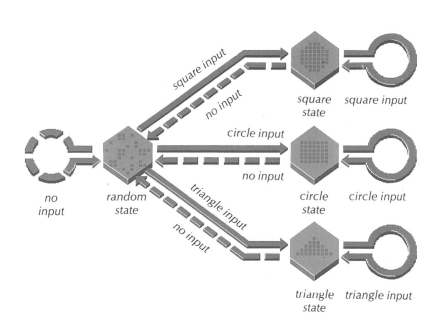

square input

no input

no input

circle input

no input

triangle input

no input

no input

random state

square state

square input

circle state

circle input

triangle state

triangle input

Below: Creating an internal image. Compared with those shown in previous illustrations, this arrangement incorporates two new features. The information representing the image on the screen is now being fed into both the address terminals and the data-in terminals of the net. This means that the appearance of a new image on the screen will cause the system to learn a state that actually represents what it is 'seeing'. Secondly, the output terminals have now been connected up to a display screen and the image on this screen is being fed back into the net – as a result there is now an internal or state image which continually circulates within the system. In fact, since the arrangements for connecting the output terminals duplicate those used to connect the data-in terminals, the internal image is a literal representation of the input image. But while this is convenient in that it allows the internal state of the net to be easily monitored, it is not essential. Even if the connections of the output terminals were rearranged so that the internal image was no longer recognizable to an observer, it would still be a perfectly valid representation of the input image so far as the system itself was concerned. Indeed, the internal image would be no less 'real' if it existed only as a pattern of signals in a bundle of wires linking the net's output terminals to its input terminals.

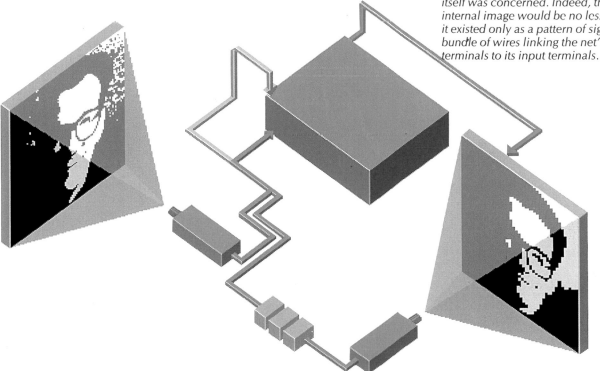

also that when the input is removed the continuing feedback ensures that the 'decay' of state J will be a gradual process. In effect the net will move from state J back to a random state via a series of intermediate states that become progressively 'less J' and 'more random'.

This phenomenon is very reminiscent of our own short-term memory. For our ability to remember, from moment to moment, what we have just seen or heard itself depends upon those images or sounds being fed back within the brain. The mechanism becomes particularly obvious in the case of 'meaningless' strings of digits, such as unfamiliar telephone numbers, which we find it hard to memorize, even for a few seconds. To make good this deficiency we will often provide ourselves with a sort of external feedback loop, continuing to mumble a number that we have just looked up over and over again while we reach for the telephone and prepare to make the call.

It is also significant that, just as we must look long and hard at something we particularly wish to commit to memory, so the longer WISARD looks at John Smith, the clearer its idea of him becomes. For in rather the same way as the image of the histograms served, when fed back into the net during the training process, to make the two white dots more easily distinguishable, so the internal image of John that is now travelling round the feedback loop will further clarify and refine state J with each successive cycle. The result is that WISARD now 'polishes up' its own internal state by eliminating the effects of noise and generalizing the changes that occur when John changes his expression or moves his head thus combining a sequence of input images into a single 'state image' (see opposite).

This process has some extremely interesting consequences, for it must be remembered that the RAMS are not only learning to respond to the input patterns that represent what the camera sees, they are also being set to respond to the feedback patterns that represent the internal state image – or, more accurately, they are learning to recognize the combination of the two. As a result, if we imagine that WISARD has now learnt to recognize a second face, that of Peter, and has therefore learnt a second internal state, state P, in addition to J, we will find that when it sees a third, unknown, face, it will be driven into one or other of these two 'known' states. Which it ends up in will depend upon whether the newcomer most closely resembles John or Peter. In effect, when exposed to an unknown image, the net is now driven by its own feedback into one of its learnt states, the one which is 'nearest' to that image (see page 184).

This compulsion to try to classify unknown images by allotting them to the nearest familiar category can be seen as an extension of the net's powers of generalization. It also mirrors the way in which we rely upon a stock of familiar images in order to decribe novel ones. WISARD's behaviour might, for example, bring to mind the dialogue in *Hamlet* in which the Prince is teasing Polonius:

HAMLET: Do you see yonder cloud that's almost in the shape of a camel?
POLONIUS: By the mass, and 'tis like a camel, indeed.
HAMLET: Methinks it is like a weasel.

POLONIUS: It is backed like a weasel.
HAMLET: Or like a whale?
POLONIUS: Very like a whale.

FORMING LINKS BETWEEN STATES

We shall now consider what happens when, during the learning process, WISARD is exposed to two or more images one after the other. Suppose, for example, that it is shown the sequence of letters F R E D. Initially, it will learn an F state and the image of the letter F will begin to circulate in the feedback loop. But when the F is removed and replaced by the R the net will learn a combination of two patterns, that representing the internal image of the F which is

The state structure of the system shown in the previous illustration after it has learnt to recognize John's face. As before, the input of the learnt image, input J, causes the net to move into the corresponding state, in which it will remain so long as the input is maintained. But when the input is removed the system no longer returns directly to its random state. For now the internal image will continue to circulate in the feedback loop, providing the system with a sort of short-term memory which gradually fades as the internal image decays with each successive feedback cycle.

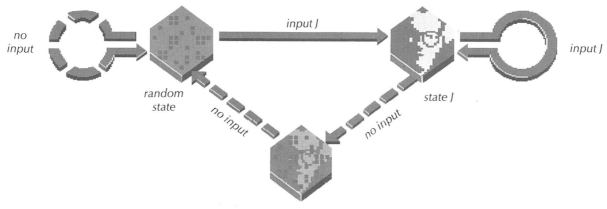

no input   *input J*   *input J*

random state   *state J*

no input   *no input*

one of a series of states that progressively become 'less J' and 'more random'

The sequence of images on the right-hand side of the illustration represents a man turning his head from left to right, the sort of sequence that is fed into WISARD when it learns to recognize a 'live' subject. As a result it will initially form an internal image that is a composite, made up of many overlapping images like those in the large picture, but as the internal image continues to circulate in the feedback loop this composite image will gradually be clarified and refined into a single state image which, in effect, represents the system's own, highly generalized, 'idea' of what this person looks like. Subsequently the reappearance of the same face, in whatever attitude, will drive the net into the internal state that represents this state image.

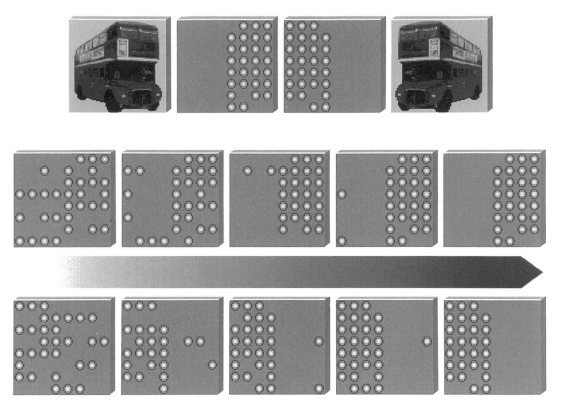

This illustration shows the responses of a small network of just 64 interconnected elements as simulated on a home computer. The net was initially taught to recognize the two patterns at the top of the illustration, representing highly simplified images of a London bus seen from two different aspects. Two apparently random patterns (those on the extreme left of the illustration) were then fed into the net in turn. In each case it was then driven, by its own feedback, through the sequence of states which follow. As can be seen, reading from left to right, these states became progressively 'more like' one of the learnt states until the net finally entered the learnt state (on the right) which was 'closest' to the random state in which it had started. It is, we might surmise, exactly this sort of mechanism which is at work in our own brains when we leap back instinctively after glimpsing a rapidly approaching shape out of the corner of an eye and then realize, a second or two later, that what we actually saw was a bus.

still being fed back, and that representing the R as seen by the camera. As a consequence, the net will pass through a transition in which, with each successive cycle, its internal state becomes 'less F' and 'more R'. And similar changes will occur when the R is replaced by the E and the E by the D.

Now the net has not only learnt internal states which represent each of the letters, it has also learnt the succession of states which are intermediate between each letter and its successor. As a result, if it is now shown the F, say, which is then removed leaving no input at all, the F state will not immediately begin to decay back to the random state; instead the net begins to move towards the R state. The point being that as the internal image of the F begins to fade the net is driven towards the known state that most closely resembles the resulting feedback pattern, and that state is the one it learnt when F first changed to R.

There is now, it seems, a sense in which WISARD can be said to have developed a set of expectations about that tiny fraction of the world which it has experienced. Its responses, that is its changes of internal state, not only mirror what the world does, they also predict what, on the basis of the machine's experience, the world is likely to do next.

But this is only a beginning, for the effect becomes even more marked if the learning process is speeded up, with the letters following each other in rapid succession. Since each letter is exposed to the camera only briefly, the net does not have time to stabilize in any one state, that is learn the pattern formed by the combination of the input image and the corresponding feedback image. Thus, instead of learning four distinct states, it learns a continuous chain of state changes in which its own response to the first input, F, is linked with the next input, R, and so on, right through to D.

Now, once primed with the F, the net's search for a known state will carry it through the F state and on into the R state and it may even, without further prompting, stumble on towards the E state (see next page). The fact that, given no further inputs, it falters and decays back to a random state at this point is a consequence of the fact that the world has failed to behave in the way that was predicted – the R and the E that should have followed the F have not materialized. Nonetheless, it is clear that if we want to describe the machine's behaviour we can no longer suppose that it is simply following rules such as:

If input F and random state, then state F next
If input R and state F, then state R next
. . . and so on.

For these rules fail to account for the fact that input F now triggers off a whole sequence of state changes. In fact, if we want to define the automaton we have created, we have to consider it not as a single automaton, but as two interacting automata. For the state structure of the machine now reflects the fact that the world, as the machine has experienced it, behaves exactly as if it, too, was an automaton – an automaton with its own set of states which represent the inputs to the machine. In fact, if we try to summarize what the machine now 'knows' we will find that we must draw up two sets of rules. The first set is simply the instructions that govern the machine's behaviour, and these are as follows:

If world state random, then machine state random
If world state F, then machine state F
If world state R, then machine state R
If world state E, then machine state E
If world state D, then machine state D

These rules can be translated into a state diagram exactly as before (see page 187).

The second set of rules, those which govern the behaviour of the world-automaton, are perhaps rather less obvious. For at first glance they seem pretty arbitrary:

If random state now, then state F next
If state F now, then state R next
. . . and so on.

But just as changes in the state of the world represent inputs to the machine-automaton, so changes in the state of the machine can be seen as inputs into the world-automaton. (This simply reflects the machine's experience that, for example, as soon as it responded to

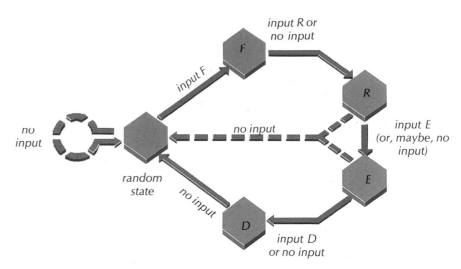

input F by moving into state F, the world changed to state R.) So it now becomes clear that the rules followed by the world-automaton can be expressed as follows:

> If machine state random, then world state random *or* state F (This reflects the fact that the machine cannot predict *when*, or even *if* the F is going to reappear)
> If machine state F, then world state R
> If machine state R, then world state E
> If machine state E, then world state D
> If machine state D, then world state random

These rules can now be translated into a state diagram for the world automaton (see opposite).

Finally, in order to summarize everything that the machine knows about its interaction with the world, we can construct a single combined state diagram for both WISARD and the world (see opposite).

ADDING MEANING

It might at first seem somewhat unsatisfactory that WISARD cannot learn a simple sequence of letters such as F R E D and repeat them without the need for further prompting; after all, we find little difficulty in committing long sequences of words, such as songs or poems, to memory. But this ignores the fact that we, too, have great difficulty in memorizing arbitrary sequences that are apparently meaningless – in fact psychological experiments have shown that, even with the vastly greater resources of the human brain, most people have difficulty in memorizing a random sequence of more than seven letters.

So what happens if we show WISARD that the sequence F R E D has a 'meaning'? We can do this in a very literal fashion by placing Fred in front of the camera while at the same time flashing up the letters one after another. As before, the machine will learn a chain

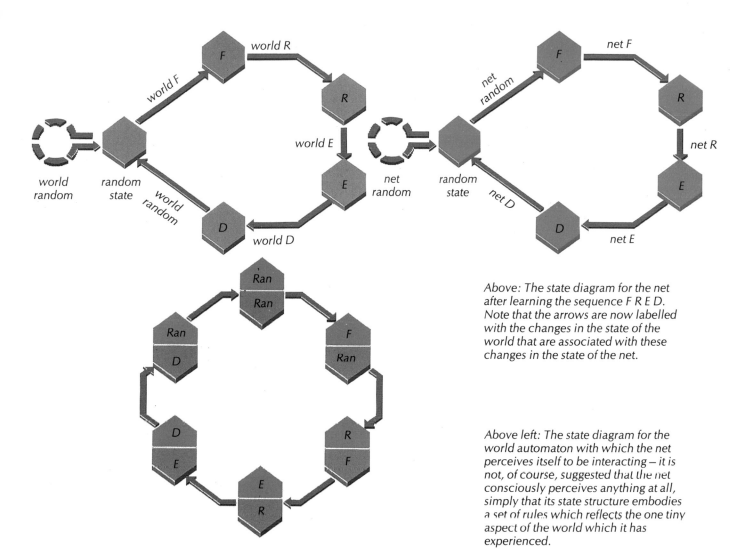

Above: The state diagram for the net after learning the sequence F R E D. Note that the arrows are now labelled with the changes in the state of the world that are associated with these changes in the state of the net.

Above left: The state diagram for the world automaton with which the net perceives itself to be interacting – it is not, of course, suggested that the net consciously perceives anything at all, simply that its state structure embodies a set of rules which reflects the one tiny aspect of the world which it has experienced.

Centre: The combined state structure for the net and the world-automaton. The labels in the top half of each node represent the state of the world and those below the state of the net. This illustration incorporates everything that the net has learnt after being trained on the sequence F R E D; note that if the net is in a random state then the world may either be in a random state or an F state – the net cannot know when or if the sequence will begin – but once the world has entered the F state the net 'expects' it to continue through R, E and D.

of state changes, but each state will now represent a letter *plus* Fred's face, so there will be an 'F plus Fred' state, an 'R plus Fred' state, and so on. We can even go a step further and, replacing Fred with his dog Fido, run through the sequence F I D O.

Now, supposing that the letters are large enough to form a substantial proportion of the total input pattern, the reappearance of either element (Fred or one of the two sequences of letters) will produce an input pattern sufficiently close to the ones which were learnt for the net to recognize it, thanks to its built-in capacity for generalization. It will therefore embark upon one of the two chains which it has learnt, and, since the world now continues to behave as predicted (that is to say either the image of Fred or Fido or the sequence of letters continues to appear), it will follow it through to its conclusion. Thus, on being shown Fred, the net will traverse the chain 'F plus Fred', 'R plus Fred' . . . . and the sequence F R E D even when not accompanied by Fred himself will set it off along the same chain. Similarly, on being shown either Fido or the sequence

F I D O it will traverse the chain 'F plus Fido', 'I plus Fido' . . . . So we can now say that Fred's face 'reminds' WISARD of his name, and that when it sees his name it 'thinks' of his face.

The intriguing question is what happens if the machine simply sees the letter F, which might be the beginning of either of the two sequences. And the answer is that, just like a human being in similar circumstances, it waits to see what will happen next. In fact the machine has now 'discovered' something well known to all human beings, that it is not always possible to predict with certainty whether the world will behave in one way rather than another, and this is reflected in its state diagram (see below) which now contains an OR branch.

However, the main point to be made about this last experiment is that it clearly demonstrates that WISARD's memory, like our own, is enormously strengthened by the power of association. Indeed, the way in which one image allows the machine to recover a whole chain of associated images is rather reminiscent of a very familiar phenomenon. For there can be few of us who have not had the experience of being suddenly and vividly reminded of an occasion or event that we had thought to be long-forgotten by a familiar sound or scent. In our case, we are of course well aware of the power of association — why else do we tie knots in handkerchiefs to remind ourselves that there is something we need to remember, or teach our children the alphabet by showing them picture books in which A stands for Apple and B stands for Ball? It is therefore highly suggestive, to say the least, that WISARD should be able to make use of a comparable mechanism.

At this point it may be helpful to pause and summarize what has been learnt from the series of experiments which have been described so far. We have seen, first of all, that a neural net-type structure can represent an input in terms of its own internal state, and that it can, therefore, not only recognize that input when it recurs, but can also 'remember' what it looks like. Secondly, it has been shown that, with the addition of a feedback loop, the net

The state diagram for the net and the world after training on Fred and Fido and the associated sequences F R E D and F I D O.

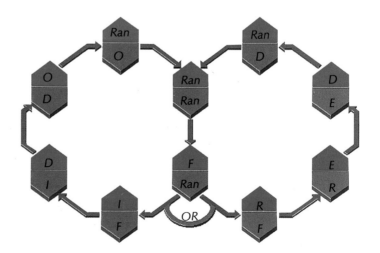

generates internal, or state, images which could be considered akin to the mental images formed in the brain. Further, the net now becomes an automaton with a whole set of internal states, each representing a known image, and the recurrence of a known image will cause the net to move into the corresponding internal state, that is to regenerate the appropriate internal image.

We have also seen that, under certain circumstances, the net can learn to traverse the chain of state changes that represent a whole sequence of inputs. At this point it could be argued that the net is capable of inductive learning, albeit of a very rudimentary kind. For its state structure now represents not only a set of instructions governing its own behaviour, but also a set of rules, or statements, which describe the behaviour of the world in so far as the net has experienced it. Or, to put it in our own terms, the net now has 'expectations' about the world's future behaviour which reflect its very limited experience of the world's past behaviour. Finally, we have seen that by presenting images in association with each other it is possible dramatically to improve the net's ability to remember and recapitulate a sequence of inputs.

MOVING CLOSER TO THE NATURAL VISUAL SYSTEM

We shall now move on to consider two further ways in which feedback may be used to bring WISARD's performance a little closer to that of our own visual system. The first deals with a problem which is known, technically, as invariance. The point is this: despite the net's capacity for generalization it is quite apparent that its ability to recognize an object such as, say, a spoon or fork is dependent upon the object always being presented in approximately the same orientation. For the input patterns produced by such objects will obviously become unrecognizable if they are turned the other way round. On the face of it this problem might seem to provide a clinching argument in favour of the algorithmic approach employed by the top-down school. It is, after all, relatively easy to account for our ability to recognize such objects regardless of their orientation if we suppose that we apply some set of formal rules, such as 'If it has prongs at the end it is a fork, but if it has a bowl at the end it is a spoon.'

The only alternative, if we insist on sticking to the notion that visual recognition is essentially a matter of pattern matching, is to suppose that we are somehow capable of rotating an image 'in our heads', rather as we might turn a piece of a jigsaw puzzle first this way and then that in our hands in order to see if it fits. There is, in fact, a good deal of evidence to support this idea. For example, while changes in orientation present no difficulty in the case of things like spoons and forks, which we are accustomed to seeing from many different viewpoints, we *are* often thrown, if only momentarily, by familar images, like faces, which we consistently see in just one orientation, when they are presented, say, upside down. To verify this observation, try identifying the face on the next page without turning the book round.

Interestingly enough, it is comparatively easy for WISARD to learn to rotate its own internal images. For if it is shown a sequence of images representing successive steps in the complete rotation of, say, a fork (see below), it is clear that the chaining mechanism described above will come into effect and as soon as the machine sees another fork it will recognize it, however oriented, and start to rotate its own inner image of it. But this, it may be objected, is no more than a clever trick; the machine is not going to be very useful if everything it is required to recognize has first to be slowly turned through 360 degrees and if, as a result, all it knows about the world is that everything in it rotates.

However, if we persevere, and expose the net to a series of such sequences, using different objects each time, we will soon find that it has learnt to rotate any and every image which it encounters, no matter whether the image was known to it or not. Now, if we imagine a system composed of two interconnected nets, one of which specializes in rotating its own inner images while the other is trained to recognize those images in just one orientation, we can see that together they might well overcome the problem of invariance. For it would be a comparatively simple matter to arrange things so that if a new image failed to elicit a response from the 'recognition net' it would be passed on, so to speak, to the 'rotation net' which, having turned the image through one quadrant, would then feed it back into the 'recognition net', and so on, until every possible orientation had been tried and the image had either been recognized or rejected.

There is, however, a second problem. Unless an object is

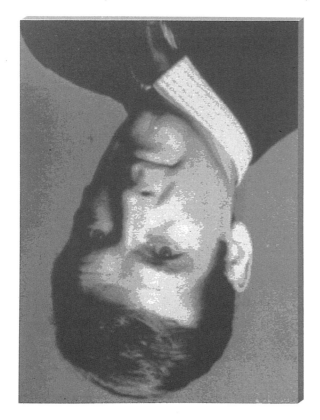

Roger Moore as James Bond 007.

Right: The problem of invariance can be overcome by training the net on a sequence of images such as these, representing successive stages in the rotation of an object.

consistently presented in the centre of the camera's visual field, WISARD's ability to recognize it will depend not only upon its orientation but also upon its position. In our case, of course, this problem does not arise in quite the same form, for we can move our eyes in order to look straight at whatever it is that interests us. In fact, our own visual system deals simultaneously with two quite distinct sets of inputs. There is, first of all, the image captured by the fovea (the region in the centre of the retina of the eye where the light-sensitive rods and cones are closely concentrated). But while this represents the input upon which our attention is, quite literally, focussed, we also remain aware of the input from surrounding areas of the retina which provides us with our peripheral vision. We are aware, that is, in the sense that our attention will immediately switch if, 'out of the corner of our eye', we detect anything interesting or untoward going on.

We are also able to concentrate on that area of an image that currently concerns us – one sentence in a paragraph, say, or the expression on another person's face – while at the same time retaining an awareness of other objects or events. Even when we are walking along the street, thinking of nothing in particular, our eyes are continually flicking this way and that. This process, known as 'saccadic eye movement', is a product of feedback signals within the brain that involve not only the visual cortex but also the organ, the superior colliculus, which actually controls the muscles that rotate the eyeballs in their sockets.

By use of a technique known as 'windowing' WISARD, too, can be equipped to deal, at one and the same time, with both a peripheral and a closely focussed field of vision. The technicalities of this arrangement, which involves the use of a framestore, need not concern us overmuch. The essential point is that the net now sees two patterns of input simultaneously: the first represents everything within the camera's field of view, while the second represents a 'window' of high resolution within that area. The crucial point is that by teaching WISARD to move the window around the overall image that represents its peripheral field of vision we can, in effect, train it to find and concentrate upon those features that are significant.

In order to keep the explanation as simple as possible we will consider the arrangement shown on the next page. Here, the net's internal image, representing both the entire field of view and the window within that field, is fed into a control mechanism that translates changes in output into movements of the window. This creates a new feedback loop, for every time the control mechanism moves the window it changes the input pattern which, in turn, generates a new output. But WISARD cannot be expected to know what use it should make of its window without some sort of training. So, in addition to being connected, as before, to a matrix representing the input image, the data-in terminals are also linked to a joystick control. By moving the joystick the operator can change the pattern of input at the data-in terminals so that the window 'appears' to change its position, and this, in turn, results in a corresponding change in the output pattern which actually controls

WISARD with window control. The input image is now fed into a framestore, on the right of the illustration, where one small area, or window, is isolated. The information representing both the image and the window is then fed into the net. By manipulating the joystick connected to the data-in terminals, the operator can determine which RAMS in the net are addressed by the window input and thus generate the output signals that drive the window control mechanism (the black box on the right). Signals from the control box are then fed into the framestore, causing the window to move in the direction indicated by the operator. As a result of this training process the net will learn to move the window around an image in a predictable fashion, to follow the edges of objects, for example.

the window's movement. Thus the operator can move the window around in very much the same fashion as a player uses a joystick to move the cursor around the screen in a video game.

Clearly, for reasons we have already explained, the changing sequence of input patterns generated by the moving window will generate a chain of state changes within the net – for movements of the window are perceived by the net as changes in the state of the world which are interlinked with the consequent changes in its own internal state. So if, for example, the window is steered round the periphery of a triangle the net will develop a state structure which reflects its 'expectation' that, whenever the triangle reappears, the window will retrace its path. But the information travelling around the feedback loop no longer represents an internal image; instead it consists of the signals which control the movement of the window. It follows that when the triangle does reappear and the net starts to traverse the sequence of state changes which it has learnt, the resulting outputs will actually cause the window to follow the predicted path.

What is even more intriguing is that if this teaching process is repeated with a variety of images of different shapes and sizes the net will generalize the whole range of inputs and will, as a result, learn to guide its window around the edge of any image whatsoever. It is not difficult to see that, if the teaching program was further elaborated, WISARD might well be trained to respond to those features, such as a sudden movement, which tend to catch our own attention even when glimpsed only out of the corner of the eye.

No less interesting is the fact that, once trained to follow edges, WISARD begins to be subject to a number of familiar optical illusions. Presented with the two sets of elements shown here, for example, we have no difficulty at all in seeing that they both represent triangles, indeed we 'fill in' the missing lines almost without being aware of having done so. Confronted with similar visual clues WISARD, too, will now 'see' a shape and move its window along the path where it 'thinks' the edges should be.

These last two chapters have, we hope, demonstrated that a bottom-up approach has something novel and potentially very valuable to offer in the field of artificial vision, and elsewhere for that matter. There is, for example, no reason why similar methods should not be applied to language. Indeed, as we shall see in Chapter 11, in the United States the so-called 'new connectionists' are already proclaiming, perhaps rather prematurely, that the development of neural net-type structures will produce a major breakthrough in all branches of artificial intelligence.

But the two approaches, bottom-up and top-down, and the two classes of hardware, neural nets or 'connection machines' and more orthodox kinds of computer, are best seen as complementing each other. We shall, therefore, conclude this chapter by looking at one possible combination that seems to offer great promise.

This involves using an array processor such as CLIP (see page 126) as a 'front-end' for an adaptive pattern-recognition device such as WISARD. The role of the array processor, which can, as we have already seen, implement edge-finding and similar algorithms at great speed, would be to translate input images into something akin to Marr's primal sketches before passing them on to the pattern-recognition device. The result would be a system which operated on principles much closer to those which, Marr suggested, must be followed by the brain itself. For the actual contents of the system's visual memory, the internal images represented in the state structure of the neural net, would be simple graphic prototypes, which would be clearly differentiated and easily matched. It would also be possible to extend the system further by adding another element, a knowledge-based system which would make it possible to interpret the responses of the pattern-recognizer and translate them into written or spoken form.

The exploitation of such possibilities may lie some way into the future. We mention them here only to make the point that artificial intelligence is likely to develop far more rapidly and fruitfully if both 'top-downers' and 'bottom-uppers' adopt an open-minded attitude and look for ways of cooperating rather than digging themselves even deeper into their already entrenched positions.

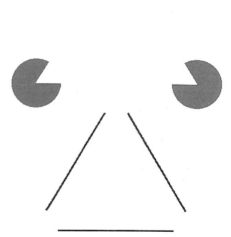

We have no difficulty in recognizing that both these patterns represent triangles. A net that has been trained to move its window around the edges of a shape will, in effect, be subject to just the same illusion in that its window will follow the outline of either of the two illusory 'triangles' even though most of the sides, in one case, or the corners, in the other, are missing.

CHAPTER 11

THE MYTH OF THE SUPER-INTELLIGENT MACHINE

There is no principle of science or engineering that prevents us from making intelligent computers that are infinitely smarter than ourselves. . . . We must ask ourselves what such machines will be doing in the future. . . . They may take away some of our (nuclear) toys, they will solve weighty problems that we ourselves have been unable to solve. They will talk to us only to amuse themselves and so, in some sense, keep us as pets.

This statement was made by Professor Edward Fredkin in the course of an interview which was broadcast on BBC television in October 1983. As the manager of the Artificial Intelligence Laboratory at MIT, Fredkin represents one of the world's leading centres for research into artificial intelligence and viewers must, presumably, have believed that this vision of the future was based on a sober and authoritative assessment of the scientific possibilities. If so, many of them must have felt deep disquiet. For although Fredkin himself seemed to view the prospect that he outlined with equanimity, if not relish, his words could hardly have failed to arouse suspicion and apprehension in the minds of a lay audience.

Such feelings are understandable. Over the past three-quarters of a century, and more especially since the dreadful dawning of the nuclear age over Hiroshima, people have come to see scientific research and technological advance as processes that are as likely to lead to evil as to good. They have also come to suspect that scientists themselves are irresponsible, in that they will, if given the opportunity, recklessly pursue what they believe to be 'the interests of science' without pausing to consider whether these coincide with the interests of mankind.

In the case of computer science in general, and artificial intelligence in particular, such suspicions are likely to fall on fertile ground, already well-prepared by novelists and film-makers who have presented us with so many grim, futuristic visions of a world dominated by machines. Thus, when an authoritative figure such as Fredkin blandly forecasts that humanity will shortly relinquish responsibility for its own future to a race of super-intelligent machines, most people are likely to conclude that something very nasty indeed is stirring in the artificial intelligence laboratory.

It should, therefore, be stated quite bluntly that a large majority of those working the field of artificial intelligence would regard Fredkin's pronouncement as outrageous and damaging nonsense.

To take this view is not necessarily to dispute Fredkin's claim that 'There is no principle of science or engineering that prevents us from making intelligent computers that are infinitely smarter than ourselves'. But the claim itself is virtually meaningless. There are, after all, very few things that we actually know to be beyond our reach because they would contradict the principles of science or engineering – a perpetual motion machine is one, a vehicle that travels faster than light is another – but there are, none the less, many things we do not yet know how to accomplish – from curing cancer to harnessing nuclear fusion. The real point is that, on existing evidence, building super-intelligent machines quite clearly falls into this latter category.

COUNTING CHICKENS BEFORE THEY HATCH

One reason for treating claims like Fredkin's with a healthy degree of scepticism is that we have, so to speak, been here before. As early as 1959, for example, the creators of LOGIC THEORIST, Herbert Simon and Alan Newell, were forecasting that 'within the visible future' artificial intelligence would produce computers with processing powers 'co-extensive with the range to which the human mind has been applied'. By 1970 Marvin Minsky was willing to be even more specific: 'In from three to eight years we will have a machine with the *general* intelligence of a human being'. Indeed, so confident were some of the prophecies made by the artificial intelligentsia during the 1960s that, had they turned out to be well-founded, super-intelligent machines would already be an established fact of life. We are, therefore, entitled to ask why we should take such views more seriously this time around. Has anything changed over the past fifteen years that might justify this renewed optimism?

The answer generally given is that the development of expert, or knowledge-based, systems represents a major breakthrough for artificial intelligence; all the years of research have at last been justified by the creation of a marketable product. And that is only the beginning. The knowledge-based system, it is claimed, has opened the way to a transformation of society, a second industrial revolution. In future, knowledge, not oil or steel, will be the fundamental economic resource and computer systems, not factories and power stations or roads and railways, will be the essential means of production and distribution.

Moreover, argue prophets of artificial intelligence such as Edward Feigenbaum, this is not simply a utopian vision. It is a view of the future that has apparently been endorsed in a most practical way by the Japanese, whose project for the development of 'fifth generation' computers amounts to an audacious attempt to leapfrog into the new age ahead of their competitors.

For the whole concept of a fifth generation is based upon the premise that artificial intelligence has at last come of age. Up to now, the transition from one generation of computer to the next has been marked by advances in hardware. The valve circuits of the first generation were replaced by transistors, then came the first integrated circuits, chips containing small numbers of transistors and other electronic elements and finally, from about 1970 onwards, a fourth generation based on Very Large Scale Integration

(VLSI) began to take over. But although the struggle to fit more and more elements onto a single chip continues the fifth generation, as the Japanese see it, will be distinguished from its predecessors by virtue of its ability to manipulate knowledge rather than merely processing information. The emphasis, in other words, has been placed on developing the techniques required to handle very large knowledge bases and inference mechanisms capable of operating at enormous speed. If new hardware is needed, it is basically because programs of the size and complexity that are envisaged would be impossible to run on existing machines.

It took a year or two for the full implications of the fifth generation project to be grasped in the United States and Western Europe, but when they sunk in it was recognized that this was a challenge that could not be ignored. As a result, artificial intelligence, or rather those branches of it which are relevant to knowledge-based systems, has become a subject of concern to governments, banks and industrialists in all the developed countries of the world.

There is, therefore, no disputing that something has changed. But the fact that these developments are likely to impinge dramatically upon all our lives between now and the end of the century makes it all the more important that we should not misunderstand their nature.

In this book we have examined most of the techniques which are now coming together in the new generation of 'intelligent' computers – the ways of structuring a knowledge base, the problem-solving algorithms and the inference mechanisms which are used to construct a chain of reasoning, the language-using programs and the vision systems which facilitate communication between man and machine. We have seen that, in certain very limited respects, computers have become intelligent, in the sense that they have shown that they can do things which, if done by people, would be said to require intelligence. But we have also seen that the methods used are highly mechanical and can only be implemented success-fully thanks to the ability of the machines to operate at enormous speed and to follow logical rules slavishly.

It is certainly fair to say that these sort of techniques, sometimes grouped together under the heading of 'automated reasoning', may eventually produce machines with a capacity for manipulating logical rules that will match, or even exceed, our own. But logic is just one aspect of human intelligence, and one whose importance can easily be overrated. For, as we have tried to show throughout this book, factors such as intuition and flair play a very large part in our thinking, even in areas like science where logic ostensibly reigns supreme. For example, most of the scientists who have recounted how they came to make an important discovery or to achieve a significant breakthrough have stressed that when they found the answer to the crucial problem they intuitively recognized it to be *right* and only subsequently went back and worked out *why* it was right.

In fact, knowledge-based systems are likely to be most useful precisely because they complement human intelligence rather than competing with it. Their strengths – the ability to store and retrieve large amounts of data with faultless accuracy, the capacity to follow the chain of reasoning that derives from a given set of axioms with total precision and without deviation or distraction – are often our weaknesses. But if we were to conclude that they are therefore 'more intelligent' than we are, we would be adopting a singularly narrow and impoverished definition of intelligence.

This is not to belittle the achievements of artificial intelligence, but simply to point out that there are many important aspects of human intelligence which still remain elusive and mysterious and which we cannot account for within the framework of any existing logical calculus. In particular, the brain is extraordinarily effective at making guesses based on experience, at retrieving knowledge from memory without the need for exhaustive searches, at perceiving analogies, at forming associations between seemingly unrelated items and at making sense of its experience even on the basis of imperfect and incomplete data.

If we want to build machines that are equally competent – or even if we simply want to understand and explain our own competence – then it seems likely that we will need to discover a good deal more about the brain and particularly those aspects of its performance that cannot be duplicated by the application of formal logical rules. This is an area which science has barely begun to investigate, in which we scarcely know how to ask the questions, let alone where to find the answers.

Yet all the signs are that a serious assault on the problem is at last being mounted. From different directions, using different weapons and adopting different tactics, neurophysiologists, psychophysicists, cognitive scientists, brain biochemists and even computer scientists are closing in on the brain, seeking an explanation for its extraordinary competence.

THE NEW CONNECTIONISM

Among the computer science contingent in this investigatory army a new watchword has come to the fore within the past few years – 'connectionism'. Roughly speaking, a 'connectionist' is someone who is interested in systems that are made up of many simple, interacting computers. This is, however, a theme upon which it is possible to play a wide range of variations. Some of the research, such as the WISARD project described in Chapters 9 and 10, is avowedly based on bottom-up principles; in other cases the aim is to develop massively parallel architectures which will allow very complex algorithms, such as those proposed by David Marr (see Chapter 8), to run in real time.

But all connectionist systems share one intriguing feature, their 'intelligence' derives, at least in part, from the way in which the elements are interconnected rather than being entirely the product of programming. And much of the current interest in connectionism is due to the fact that the brain, too, is a system in which intelligence is an 'emergent property'. For however much importance we attach to education, both formal and informal, it is clear that in our own case intelligence is something that all brains 'have', a product of the evolutionary processes which created the structure of the organ, rather than a 'program' which is loaded into it.

As has already been explained, the idea of building brain-like machines is not a new one; it has been in the air ever since 1943 when McCulloch and Pitts produced their logical model of the neuron. But after the publication of Minsky and Papert's work on the Perceptron in 1969 (see Chapter 9) the prospects of using neural net-type structures as a basis for computer architectures looked exceedingly dim, and work along these lines virtually ceased. There were, however, a small minority of researchers who continued to wrestle with the theoretical issues. After all, the fact that Minsky and Papert had exposed what seemed to be fundamental shortcomings in the capabilities of Perceptrons did not alter the fact that the brain was made up of millions of interconnected cells and that their interactions somehow generated an intelligence which far outstripped that of the orthodox computer.

One of those who struggled on with dogged determination, seeking to provide a mathematical explanation for the workings of neural nets in the brain, was John Hopfield of the University of California at San Diego. And it was very largely as a result of his work that, in the early 1980s, interest in the computational properties of neural networks began to revive, giving rise, in due course, to the movement known as the 'new connectionism'.

Among those who have consolidated and built upon Hopfield's work are Geoffrey Hinton of Carnegie Mellon University and his colleague Terry Sejnowski of Johns Hopkins. They defined a device, which they christened a 'Boltzman machine' after the nineteenth-century Austrian physicist, Ludwig Boltzman. So far at least the Boltzman machine runs only as a computer simulation, but it has already created much interest and excitement because it has shown that, far from being an unavoidable nuisance, 'noise' (the random interference which distorts the signals in a system) may have a vital role to play in connectionist structures.

Boltzman's great contribution to physics was a law which related the energy of a molecule to its absolute temperature; as the temperature rises, so the random vibrations of the molecules in a gas will increase and its pressure will grow. The Boltzman machine was so-named because its behaviour changes in an analogous fashion according to its 'computational temperature'. Briefly, a Boltzman machine consists of a number of elements linked together by connections that may be given variable 'weights'. By 'clamping' elements (forcing them to fire, as it were) both inputs and outputs of information can be represented. The machine will then adjust the weighting of its connections so that a recurrence of the input will again produce the corresponding output (see opposite).

When the machine is 'taught' to relate an input to an output in this way it is in fact modifying its own state structure so that the input will in future drive it into a 'learnt' state and, since the output is a function of the system's internal state, cause it to produce the appropriate output. The state structure of a net of any size will,

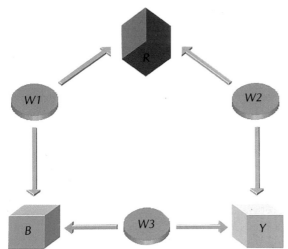

The three coloured boxes (above) labelled B, R and Y (for blue, red and yellow) are neuron-like elements which at any instant may be either firing (outputting a 1) or not firing (outputting a 0). The blue discs, W1, W2 and W3, represent variable 'weights' which are applied to all firing signals transmitted along a connecting wire – i.e. if R and B are both firing and W1 = +2 then R will receive a +2 input from B, and B will receive a +2 input from R. Each element will fire if, and only if, the sum of the signals it receives from other elements is positive. To illustrate how such a system works, let us suppose that W1 = +1, W2 = +4 and W3 = −2. We can now construct a state diagram that shows how the machine will behave under all possible circumstances.

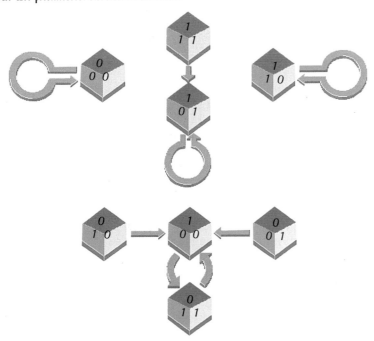

The illustration on page 199 clearly shows that, whatever state the machine starts in, it will always end up either in one of three stable states (R0B0Y0, R1B1Y0 and R1B0Y1) or in a cycle in which it alternates between state R1B0Y0 and state R0B1Y1.

The presence of noise, which causes elements to fire when they otherwise would not fire and vice versa, will obviously have the effect of driving the machine out of its present state and restarting it in a new, randomly-selected state. Since the probability, P, that the machine will end up in one particular stable state (or the cycle) is directly related to the number of starting states which lead to that stable state, we can say that if noise is introduced into the system the probabilities of it ending up in one of the three stable states or the cycle are as follows:

For state R0B0Y0 $P = \frac{1}{8}$
For state R1B1Y0 $P = \frac{1}{8}$
For state R1B0Y1 $P = \frac{1}{4}$
For the cycle R1B0Y0/R0B1Y1 $P = \frac{1}{2}$

It should also be clear that if the weights were changed the state diagram would also change and with it the range of states and/or cycles in which the machine could end up and the probability factor associated with each of them. A little work with pencil and paper will, for example, confirm that if $W1 = -2$, $W2 = -1$ and $W3 = +2$, then the machine will always end up in either the stable state R0B0Y0 ($P = \frac{3}{8}$) or in the cycle R0B0Y1/R0B1Y0 ($P = \frac{5}{8}$).

Although this example is too small to illustrate the phenomenon, a network of this type has one very important characteristic – it will always go from a high energy state to a low one (a high energy state is defined as a state in which the sum of all the weights between pairs of active elements is a large minus quantity and a low energy state as one in which the sum of the weights between active elements is a large positive quantity – in other words, the energy expended by the net can be thought of as the force needed to operate negatively weighted interconnections). It follows that the most stable states in the state structure of such a machine are its minimum energy states. The basic idea of a Boltzman machine is that it should learn to relate certain patterns of input to specific outputs. Inputs and outputs are represented by 'clamping' elements or sets of elements – i.e. forcing them to fire or not to fire. In the case of our machine, for example, we might make elements R and B fire to represent the input 11 and prevent element Y from firing in order to represent output 0 and, as a result of a series of such exercises, we might hope to teach the machine to output 0 whenever the two input digits were the same (i.e. 11 or 00) and to output 1 whenever they were different (i.e. 01 or 10).

Unfortunately it is not possible to illustrate the learning mechanism in detail by continuing with this example, for it depends upon the presence of elements intermediate between those which receive the inputs and those which produce the outputs. But the essential idea is that once input and output elements have been clamped the network is run in the presence of noise (in fact the logical functions of the elements are modified by introducing a probabilistic factor) until it achieves a minimum energy state, and the weights attached to the connections between active elements are then increased by a given amount. Next, the inputs, but not the outputs, are again clamped and the process repeated except that this time, once a minimum energy state has been achieved, the weights attached to connections between active elements are decreased by the same amount as was previously added. As a consequence, if the second set of inputs drove the net into the 'right' internal state, causing it to produce the 'right' output, all the weights will have returned to their former value, but if the output was 'wrong' some of the weights will have been permanently altered.

If the net is put through a series of these exercises its state structure will be modified so that the most stable states are those which relate the learnt inputs to the corresponding outputs and, most importantly, it will also achieve a high level of generalization, i.e. it will be able to recognize a whole range of similar but not identical patterns of input.

however, include states, or cycles of states, which are stable (i.e. they lead back to themselves) even though they do not represent 'known' inputs – they are, so to speak, *culs de sac* in the net's state structure into which it may accidentally stray while in quest of a learnt state. But by increasing the amount of noise in the system, or raising the computational temperature, the net can be shaken out of these holes and freed to continue towards its learnt state.

In a vivid analogy Hinton and Sejnowski compare the state structure of a Boltzman machine to a bumpy surface upon which a ball bearing, representing the current state of the network, can roll freely in any direction. The surface contains one or more deep holes, representing its learnt states, as well as many minor pits and ruts. Once set in motion, the chances are that the ball will roll into the nearest 'local minimum' and get stuck there; but if the surface is continuously vibrated, then the ball will be shaken free and will eventually find its way into the deepest hole.

In theory at least, structures of this kind have enormous potential for storing vast amounts of information and recalling it speedily. For, given one input, they could retrieve a vast amount of associated data without going through formal, algorithmic search procedures; instead they would be driven through the appropriate sequence of internal states by the inexorable logic of the weighted interconnections that had been set up when the information was taken into store. Indeed, working with a conventional computer that had the capacity to handle formal languages, a Boltzman-like system could well remove some of the bottlenecks which currently limit the size and scope of expert systems.

Another promising connectionist venture has been spawned by the MIT Artificial Intelligence Laboratory, where a number of faculty members set up a company called Thinking Machines Inc to construct a device which they have christened the 'connection machine' (see opposite). Largely engineered by Daniel Hillis, the connection machine consists of a 'pool' of 64,000 processors that may be interconnected in any way the user pleases. In order to facilitate the task of setting the machine up, a special version of LISP has been developed which operates as a sort of 'hardware compiler', translating the programmer's instructions so that specific functions are allotted to each processor and the necessary interconnections are established between processors.

The connection machine greatly increases the speed at which conventional programs, such as Marr's visions algorithms or rapidly changing, high resolution graphics, can be run. It will also be extremely valuable to those who wish to study brain-like connectionist networks, in that it allows such systems to be simulated far more readily than is the case with a conventional computer.

There are, however, worrying signs that connectionists may fall prey to the sort of *hubris* that has affected Fredkin and others. Soon after the connection machine was publicly unveiled, for example, Daniel Hillis was seen on television arguing that the way now lay open to the construction of machines 'smarter', by several orders of magnitude, than the smartest human being.

Any such notion is, of course, absurd. Connectionists are as yet only at the beginning of their enquiries and there is all the difference in the world between studying intelligent behaviour with the help of a novel, highly competent and extremely fast computer and actually building an intelligent computer. Before such hyperbole can be taken seriously, connectionists will have to overcome massive problems. To take but one example, no one has seriously begun to consider *how* these systems might absorb and organize the vast amounts of knowledge they would require if they were to become 'smart'.

WHERE DO WE GO FROM HERE?

Given the money and resources currently being invested and the level of expectation that has been aroused, it seems likely that we will all be hearing and reading a good deal about artificial intelligence in the course of the next ten years. Inevitably, there will be more talk of super-intelligent machines, of computers which will out-think and therefore supplant human beings. But a sober assessment of the present 'state of the art', together with the market forces which are increasingly likely to determine the course of future development as the emphasis switches from pure research to practical applications, suggests a rather different scenario. What we should be looking forward to is not the day when machines start to treat us as pets, but a time when they will have become sufficiently intelligent to make it worthwhile for potential users to give them houseroom.

In order to keep things in perspective, it is important to remember that other areas of computer science such as office automation, home computing, or even computer-aided design and robotics which were late starters when compared with artificial intelligence

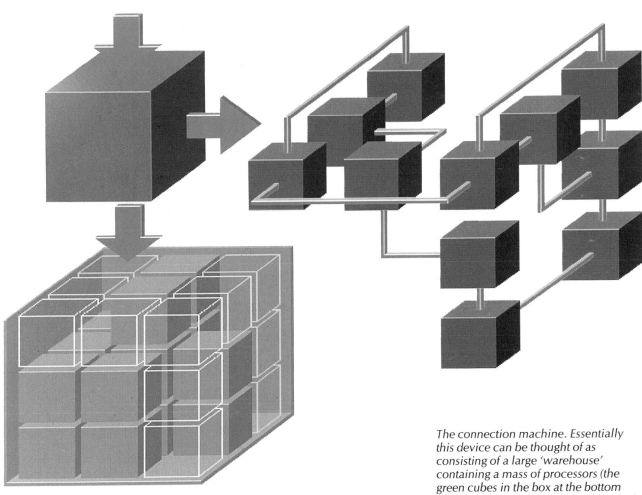

The connection machine. Essentially this device can be thought of as consisting of a large 'warehouse' containing a mass of processors (the green cubes in the box at the bottom left) and a program controller (the black box at the top left). When instructions defining a task are fed into the program controller it assembles some or all of the processors into a network (the interconnected red cubes on the right) which it has, as it were, specifically designed to perform that particular task. In reality, of course, bits of hardware are not actually moved about; instead the program controller simply sets up the appropriate pattern of interconnections between processors and provides each processor with a program that enables it to perform its allotted role.

have so far had a far greater impact on both our private and our working lives. And most of the work now being done on the practical applications of artificial intelligence is in fact directed towards widening the scope of these existing technologies and making them easier to use. To take just one example, the three largest projects in the Alvey Programme (the British counterpart of the Japanese fifth generation programme) involve constructing a computerised database to store legislative information for the Department of Health and Social Security, devising a knowledge base that can be added on to existing computer-aided design systems and designing a speech-driven word processor capable of handling a vocabulary of up to 20,000 words.

What these ventures, and many other similar ones currently underway elsewhere in the world, have in common is that they are intended to produce new tools that will complement and sup-plement human skills. Such tools will undoubtedly change the way we live and work, but if they threaten us the threat is no different from that posed by other technological developments.

There is indeed one sense in which artificial intelligence may make the next generation of computers considerably less threat-ening than their predecessors, in that, for the first time, it will allow us to dictate the terms upon which we deal with a new technology rather than vice versa. The Japanese, for example, have recently announced that they are beginning work upon what they call the 'sixth generation' and that the emphasis of their research is switching from the problems of eliciting and storing knowledge to the problem of making that knowledge accessible.

For it is widely recognized that the knowledge-based system will only realize its full potential if the knowledge it contains is available to anyone and everyone who requires it even if they have no specialist knowledge of computers or computer languages. As a result, the need to improve what is known as the 'man-machine interface' (the term is itself an excellent example of the kind of jargon that makes the world of computers seem alien and forbidding to the layman) has now become one of the main focusses of research. The aim is not only to produce systems which can understand and generate natural language, so dispensing with the need for all communications to be couched in standard form, but also to make the machine's internal processes 'transparent' to the user and to enable the machine to adapt to the user's needs and style.

In other words, no matter what is actually going on inside the machine, it will appear to the user that the reasoning processes it is following are comparable to his own and it will make an attempt to 'understand' what he is driving at, even if his questions seem illogical or obtuse. To take a simple example, instead of simply flashing 'syntax error' on the screen when confronted with an 'ungrammatical' imput, the machine might be able to work out what the user was likely to have meant and then ask for confirma-tion.

Another indication that artificial intelligence may encourage what might be called the 'democratization' of the computer is the fact that

204

expert systems are increasingly being written specifically for the small business or even the home computer enthusiast. Even five years ago it was axiomatic that artificial intelligence was a field which required the use of a mainframe or at least a large minicomputer, but personal computers have now developed to the point at which their memories are large enough to support an expert system which is non-trivial and several software companies already have products on the market. Some of these are ready-made systems designed for the user who wants to have access to existing expertise in some field, others are 'shells' which allow the user to construct a system that will meet his own particular needs.

What these and other developments suggest is that artificial intelligence is emerging from what might be called its 'manic depressive phase' and is now taking a more practical and realistic view of its own future. Already there is less talk of machines that could, in principle, solve 'weighty problems that we ourselves have been unable to solve', and more discussion of how machines might, in practice, be able to solve some of the mundane problems which we find it tiresome or time-consuming to deal with. Instead of dreaming of vision systems that could operate a hundred times faster than the human eye, researchers are now seriously tackling the job of designing equipment that can distinguish a good weld from a bad one as rapidly and reliably as the average quality control inspector.

This may strike some as a curiously down-beat note on which to conclude the book about a field which has been the subject of so much extravagant speculation. But, as we have tried to make plain throughout, most of this speculation has been ill-informed or ill-judged and has served only to arouse expectations that could not be fulfilled and fears that were not justified. We will only make full and proper use of artificial intelligence if we understand its limitations as well as its potential. We hope that this book has explained something of both.

INDEX